- the myths and realiti[es] and influence of PAC[s]

- the vanishing funds f[or] the presidential campaigns

- the new middlemen and brokers (e.g., the case of Charles Keating)

- the major options for reform: private versus public funding

- the political deadlock over reform: parties, public opinion, and the interests of incumbents

- the possibility of new levels of competition and spending in 1992

Sorauf argues that the American system of campaign financing has become increasingly stable and institutionalized during the last sixteen years, and that the major players in the system—PACs, individual fundraisers, party committees, and incumbent candidates—now behave in fairly predictable ways. His book is a fresh and persuasive account of the importance *and* the limits of money as a base of political influence in the United States.

Frank J. Sorauf, Regents' Professor of Political Science at the University of Minnesota, is the author of the classic *Party Politics in America*. In 1990 he was the recipient of the Career Award given by the section on Political Organizations and Parties of the American Political Science Association for a lifetime of professional and scholarly contributions to the field.

Inside Campaign Finance

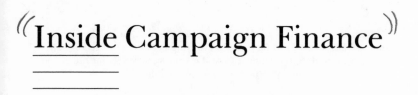

Inside Campaign Finance

Myths and Realities

Frank J. Sorauf

Yale University Press

New Haven and London

Set in New Baskerville type by Rainsford Type, Danbury, Connecticut.
Printed in the United States of America by Vail-Ballou Press, Binghamton,
New York.

Library of Congress Cataloging-in-Publication Data

Sorauf, Frank J. (Frank Joseph), 1928–
Inside campaign finance : myths and realities / Frank J. Sorauf.
p.   cm.
Includes bibliographical references and index.
ISBN 0-300-05726-1
1. Campaign funds—United States.   I. Title.
JK1991.S67   1992
324.7′8′0973—dc20   91-44246 CIP

The paper in this book meets the guidelines for permanence and
durability of the Committee on Production Guidelines for Book Longevity
of the Council on Library Resources.

10 9 8 7 6 5 4 3 2 1

To a decade of research assistants,

with gratitude

Contents

Preface

When I returned to teaching in the late 1970s after a tour of duty in academic administration, I planned to resume the research in political parties and judicial politics that I had left six years earlier. That attempt to go home again was thwarted by an invitation in 1981 by the Twentieth Century Fund to staff a task force examining the implications of the growth of PACs in American campaign finance. The work for the fund was a crash course on campaign finance, a stimulating experience in itself, and the beginning of a decade of work on the subject. This book is the culmination of that time of studying and writing about campaign finance.

Such a mid-career change to a new research topic was possible largely because I have had the dedicated service of seven superb research assistants. All seven of them were then undergraduate majors in political science. Some have worked one year, some two, but all with intelligence, responsibility, and good cheer. They have mediated my dealings with computers of various sizes, and to do so, all of them mastered the logic and complexities of Federal Election Commission data. They have also run down countless facts and footnotes in the library, combed through periodicals and newspapers, compiled bibliographies, generated charts and graphs, and done all of the other things that made it possible for me to write several books and a number of papers while carrying on the other duties of a professorial life.

So, I dedicate this book to the seven of them as a token of my very great gratitude. In chronological order they are: Wallace Hilke, Stephen Ansolabehere, David Linder, Tracy Tool, Scott Wilson, James Audette, and Peter Radcliffe. Because the problem of getting this book together in a relatively short time fell during Peter's watch, I want to express my special thanks to him. It could not have been done without his help.

Many other people have contributed to the writing of this book. My friend Gerald Elliott continues to be the peerless source of Washington information. Everyone I deal with at the Federal Election Commission is helpful, but I am especially indebted to Bob Biersack and Kent Cooper, who always go way beyond the call of duty. Also in Washington, Chuck Alston has generously shared his knowledge and insights with me, and Joe Cantor of the Congressional Research Service was unfailingly helpful. Besides these people I am also grateful for the assistance of too many other Washingtonians to mention by name.

My association with the people at Yale University Press has been pleasant and productive, and I thank them collectively. It was an especial pleasure to work again on a project with John Covell. I also appreciate the comments of two anonymous readers the Press secured for the manuscript. The whole experience has once again made me optimistic about book publishing.

Here in Minneapolis my colleague Phil Shively read part of the manuscript and made exceptionally valuable comments on it. Mary Ellen Otis handled the production of the manuscript with her usual skill. Others—friends, colleagues, librarians, machine wizards—have been helpful and supportive in countless ways. With so much skilled and generous assistance, there should be no shortcomings in the book. But I fear there are, and they are entirely of my contriving.

Chapter 1 _____
_____
_____

_____

The First Ninety Years

Americans have two contradictory reactions to the way they finance political campaigns. They remain deeply suspicious of wealth as a campaign resource. The impression persists that campaign money can buy elections and that it can similarly buy public officials. Many Americans believe that monied interests do in fact make the purchases, and commentary about campaign finance repeatedly turns to clichés like "war chests" and "the best Congress money can buy." Yet at the same time, millions of Americans, perhaps as many as 20 million in an election year, contribute willingly, even virtuously, the cash that makes the funding of American campaigns so feared and despised. Thus Americans both nurture and distrust a system of campaign finance, a system that they reject, even scorn, while making it the most broadly based in the world. Perhaps the major result of these paradoxes and anomalies is our collective inability to agree on the reality of American campaign finance and its consequences. It is hard enough to grasp the details of so technical a subject, especially in sorting out the routes and magnitudes of so much campaign money, but it is even harder to pierce

1

the myths that surround the money's impact and consequences.

If there is any constant in the confusions about American campaign finance in the twentieth century, it is in the repeated attempts to reform it to rely on the small sums of ordinary citizens. The history of those attempts is not a happy one, and yet we have not given up. American optimism about the efficacy of reform, ironically, has run as deep as American distrust of the cash we have tried vainly to reform. So the reformers have persisted throughout the century, their efforts often limited to half-measures and just as often greeted with knowing winks. The last great reform dates from 1974, the immediate consequence of Watergate and the misdeeds of Richard Nixon's Committee to Reelect the President. That legislation, by far the most comprehensive attempt yet to tame campaign money, defines the beginning of the contemporary period or regime in American campaign finance. Congress's hopes for it can best be understood in the light of what preceded it.

From 1907 through Watergate

For most of the twentieth century American campaign finance was ruled by the political parties and their sleekly affluent "fat cats." The parties dominated finance because they dominated the campaigns themselves. They either chose the candidates or provided the votes for their nomination in primary elections, and they managed the full span of the campaigns, from the circulation of nomination petitions through the hosting of the election-night celebrations. Their minions canvassed the wards and precincts for the same information that telephone polls now inquire. Candidates spoke at party rallies and in party-affiliated newspapers, and when they needed advice they sought it from the seasoned campaigners of the party organization. Much of the party-centered campaigning needed no cash; it rested heavily on services volunteered or bartered for some party-controlled favor. But when the campaign needed cash, the party raised it—often from the candidates themselves, since providing money for the campaign, either from acquaintances or from one's own resources, was frequently a condition of receiving the party's nomination.

When cash in large sums was needed, the parties went to men of wealth, the storied fat cats of party and campaign lore. In the street vocabulary of party politics in the nineteenth century, "fat" was money and aggressive fund-raising was called "fat-frying," presumably a reference to rendering fat.[1] Some local campaigns did without the fat cats, but attempts to raise substantial sums from small contributors rarely made the big contributors superfluous in national politics. Louise Overacker, in an early and important study of money in American campaigns, reported that in 1928 some 69.7 percent of the receipts of the Democratic National Committee and 68.4 percent of the receipts of its Republican counterpart came from contributions of $1,000 or greater.[2] In the late 1920s, a less political family could have bought two of Henry Ford's Model T's with a thousand-dollar bill.

The reign of the parties and the big contributors continued well into the 1950s and 1960s, but important changes were afoot both in the campaigns themselves and in their financing. Whereas in 1952 only 34 percent of American households had a television set, 92 percent did by 1964. Campaigning was never the same again, both for the growing number of political commercials and for the restructuring of campaigns to produce sound bites and gripping pictures for the nightly network news. Not surprisingly, it was in the first full flush of television expenditures for campaigning, during the 1960s, that the costs of campaigning first rose at a rate sharply greater than that of inflation. Herbert Alexander estimates that spending in all American campaigns rose from $200 million in 1964 to $425 million by 1972.[3] A new era had arrived.

In the race to provide the fuel for the new electronic engines of campaigning, the big contributors remained essential. To be sure, there were some successes in raising smaller sums of money, and three unsuccessful presidential candidates led the

way. Barry Goldwater, despite his landslide loss to Lyndon
Johnson in 1964, raised $5.8 million from 410,000 contrib-
utors in direct-mail appeals. Four years later, George Wallace's
rebellious third-party candidacy raised $5.8 million—three-
quarters of his funds—in sums of $100 or smaller, and George
McGovern, another landslide loser (to Richard Nixon in 1972),
received almost $15 million in sums averaging $20 from two-
thirds of a million supporters. But broadly based fund-raising
was, it seemed, for losers running ideological campaigns of
the left or right. The winning major-party candidates and
organizations stayed with more traditional ways. In fact, in
1968 Chicago insurance executive Clement Stone and his wife,
Jessie, set a record that seems destined to endure, giving $2.8
million to Richard Nixon's first presidential victory.

At the same time, an even more fundamental, if less visible,
change was under way. The political parties, long the focus
and the main agent of America's electoral politics, began to
lose their vaunted role. The party organizations of the country's urban centers began to crumble until by the 1970s there
was little more than Richard Daley's increasingly anachronistic
machine in Chicago. Just as important, voters reduced their
emotional commitments to the parties; fewer and fewer
thought of themselves as loyal "members" of a party, and more
and more split their tickets at the polling place. And as if to
replace the parties in campaigns, there arose a clan of campaign specialists for hire: media consultants, polling experts,
organizers, even tutors in the art of using television. Children
of electronic politics, the new specialists vaulted past the parties as the masters of the new campaigning in less than a generation.

Whereas the people and events of the old campaigning had
pivoted around the political party, the new configuration centered on the candidate. Liberated from the control of the
party, candidates could run their campaigns and make their
own personally tailored appeals. They could in fact rent most
of the old party services from the new specialists. The new
technicians not only felt the public pulse, but they also did so

with greater sophistication than had the earlier precinct workers; one could even rent the organization necessary to arrange
rallies in shopping centers or coffee parties in suburban
homes. In the process the old economy of gifts and barter
became a cash economy. To rent media time and the new
campaign technocrats one needed cash—lots of it. And so the
burden of raising campaign money passed from party to candidate, and the fat cats became as important to the candidates
as they had been for the parties. Moreover, because it was so
candidate-centered, American campaign finance became
much more campaign-specific, and, thus, much more expensive. All that seemed clear as the nation approached the Nixon-
McGovern campaign in 1972.

There had, of course, been sporadic but determined attempts to legislate limits to the funding of campaigns, beginning in the period between 1890 and World War I. That such
reform and regulation should have begun in the heyday of
the Progressive movement was no accident, for its political
rhetoric had long featured attacks on the political power of
big money. After a rash of legislation in the states largely
aimed at publicity about the sources and sums of campaign
money, Congress took its first reforming step in 1907. React-
ing to the growing political power of the new corporate wealth,
it outlawed contributions to congressional and presidential
candidates by banks or corporations. In a reform history in
which there are few enduring landmarks, that ban on direct
corporate contributions in federal elections stands to this day.

The results of Congress's other reforms were less enduring.
It joined the "control through publicity" movement, another
tenet of the Progressive faith, by passing a halfhearted disclosure law in 1911, and in that same year it enacted limits on
candidate spending for House and Senate campaigns. Then
it returned to reform in the unpromising years of the 1920s
with legislation in 1925 to reinforce reporting requirements
and raise spending limits. The spending limit for a House
seat, for example, was set between $2,500 and $5,000 depending on the number of votes in the district in the previous

election. Further legislation in 1940 added contribution limits to the arsenal of regulation for the first time; individuals were limited to contributions of $5,000 to a candidate for the presidency or Congress. During World War II the long-standing ban against corporate contributions was extended to labor unions.

All of this regulation scarcely impeded the flow of campaign money. Much of the reform legislation, both of Congress and the states, seems to have been passed with the loopholes tailored in. Contribution and spending limits applied only to the candidates themselves; other committees set up to assist their campaigns, often called "volunteer" committees, were unaffected by the limits. Moreover, neither the states nor the Congress set up special agencies to oversee compliance with the laws or to make financial reports public. In fact, the required reports of candidates and party committees under federal law were deposited with the staffs of the House and the Senate, rarely to be exhumed from unmarked boxes in inaccessible closets. As for the investigation and enforcement of violations, the responsibility fell to a Justice Department whose traditions and budgets had not prepared it for riding herd on candidate spending. Not surprisingly, there were no prosecutions under the 1925 law, from its origin to its repeal in 1971.

So, as the nation approached the pivotal election of 1972, the regulation of the financing of American elections had a long history of futility and the cynicism that futility breeds. Candidates increasingly had seized control of their campaigns, but they were as dependent on the fat cats as the parties had been. Richard Nixon moved confidently into his reelection campaign against George McGovern, a candidate carrying the twin burdens of an unabashedly liberal-reformist program and a party divided over the lingering war in Vietnam. Campaign spending continued its upward climb. The Nixon campaign raised a record $63 million, and the Clement Stones again led the list of contributors with $2.14 million. As it turned out, the events of 1972 were a last hurrah for the old ways of campaign finance.[4]

Watergate and Its Aftermath

Both the events and the effects of the Watergate scandals extended far beyond campaign finance. Starting in June 1972 with what seemed to be an isolated break-in at Democratic National Committee offices in the Watergate complex, investigators slowly unraveled a tale of abuses of executive and political power that touched campaign finance only in minor, though substantial, part. Amid the stories of break-ins, of underhanded political knavery (the "dirty tricks"), of enemy lists in the White House, of lying to the Congress and federal investigators, and of an unexampled venality in the Oval Office, there were also the gamy stories of illegal campaign money: political money laundered to conceal its illegal corporate or foreign origin, secret and unreported funds, and funds raised in exchange for favorable government action. Public outrage and humiliation followed the revelations and spurred a remarkable flowering of legislation designed to improve American political ethics. Not the least of those efforts were the extensive amendments in 1974 to the earlier Federal Election Campaign Act (FECA) of 1971.

The 1971 legislation stands as evidence that the reasons for reform ran earlier and deeper than the traumatic events of Watergate. The rising costs of campaigns, blamed then almost entirely on the new use of the mass media, certainly lay behind the 1971 legislation, and so did a gnawing fear within the Democratic party that it had lost the money chase to the Republicans. In 1971 the Democratic party was still struggling to retire a debt of more than $6 million incurred in Hubert Humphrey's loss in 1968, and Democrats began to fear that their old ability to raise big money as a party—a skill based heavily on party control of public spending in the cities—would not transfer to their candidates. So, the Congress acted to cap the rising costs of campaigning by attacking spending on the media. The 1971 FECA limited media-advertising expenditures in congressional campaigns to $50,000 or ten cents per voting age resident, a formula that permitted senatorial candidates in California to spend almost $1.4 million. The Congress acted, too, to build a fund for the public financing of presidential campaigns; it agreed to postpone spending it until 1976, however, in order to neutralize Richard Nixon's opposition.

After the revelations of the Watergate investigations opposition to reform fell away. The nation's leading opponent of campaign finance legislation left the White House in disgrace, and even the Republicans in Congress warmed to reform. So potent a creator of support and a catalyst of legislation were the events of Watergate that at least half of the states also toughened their regulation of campaign finance. The tremors of Watergate were felt even in Canada. Explaining the passage of 1974 Election Expenses Act, two of the most authoritative scholars of Canadian campaign finance concluded: "Public discussion of party finance and election spending had become much more widespread in Canada and was further stimulated by Watergate revelations, which began to excite public opinion on both sides of the American border. It is difficult to estimate how much events in the United States influenced the Canadian government, but it is clear there was a desire to act before public suspicion about party financial activities was heightened even further."[5] Indeed, Canadian and U.S. regulation of campaign finance still rest primarily on legislation passed in the aftermath of Watergate.

Although technically Congress's work in 1974 was a series of amendments to the FECA of 1971, in reality it was a new and comprehensive piece of legislation, the first attempt at an all-inclusive, integrated system of regulation for congressional and presidential campaigns. If the history of reform since the early years of the century had taught any lesson, it was that tentative, piecemeal regulation was doomed to fail. The 1974 amendments began by concentrating responsibility for a candidate's getting and spending in one registered committee for which the candidate was responsible. The Congress then erected a set of limits on all contributions and on all spending in the campaign—by individuals, by political action committees, by party committees, and by all candidates. The 1971 limits on media expenditures were scuttled, but the reporting requirements were kept and even stiffened. Finally, the Congress created an administrative agency, the Federal Election Commission (FEC), to oversee the gathering and publicizing of reports and the enforcement of regulations it created.

The FECA after the 1974 Amendments

In passing the 1974 amendments to the Federal Election Campaign Act, Congress created for the first time a comprehensive structure of regulation for American campaign finance. It incorporated a number of features from the regulatory past—the ban on union and corporate contributions, for example—and it strengthened the reporting requirements while creating an agency, the Federal Election Commission, to enforce and administer the legislation.

For both the public and the political participants, however, the new FECA was primarily a structure of limitations on the movement of money and a venture into the new world of public funding of presidential politics. It included these provisions:

Limits on contributions:
- Individuals could contribute a maximum of $1,000 per candidate per election. In this and all other limits the primary and general elections came to count separately; thus the limit was in effect $2,000 per candidate in a two-year election cycle.
- Individuals were also limited to a calendar-year total of $25,000 in all contributions, with sublimits for the year of $20,000 to national party committees and $5,000 to a PAC or any other party committee.
- Political action committees (PACs) and party committees were limited to contributions of $5,000 per candidate per election (or $10,000 in the cycle).[6]
- Party committees, too, could contribute no more than $5,000 per election to a candidate. The major party sena-

torial campaign committees, however, were permitted to contribute $17,500 to each of their party's senatorial candidates.

Limits on spending (all except the first were struck down in Buckley v. Valeo)*:*

- Different formulas governed the spending of political party committees "on behalf of" their candidates for the Congress. Committees were limited to $10,000 in spending for House campaigns, indexed to 1974 dollars (value in 1991: $26,500). The minimum limit for Senate campaigns was set exactly at twice that; an adjustment formula raised the limit for races in the more populous states, with the California limit in 1991 rising to $1,166,493.
- Candidate expenditures were limited in two ways. Candidates and their families were limited to $35,000 per year (Senate) or $25,000 (House) in contributions to their own campaigns. Their campaigns for a House seat were limited to $70,000 in total spending; Senate campaigns could spend the greater of either $100,000 or 8 cents times the voting-age population of the state, both totals indexed to 1974 dollars.
- Independent spending by groups and individuals to support or oppose a candidate was limited to $1,000 per candidate per election. Such spending was "independent" if it was made without the cooperation or knowledge of the candidate.

Public Funding of Presidential Elections:

- Candidates for the presidency established eligibility for federal matching of all individual contributions of $250 or less; spending limits were set in each state as well as an overall national spending limit of $10 million in 1974 dollars.
- Full voluntary public funding was instituted at a spending limit ($20 million in 1974 dollars) for major party candidates in the post-convention, general election campaign.

Like most grand reformist victories, however, the 1974 reworking of the FECA in reality addressed old problems and

issues. Reform almost inevitably lags behind because reforming coalitions are built on grievances and problems with histories; moreover, forward-seeing reform is thwarted by the
sheer difficulty of seeing forward. Thus, the 1974 rewriting
of the FECA was primarily an attack on the domination of
campaign finance by wealthy individuals in the past. Ignored
or overlooked were the two emerging developments in American politics that soon would push reform off the course the
reformers had set.

Only later in the 1970s did it become clear, first of all, that
the Supreme Court was bent on applying more of the First
Amendment's protections to political parties, campaigns, and
electoral politics. In 1976, less than two years after the epochal
amendments to the FECA, the Court heard a broadside attack
on their constitutionality in the case of *Buckley* v. *Valeo*.[7] In
deciding it, the Court held for the first time that the giving
and spending of campaign money was protected by the First
Amendment. "Money talks" was elevated from popular saying
to constitutional principle, and the power of Congress and
state legislatures to regulate campaign finance was thereby
severely narrowed. While the Supreme Court upheld the
FECA's limits on contributions, it struck down all of its clauses
limiting expenditures except those by political parties. Congress's grand scheme of regulation was savaged, and so
were similar provisions in state laws. The decision was very
much of a piece with the Court's other rulings of about the
same time using the First Amendment to strike down state
restrictions on access to the ballot, control of voting in party
primaries, and the very structure and operation of party
committees.[8]

Furthermore, as the decade of the 1970s unfolded, it also
became clear that the growth of interest groups was transforming American politics. If Americans were loosening their
ties to political parties, they were more and more enthusias-
tically joining groups—professional and occupational groups,
neighborhood groups, groups mobilizing support on morality
and life-style issues, groups working for the rights or equal

status of some set of Americans, groups supporting every imaginable cause or issue. The number of registered lobbyists before the Congress rose from 1,317 in 1974 to 1,970 in 1982, and one study of groups with a Washington presence found in the mid-1980s that 40 percent of them had been established after 1960.[9] American adults had come to prefer the representation of narrowly defined interests and enthusiasms, even those of single issues, to the untidy and sprawling agendas of the political parties. The new FECA could hardly escape the impact of such an atomizing of American politics, and almost immediately the campaign-funding arms of the groups, the political action committees, began to proliferate. It was, momentously, the first invasion of American electoral politics by interest groups across the whole spectrum of issues and ideologies.

So the FECA was launched, only a tattered remnant of its original self after *Buckley,* into an electoral politics no longer dominated by parties, facing new interventions from groups, and dominated by the unrestrained spending of candidates freed to acquire all the new arts and skills of campaigning. It is no wonder that the framers of the 1974 legislation saw the future of campaigning only dimly and that, in retrospect, the unfolding of the new regime in campaign finance seems now to confirm the existence of some law of unintended consequences in the writing of complex regulatory legislation.

The New Era in Campaign Finance

In one sense we have experienced a single era or regime in campaign finance since 1974. The governing legislation, primarily the work of that year, stands relatively unchanged except for its devastation in *Buckley* v. *Valeo*. To be sure, Congress added other limits on contributions in 1976—limits on individual and PAC contributions to party committees, for example—and in 1979 it exempted some state party expenditures from federal spending limits in order to help those parties regain a place in presidential campaigning. But the basic regulatory outlines set down in 1974 have remained substantially unchanged through the 1990 campaigns. The brief span of those years easily suggests a single history, a single response to a relatively stable regulatory environment.

Yet even within so short an era or epoch, shifts and changes in many of the most important indicators of the movement of political money in congressional elections are apparent between 1976 and 1990.[10] Most surprising of all, the shifts seem to take place in or after the 1984 elections. So, while one finds a single regulatory era or regime since 1974, two clear subperiods can be marked in the flow of money.[11]

The trends and shifts since 1974 are of two main kinds, each with its own particular break after 1984. First are the trends of growth—the growth of PACs and of total sums spent in congressional elections, for instance—in which one sees often staggering increases starting in the middle 1970s and sharply leveling off in the mid-1980s. Second are the trends of distribution—as in the sums going to different kinds of candidates—in which redistribution begins or sharpens in the years around 1984. In short, the sharp growth of money in the late 1970s and the early 1980s, and the apocalyptic predictions based on it, seems to have been temporary, a trend now overtaken by new events and a maturing of the FECA regime.

When the Federal Election Commission reported that both receipts and spending by congressional candidates in the 1990 elections were below totals in the 1988 campaigns, some of the American media finally took notice. The growth of spending in all congressional races had decreased between 1986 and 1990 by 1.3 percent, but with inflation taken into account, the drop in constant dollars was one of 17.2 percent. The drop in Senate spending of 28.7 percent overshadowed the 7.1 percent decline in House spending (fig. 1.1). In some years campaign spending in Senate and House races even moved in opposite directions, and one could also find explanations for this or that dip from one cycle to another: weak candidates, lack of competitive races, or the particular mix of Senate races

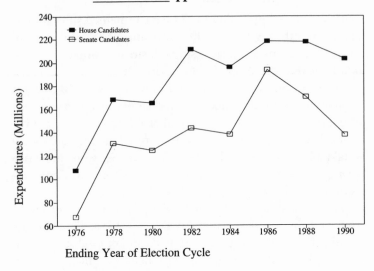

Figure 1.1
Expenditures of All Congressional Candidates: 1976–1990
(Constant Dollars)

in a given year. And clearly the surges in spending were greater in nonpresidential years. The central fact remains, however, that total cash outlays have now achieved, at least for the short run, a somewhat tentative stability, which contrasts dramatically with the stunning growth until the mid-1980s.[12]

There is one measure of spending that continues to show increases, and for that reason it has become ever more popular: the average expenditure of victorious House candidates. The rise in their spending is continuous from $178,000 in 1980 to $410,000 in 1990; if one measures in constant dollars, however, even the winners' spending shows a decline between 1988 and 1990.[13] Moreover, the increase in the spending of winners becomes a cause in itself, or at least the occasion for tendentious rhetoric. Such phrases as "the price of admission" and "the cost of winning" proliferate. In truth, the rise indicates little more than the increasing ability of incumbents to win reelection and to raise and spend money in their reelection

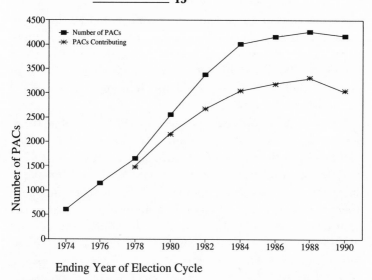

Figure 1.2

Ending Year of Election Cycle

Figure 1.2
Number of PACs Registered with the FEC and Number Making
Contributions: 1974–1990

campaigns regardless of the extent of the competition they
face. Their campaign outlays are much more accurately, if
much less dramatically, called their expenditures.[14]

The growth of PACs from 1974 through 1990 followed a
similar pattern: steep upward climb followed by a leveling off
in the mid-1980s. The shape of the curve is the same whether
one measures growth in the number of PACs registered with
the FEC or the considerably lower number of PACs active as
contributors in a two-year election cycle (fig. 1.2). Spurred by
the generous contribution limits of the FECA and by a subsequent FEC decision permitting parent organizations to pay
overhead and administrative costs for their PACs,[15] the number
of PACs rose from 608 at the end of 1974 to 4,009 at the end
of 1984. Six years later the total had edged up only to 4,172
after a series of small upward and downward fluctuations in
the intervening years. The total sums PACs contributed to candidates for the House and Senate leveled off in much the

same way, but just a bit later. PACs contributed $55.2 million to all congressional candidates in 1980 and $139.4 million in 1986. The total then rose only by 11.8 percent to $155.8 million in 1988 and by 2.2 percent to $159.2 in 1990. In constant dollars, however, PAC contributions declined by 4.2 percent between 1986 and 1990.

Presidential campaigns present a special case. Public funding at 100 percent of the spending limit is available for the candidates of the two major parties, and all of them—Carter and Reagan (each twice), Ford, Mondale, Bush, and Dukakis— have accepted the public money and the attached limits on their spending. Since the spending limits are indexed to the Consumer Price Index (CPI), the direct spending in the general election campaign has not changed in constant, inflation-adjusted dollars. The other part of the presidential campaign, that before the party conventions meet to choose their candidates, is governed by its own quite different form of public funding. Since the complexity of its financing defies the quick summary this overview requires, it must wait until later (see chapter 5).

As the growth of money and its sources slowed, its redistribution began in earnest. House and Senate incumbents in 1978 raised only 38 percent of all the money raised by all candidates for the Congress; that proportion rose steadily to 62 percent in 1990. More to the point, it increased only from 43 to 49 percent from 1980 to 1986 before taking off to 56 percent in 1988 and 62 percent in 1990. House incumbents fared even more famously in the same period. What was a 1.5 to 1 advantage over their challengers in receipts in 1978 became a 3.7 to 1 spread by 1990 (fig. 1.3).

The changing distribution of funds to the candidates of the two major parties is more complicated. The line of the percentage of funds going to Democrats is indeed a somewhat meandering and shallow U-shaped curve. Democratic candidates for the Congress accounted for 53.0 percent of all candidate receipts in 1978 and 53.6 percent in 1990, but in between those years the Democratic share dipped somewhat.

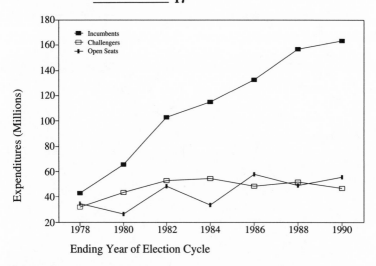

Figure 1.3
Expenditures of All House Incumbent, Challenger, and Open-Seat
Candidates: 1978–1990

Overall percentages, however, conceal the fact that there are
more Democratic than Republican candidates for the House
in the general elections; Republicans leave incumbents un-
challenged more often than do Democrats. Median figures for
the candidates of the two parties solve the problem (fig. 1.4),
and they reveal a closeness between the two parties giving way
to increasing Democratic dominance in 1988 and 1990. Obviously the flow of money to the majority Democrats reflects
their larger number of incumbents. The differences between
Democratic and Republican candidates for the Senate shift
with the mix of seats up for election in any given year.

The muted differences between Democrats and Republicans in the aggregate are, however, precisely to the point.
First, in the 1990s the candidates of the two parties fluctuate
around the point of parity, even though majorities had not
yielded the Democrats anything approaching parity with Republican candidates in the 1960s. That earlier failure to convert majority status to financial health was in fact a major cause

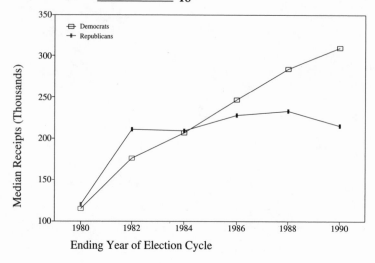

Figure 1.4
Median Receipts of House Major-Party, General-Election
Candidates: 1980–1990

for Democratic pessimism about campaign finance as late as
the 1970s. Second, the virtual parity sharply contravenes another article of the conventional wisdom: that Democrats are
greatly impoverished in facing the candidates of an affluent
and generous Republican party. The talk about the financial
superiority of Republican congressional candidates is very
much out of date, at least as long as Democrats continue to
enjoy majority control in the House and the Senate.

All of these trends invite refinement and elaboration. In
some of them there are important differences between the
patterns of House and Senate candidates; in others there are
just as surely differences between different kinds of PACs—
between labor and corporate PACs, for example. Clarifications
aside, two overall conclusions are clear, both of them again
quite different from the conventional wisdom of the day. First,
the realities of American campaign finance have changed
course dramatically in the decade of the 1980s; there has been
fluctuation and even stability rather than the upward line of

inexorable trends. Second, the good guys and the bad guys, the predators and the victims, are far harder to recognize than the wisdom would have it. PACs do not monopolize the funding of congressional elections, for example, nor do Democrats cower before the accumulated wealth of Republican candidates.

The appearance of so many changing patterns in campaign finance at approximately the same time invites interpretation and explanation. What indeed is the relationship between the end of growth in campaign money and the redistribution of it to incumbent candidates? Only the hopelessly incurious would not wonder whether the increasing financial security of incumbents is a result or cause of the diminishing supply of money. And what does one gain in explanation when one introduces other actors in campaign finance, such as the increasingly powerful party campaign committees in the two houses of Congress? Those matters and the development of a more densely textured picture of American campaign financing are in fact what much of the rest of this book is about. For now it is enough to underscore the two identifiable phases in the short history of campaign finance since 1974.

Behind the emerging stability in American campaign finance is an impressive amount of political learning and adaptation. Education into new regulatory regimes is quick and intense. After 1974 the major actors in funding campaigns, contributors and candidates alike, found themselves in a new environment, spotting new hazards and limitations and seizing new opportunities. With experience came political learning, and with that learning came reaction and adaptation to the regulatory regime. The initial euphoria, for instance, over discovering a new political tool—a political action committee—yields to a more sober assessment of experience about what the tool can and cannot accomplish. Realism increasingly defines and limits expectation; PACs encounter the realities of incumbent advantages and challenger futility. The regulatory regime and actors within it eventually settle into a more regularized, a more institutionalized stability. PACs abandon their euphoria, and PAC growth ceases; the sums of money entering the system from individual donors similarly come to a more realistic stability. That such political learning flourishes in American campaign finance is not surprising; that it came so quickly is the cause for surprise.

Political Images and Surroundings

The legal framework most easily defines the post-1974 regime in campaign finance, but the politics and public opinion that formed around it is no less defining. Today's opinion about campaign finance retains the two central premises of the populist and Progressive worldview: a fundamental and implacable distrust of political money, and a disposition to attribute much, even too much, that happens in American politics to it. It is probably no exaggeration to say that Americans are now just as committed to the Progressive worldview as they were in the early years of the twentieth century. The mass media reflect it regardless of their political party preferences; newspapers from all parts of the political spectrum plead for drastic reforms of the status quo in campaign finance. One has to search long and hard these days to find a kindly word, even a neutral word, for PACs in either print or electronic media. But the media are not alone in their perceptions of contemporary campaign finance. For the first time in American history a like-minded movement to reform it is also alive and active.

Unquestionably at the forefront of the movement is Common Cause, John Gardner's "people's lobby" founded in the early 1970s, the time of reborn stirrings of reform in campaign finance. The rewriting of the FECA in 1974 was in fact the great defining political victory for Common Cause. In every way present at the creation, Common Cause helped define policy options and mobilize support for amending the FECA. Only the dashing of its hopes for public funding of congressional elections diluted the sweetness of its success. Common Cause has never surrendered on the public-funding question, and it continues to battle for it into the 1990s. Even though its membership has declined in numbers and militancy from the high water mark of 350,000 members in 1974, it remains the dominant voice in the chorus for reform. Its press releases still find a welcome audience among journalists, and although it has nettled members of Congress for suggesting their "purchase" by monied interests, its credibility outside of Washington remains unimpaired.[16]

Common Cause does not labor alone. Enlisted in the cause of reform are a number of other good-government, public-interest, or citizens' groups. The Center for Responsive Politics, for example, was founded in 1983 as a privately funded institution conducting research on congressional and electoral issues, with campaign finance as one of its major concerns. Its general position about campaign funding is not greatly different from Common Cause's; its 1988 publication *Spending in Congressional Elections: A Never-Ending Spiral* bears an illustrative conclusion in its subtitle.[17] Ralph Nader's Congress Watch and Public Citizen have been similarly active on campaign finance issues; their views are thoroughly representative of their founder's. And Philip Stern's Citizens Against PACs has produced Philip Stern's book *The Best Congress Money Can Buy*.[18] It, too, wears its heart in its title. Almost all of these groups have been supported by national foundations, whose record for sympathy with neo-Progressive reform is old and well established. The Center for Responsive Politics, for one, gets 80 percent of its funds in foundation grants; its proposed budget for 1988 was $450,000.[19]

And the foundations themselves? In the first paragraph of its August 1991 announcement of a grant program on U.S. elections, the John D. and Catherine T. MacArthur Foundation observed, "There is strong evidence, too, that the way in which campaigns are financed works against democracy and the practice of good government." There are, to be sure, foundations on the right that would deregulate campaign finance—the Cato, Heritage, and James Madison foundations chiefly—but their impact is not yet a match for the reformist groups.[20]

There do not appear to be many foundations that maintain detachment or an open mind on the subject.

Between the offsprings of Progressivism on the one side— the media, the public-interest groups, and the foundations— and the deregulators on the other, the defenders of the status quo have been virtually mute. The Public Affairs Council, an association of corporate public or governmental affairs officers, and the National Association of Business PACs (NABPAC) have spoken out on behalf of PACs, and the labor movement, especially through the AFL-CIO's Committee on Political Education (COPE), has done so too, if less publicly. Even less publicly, an all-star Ad Hoc PAC Coalition began in 1991 to protest the treatment of PACs in the bills before Congress; the coalition included four of the top six contributors to congressional campaigns in 1990: the PACs of the National Association of Realtors, the American Medical Association, the National Education Association, and the National Association of Letter Carriers. Then in the summer of 1991 a number of PACs placed similar pro-PAC ads in the reading material of Washington insiders, *Roll Call* and *National Journal* most conspicuously; all used the same concluding, boldface motto: "Political Action Committees: My Choice for a Stronger Voice." The PAC voices, however, rarely carried beyond Washington.

The positions of Democrats and Republicans in the debates over campaign finance once were clear and predictable. In the years after World War II the Democrats, as the party historically opposed to the interests of money and wealth, were the party of reform. Certainly it was the party favoring public funding, both out of a willingness to seek governmental solutions and out of a desire to catch up with Republican funding. The Republican party had its share of reformers in its liberal or moderate wing; Senator Charles Mathias of Maryland exemplified them in the 1970s and 1980s, but with his retirement and the general loss of Republican moderates reformism in the party atrophied. Mainstream and conservative Republicans, far less touched by the traditions of Progressivism and populism, accepted the outcomes of the FECA with much greater equanimity.

Recently, however, such generalizations have been blurred and complicated in the congressional battles over reform. Each party in each house of the Congress has developed a party position about reform that artfully combines political philosophy, electoral self-interest, and the cultivation of public support. Faced with Democratic majorities in both houses and with an electorate unhappy generally with the status quo in campaign finance, Republicans have fashioned their own reform packages, if somewhat joylessly, and left the nay-saying to the Republican in the White House.

Perhaps the most singular aspect of the debate over the status quo in campaign finance is its one-sidedness. In the country as a whole there is literally no public defense. The response to the proposals of President George Bush and both parties in the Senate in 1991 to abolish some or all PACs was deafening silence. Outlawing their political activity has not spurred the millions of PAC contributors to even so much as a whimper of protest in self-defense. No matter that the Supreme Court has clothed their activity with the protections of the First Amendment or that there are 5–7 million of them.[21] The 2–3 million members of the National Rifle Association won national media attention for their outraged opposition, almost simultaneously in 1991, to a very modest impediment to their ability to buy handguns.

The advantage in publicity that the reformers enjoy has generated more than political superiority; it has created a separate epistemology of campaign finance. A special knowledge about campaign finance prevails, one based on its own rules of evidence and grounded in the premise of the monetary root of all evil. One need only recall the media's belated discovery in 1990 of incumbents' ability to win reelection; it became a major theme in their coverage of that year's congressional campaigns. Incumbents seeking reelection to the House had succeeded 98.5 percent of the time in 1988 before slipping back a bit to 96.3 percent in 1990. Ergo, the reasoning went, the almost unfailing success of incumbents seeking another term was substantially the result of their growing advantage in campaign money. Such explanations overlooked the inconvenient fact that incumbents had been winning reelection to the House at rates above 90 percent for years, succeeding at an aggregate rate greater than 90 percent back in the 1950s and 1960s. They also gave short shrift to other explanations of the invulnerability of incumbents: their growing staffs, the franking privilege, their service to constituents, their name and face recognition, and their easy access to the media.

Money, then, has come to explain too much too easily in the new epistemology. At least as it confronts the facts and events of campaign finance, the Progressive worldview relies too often on a monistic explanatory system, one unified and consolidated by the driving force of money. Thus, for example, the campaign contributions incumbents receive from PACs explain the decisions members of Congress make on public policy. Leave aside all of the alternative and competing explanations. Leave aside the effects of their own values, the demands of party leadership, the preferences of the voters back home, the power of the presidency. Leave aside the possibility that money often goes to support well-established policy preferences, that money *follows* the votes. Indeed, this is the monism of a morality play, one with a simple plot, boldly defined characters, and an elemental struggle of good and evil that engages its audience in unquestioning belief.

Not by accident has the Progressive view come to dominate the American debate over campaign finance. It has the weight of history and tradition behind it, and it contains a kernel of truth. It also fits the imperatives of contemporary journalism. Television, the span of its audience's attention now calculated in seconds rather than minutes, has no capacity for coping with complex stories, especially those with no visual content. Print journalism is equally sensitive to the limited attention and background of its readership. The pressures are great on all purveyors of news to keep the stories direct and simple, certainly without the numbing mass of numbers in which the tale of campaign finance must be told. Those same pressures also dictate a search for drama and conflict in all reporting, and in the drama of campaign finance PACs provide a suitable heavy for the cast. There is little room—and little consumer tolerance—for the hedges and caveats, the uncertainties and complexities, of the academic accounts.[22]

One can only guess about the public's cognitions about campaign finance in the 1990s. Since no careful surveys have mapped the impressions or judgments of American adults, one can best infer them from the messages people receive. Reporting in the daily newspapers of the country has included few stories of stability, much less gentle downturn, in PAC and candidate spending. There was finally some attention to the 1990 FEC figures, but few of the stories reached the public outside of Washington.[23] Reporting of campaign finance on network television has reflected its notorious difficulties for the visual media.

For their part the major reform groups appear to be caught in a time warp. As late as 1991 Common Cause chose to ignore the trends since 1986; a mail appeal for funds from Archibald Cox opened this way: "The years since the Watergate scandal have seen a skyrocketing growth in contributions from political action committees—the PACs. In the 1990 elections, PACs contributed more than $150 million—more than a tenfold increase in the past 15 years."[24] Correct, to be sure, but obscuring the important point that "skyrocketing growth" ceased in the mid-1980s. The League of Women Voters in one of its direct-mail appeals in 1991 drew on the same passé "news" and the same tired verb: "PAC spending (sponsored by unions, corporations, and trade associations) has skyrocketed in Congress."[25] Among all of the "vested interests" in American politics, there appears even to be a vested interest in its reform.

In all of the messages about campaign money, PACs remain the Satan of the morality play. Small wonder that even citizens concerned about public affairs are surprised to learn that PACs contributed only about a third of the money for congressional campaigns in the 1980s. Although the rise of incumbents has won belated coverage in the media, few journalists have sorted out the shifting nature of the exchange between PACs and incumbents. How was it possible that the predatory PACs could continue to dominate such powerful and politically secure incumbents? Was there no victim for the predator, and who indeed was the predator?

Tone and rhetoric create images just as surely as do facts and information. Media coverage of campaign finance assumes the central arguments by a few coded or loaded words. Candidates have "war chests", a phrase redolent of its apparently piratical origins. PACs are "special-interest representatives" who "pour" their "millions" of dollars into those war chests. Expenditures are "careening" or "skyrocketing" out of control. Even the formerly staid *New York Times* has in its editorials taken to referring to soft money, money raised outside of the constraints of the FECA, as sewer money, no quotation marks necessary.[26]

Very few aspects of American politics fit the metaphor of Plato's cave better than the realities of American campaign finance.[27] And the plural *realities* is apt precisely for that reason. Most scholars, experts, and practitioners of the subject claim to see one kind of reality in campaign finance—a reality of endless complexity, of ambiguous causes, and of shared and dispersed influence. The reformers and the broader American public, however, see a quite different reality of enlarged, even grotesque images projected onto the wall of the cave. Theirs is a reality of dominant actors and great events, of clear and dramatic causes, a mesmerizing pageant of power and corruption. Whichever reality may be the "real" reality, there is no denying the power and dominance of the heightened images on the wall. For better or for worse, this is the reality that frames the policy debates and shapes the reformers' proposals. It is a reality difficult to square with the evidence, but it is just as difficult to ignore.

A great many themes and motifs wind through the next seven chapters, for American campaign finance is as rich and complex as all the rest of American politics. It is both a microcosm of that wider politics and an intricate political world of its own. It has its own well-defined actors and activity, its own regulatory environment, its own information and learning networks, and its own exchanges and marketplace. Yet the system never breaks away from the gravitational pull of American politics. It is as thoroughly American as the nation's disorganized parties, its media-centered campaigns, and its eccentric ways of selecting a president.

The most dominant, recurring theme perhaps is that of the dynamics within the post-Watergate regime in campaign finance. It has quickly developed a life and history of its own. An early period of optimism and growth, a period that seemed to confirm populist fears that money could accomplish anything in politics, has already yielded to a time of maturity, organization, and lowered expectations. Optimism and risk-taking have given way to institutionalization and a new realism about political influence generally and about money as a resource for it. The professionals of campaign finance, along with the newly empowered incumbent officeholders, have come in a very short time to dominate what had started out as a much more free-wheeling, donor-driven regime. And with their ascendancy and more realistic expectations has come greater caution and efficiency in the commitment of money to campaigns. With it may also come less money altogether.

Central to the changes within the regime of campaign finance has been a prodigious amount of political learning. It is most apparent in the endless and ingenious ways the participants have adapted to the regulations and limits of the FECA of 1974. They live within it as advantageously as possible, while crafting legal avoidance or alternative strategies of action where necessary. But beyond making peace with regulation, contributors and candidates alike have learned to alter their strategies and activities in response to shifts in political realities. In 1992 PACs collectively function differently than they did 15 years earlier, not only because of changes within themselves but also because of changes in electoral politics and electoral competition. So central and heightened is the learning and adaptation in all of campaign finance that they rarely slip from view in what follows.

No aspect of post-1974 campaign finance escapes the tension in its political environment between the populist-Progressive belief in the domination of political systems by money and the far more complex conclusions of the experts about political money. It is a classic example of the elite-mass, expert-amateur tensions in popular democracy, and campaign finance remains a battleground for those tensions to this day. The cynical innocence with which so many Americans view campaign finance has always colored popular evaluations of it and conventional wisdom about it. It was a force in the passage of the 1974 amendments to the FECA, and it remains a potent ingredient in the politics of reform into the 1990s. In many ways the exploration of American campaign finance is that most fundamental of all intellectual tasks: the search for reality itself.

Chapter 2 _____
_____
_____
_____

The Sources and the Sums

Some 91,600,000 Americans, only 50.1 percent of the 182,600,000 residents of the country 18 and older, voted in the elections of November 1988. Disappointing though turnouts may be these days, voting is still the most common form of political activity in this or any other democratic polity. If other forms of political activity engage smaller numbers of Americans, the numbers are nonetheless impressive. By count of the University of Michigan's National Election Study (NES), 10.2 percent of all Americans made a financial contribution to a candidate, political party, or "political group." That percentage converts to 18.6 million contributors.[1]

Alternatively, one can estimate the numbers of political contributors from the $1.7 billion that Alexander and Bauer estimate was spent in the national, state, and local campaigns of 1988.[2] If we assume that the average contribution was somewhere in the vicinity of $50 and that most contributors give at least twice, we then arrive at a total of 17 million contributors. Both this and the NES estimates may be high. Poll data classically overstates political activity—64 percent of Americans told the Michigan interviewers they voted in 1988—and the average individual contribution may well be greater than $50. The estimates are credible, however, and we can confidently project between 13 and 15 million contributors at the least. No other system of campaign funding anywhere in the world enjoys so broad a base of support. None even approaches it.

If we now see a leveling off of spending in congressional campaigns, there inevitably is a leveling off of money being contributed to those campaigns. After years of growth in the economy of campaign finance, the end of that growth cannot be without consequences for the contributors who fund the growth. Such suppositions lead to important questions. Do we see an incipient decline in the availability of campaign money that will lead to further declines in campaign spending? Within the great universe of contributors has the stability altered the overall mix of contributors? Indeed, has the end of growth altered both the quantity and the quality of contributors? Changes, even eventual transformations, in systems of campaign finance begin with the supply and the sources of the money that is both their basic resource and their political purpose.

The Flow of Campaign Money

In the voluntary, private support for American campaigning, all money originates with individuals, but their money flows in different channels. To take the $471.2 million raised by all congressional candidates in 1989–90 as an example, $249.4 million, or 53 percent, went directly from individual contributors to the candidates' committees (fig. 2.1). Another 32 percent ($150.6 million) was PAC money raised from individuals; although sponsoring organizations such as corporations or labor unions may pay the overhead expenses of their PACs, they cannot divert funds for such political expenditures from their assets or treasuries.[3] Another sliver, $4.3 million or 1 percent, came in contributions from party committees. The candidates themselves contributed $37.9 million (8 percent) to their campaigns in loans and cash contributions. These four

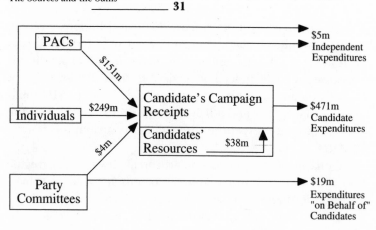

Figure 2.1
Major Actors and Flow of Money in Congressional Campaign
Finance: 1990

main sources make up only 94 percent of the $471.2 million
the candidates raised; loans from other sources and interest
earned on money in the campaign treasury accounted for most
of the remaining 6 percent.

The relative importance of these four direct channels for
volunteered money—individuals, PACs, the candidates, and
the parties—has been stable since the first reports were filed
with the FEC in the mid-1970s. Individual funding has, however, been slipping slowly in percentage, from 65 percent in
1978 to 53 percent in 1990; PACs, on the other hand, have
increased their share, from 17 percent in 1978 to 32 percent
in 1990. Party contributions and candidate self-support have
remained fairly fixed as percentages of candidate receipts.

Money from individuals feeds the expenditure totals of the
campaign in two additional ways. First, either an individual
or a group (PACs or other groups) may make expenditures in
a campaign to urge the election or defeat of a candidate,
provided that they are made without the cooperation or
knowledge of the candidate they aim to help. These "independent" expenditures totaled $4.7 million in the 1990
congressional campaigns, virtually all of that in PAC funds and

thus ultimately received as individual contributions. Second, party committees may spend "on behalf of" candidates; specialists often refer to these sums as "coordinated" expenditures because they may indeed be made with the full knowledge of the candidates who benefit. In 1990 they came to $19.3 million, a figure four and a half times greater than the sum the party committees spent in direct dollar contributions to candidates.

Unhappily, one cannot similarly break down the aggregate flows of money into election campaigns for state and local office. Alexander and Bauer estimate that campaigns for state and local office and ballot issues (such as referenda) cost $1.13 billion in 1987–88: $540 million for state elections, $365 million for local elections, and $225 million for ballot issues. Of the total for ballot issues the extravagant direct democracy of California alone accounted for $140 million.[4] And where does the $1.13 billion come from? Probably in most states from the same four sources of contributions in the same order of importance: individuals, PACs, candidates, and parties. The mix may differ in a few states, reflecting different statutory limitations and different political traditions; some of the most populous states (Illinois, Ohio, Pennsylvania, and Texas) have no statutory limitations on contributions of any kind. In some states different sources of money enter play. Public funding supports parties or candidates in at least 18 states, and some states (New York, for one) also permit direct contributions by both corporations and unions. Beyond illustrations and scraps of data, however, campaign finance is just one more aspect of state politics on which even the ordinarily brave hesitate to make more than a rough estimate.

All of these totals, to repeat, account only for the cash expended directly in campaigns for office. Larger sums of voluntary money flow to the individuals and organizations involved in them. For example, PACs contributed a total of $150.6 million to candidates in 1990, but the same PACs reported receipts from individual contributors of $372.4 million. The difference goes in part for the administrative and overhead costs of some PACs and all parties. Take the case of PACs supporting pro-life or pro-choice candidates. Since most of them have no parent organizations to pay their fund-raising costs, they may easily spend 60 or 70 percent of their receipts on the costs of the direct mail campaign itself: the postage, the rental charges for mailing lists, the printing and processing costs. They also have to pay the heat, the rent, and staff salaries. A similar logic explains the larger sums contributed to party committees ($236.2 million), whose resources also support the many year-round party activities not directly focused on the campaign.

So, although not all PAC and party spending goes for congressional elections, one can use a total of all individual funds going to them and to the candidates, including the money candidates give and lend to themselves, as a rough measure of the money flowing into national campaign politics in a nonpresidential year. That sum in 1990 came to $895.9 million, a figure a bit above the 1986 total of $885.0 million in current dollars but below it in indexed constant dollars. The 1988 total was $969.6 million, but totals historically have been noticeably higher in presidential years. The reservoir of money, then, has reached the stability that characterizes so much else in the post-1974 regime.

Who Are They and Why Do They Give?

It approaches a truism that the millions of contributors to campaigns are marked both by their affluence and their involvement in political and public affairs (table 2.1). They are better educated, earn higher incomes, and work in higher-status occupations—enjoy higher socioeconomic status, that is—than the active workers in the political parties. But they are much more similar to those party workers in socioeconomic status and political involvement than they are to the general adult public. Like the party workers, they are also more likely to be interested in the campaign and to vote in the election than is the general public.

Table 2.1

Characteristics of Contributors, Party Activists, and All
Respondents: 1990 (in percentages)

Characteristics	Contributors	Party Activists	All Respondents
Completed College	53.2	28.2	19.4
Professional/managerial	39.4	26.8	17.1
Income $30,000+	38.4	25.8	18.4
White	92.1	82.3	83.5
Republican	30.0	25.8	24.2
Very interested in politics	45.8	47.8	21.1
Voted in 1990	75.9	74.6	46.2
See differences in parties	67.7	61.6	45.2
	$N = 203$	$N = 209$	$N = 2000$

Source: Center for Political Studies, University of Michigan, *1990 National Election Study*. Data provided by the Interuniversity Consortium for Political and Social Research.

Their reasons for contributing money are as mixed and diverse as American politics. Some give because a friend or associate asks them to; political activity or involvement does not cultivate an ability to say no. Some give for nonpolitical reasons, perhaps to attend a glitzy fund-raising party or a celebrity reception. Some give to a PAC out of solidarity or identification with the union or corporation sponsoring it and out of a shared concern for its economic interests. The interests of labor unions, the tobacco industry, the American Medical Association, and countless other groups all turn on Congress's power to legislate. Other Americans give because of their commitment to a cause, an issue, or an ideology. They give money for the same reason that millions vote for candidates: to elect and reelect "right-minded" people to public office.

The most obvious, even banal, reason is perhaps the most important one: because giving is customary and expected, because it is part of a powerful and respected tradition of voluntarism. Americans support a great many local hospitals, symphonies, and emergency food shelves, as well as much of electoral politics, with their volunteered labor and money. Even though George Bush's "thousand points of light" seem not to include political volunteerism, and even though many Americans might agree with him, voluntarism in campaign finance is good, old-fashioned American voluntarism. Whether it is a matter of noblesse oblige, self-interest, civic duty, or the guilt of affluence, giving has become expected, perhaps even habitual, for millions of Americans. So central is it to the American way of campaign finance that American scholars ask who gives and why, while European observers ask why *anybody* gives.

Although contributors respond to inner motivations and political cognitions, they respond more immediately to a specific stimulus. It often is simply a request, one that comes in a lunch conversation with an old friend or in the superheated pages of a direct-mail appeal. If it is true that some people give because they are asked to give, the flow of their money depends on the number of people asking for it. With other contributors the flow depends on the persuasiveness, even the persistence of the people asking. Nothing augments the stimulus of persuasion more than the competitiveness of a campaign. Individuals, as well as organized contributors (PACs and parties), look for the candidate with a tangible chance of winning. The expectation of victory, or even its possibility, makes fund-raising easier; the competitive candidates are, in any event, apt to be better organized and more insistent. So, the question of why they give merges with the question of whom they give to. The political fortunes of the candidates define the potential contributors' chances of reaching their political goals.[5]

Nothing better demonstrates the complexity of these questions than a look at the sharply different levels of campaign funding among the American states. If one compares expenditures in the 1989 or 1990 races for the lower houses of

Table 2.2

Expenditures of Candidates for Lower Houses of Five State
Legislatures: 1990

State	Total Expenditure	Spending per Resident	Cost per Seat	Number of Seats
California	$40,964,660	$1.37	$512,058	80
Minnesota	$ 3,510,661	$ .80	$ 26,199	134
Missouri	$ 3,320,738	$ .64	$ 20,373	163
New Jersey	$ 7,653,744	$ .99	$191,344	40
Washington	$ 6,050,537	$1.24	$ 70,355	86

Data for New Jersey are from the 1989 election and are for general election candidates only.
Source: State agencies receiving campaign finance reports.

the legislatures of California, Minnesota, Missouri, New Jersey, and Washington—five states with reasonably reliable reporting of expenditures—the differences are considerable (table 2.2). They are also not easy to explain. They do not appear to be related to differences in per capita income or indeed to any other measure of affluence or disposable income. And they seem not to be related to electoral competitiveness, for the costly California legislative races are notoriously noncompetitive. Different mass-media markets would not seem relevant, for state legislative campaigns do not often use them. Do we then come down to differences in political cultures? If so, how do they affect contributing? Do they encourage or discourage contributions by structuring rewards for contributors differently, or by tolerating greater political rewards for all or some contributors? Or just by tolerating, or not tolerating, aggressive forms of fund-raising?

The fact of the extraordinarily broad base of campaign funding remains, but two nagging reservations intrude on what can easily become a celebration of American political voluntarism. First, is the giving really voluntary? Are the contributions perhaps extracted with threats of sanctions, especially job-related sanctions? That was the modus operandi of the patronage system run by the classic urban machine. A bookkeeper at city hall contributed or he lost the job the party machine controlled; often indeed the "contribution" was deducted from his paycheck for everyone's convenience. In the patois of urban politics it was called "macing the payroll," and it is still practiced today in some parts of Europe. But political patronage in public employment has shrunk almost out of existence in the United States, a victim of collective bargaining by organized public employees and the Supreme Court's increasingly dim view of political criteria for public hiring and firing. The major parties no longer raise large sums of money in the post–1974 regime, and much of what they do raise comes from phone and mail solicitations.[6]

Today's suspicions of coercion still center around the sanction of the job, but in the private rather than the public sector and among PACs rather than parties. Attention centers especially on corporate PACs, for they are the only PACs in which the employer's PAC systematically solicits the employer's employees. But there is little formal complaining, legal action, or even informal gossip to suggest widespread coercion. Moreover, corporate PACs get a higher rate of response from senior, well-paid executives than they do from more vulnerable younger personnel; they also widely report response rates no greater than 30 or 40 percent. Unquestionably, there are isolated instances of coercion; knowledgeable observers even mention specific corporate PACs "off the record." Far more common, though, are lower levels of pressure, much like the pressure to participate in United Way campaigns. Without wading into a philosophical discourse over coercion and free will, however, it appears that most contributions, even to corporate PACs, meet the ordinary meaning of "voluntary": one can refuse to contribute without risking serious personal consequences.

Harder to rebut is the attack on these cash contributions as "checkbook citizenship." These millions of contributors, the charge goes, avoid the participatory obligations of citizenship by buying their way out of them, much as some comfortable

Northerners did in paying substitutes to fight the Civil War for them. Candidates and parties, however, can no longer use the participatory activity they once did. Door-to-door canvassing, to take a single example, has fallen victim to the unwillingness of people to open their doors to strangers. Generally the decline in volunteered activity followed the decline in the parties' role in campaigns; it certainly did not cause it. Ultimately, though, the defense of checkbook participation comes down to an assertion that the standards and avenues of citizen obligation change over time and that the giving of cash is a quintessential political activity for our era. It meets the needs of the candidates and their campaigns, and it suits the resources, skills, and leisure-time preferences of millions of contributors.

New Contours for the Pool of Money

Whatever the successes in funding American campaigns with millions of voluntary contributions, there are reasons to doubt the willingness of Americans to fund electoral politics at their present level. The stakes in any such development could not be higher, for any major shrinkage in the supply of money would make campaign funds scarcer. Scarcity in turn would breed greater pressure to solicit large contributions, develop extralegal sources, devise ways of skirting the limits of the FECA. And in the absence of limits on levels of spending, scarcity would also write a scenario that the American system has so far been spared: increased contributor leverage over candidates because the contributors are trading in scarcer dollars. Such a change in the terms of the exchange would strike very few Americans as an improvement over the status quo.

The sheer sums entering the system governed by the FECA have varied little since 1986. Only when one converts to constant dollars does one see some decline. In fact, the total sums contributed to campaigns for Congress have held up remarkably well considering the inflationary shrinkage in the statutory limits on them. The $1,000 limit on individual contributions to a candidate and the aggregate limit of $25,000 per year were not indexed in 1974, and they have never been revised. Inflation, the silent regulator, has lowered their value so that by the end of 1990 the $1,000 and $25,000 limits had a real value of only about $400 and $10,000 in 1974 dollars.

Yet there are signs of softness and change in the money supply. In addition to the leveling off of the total dollars put into the system by individuals—and indeed in its slight decline in constant dollars—the receipts of congressional candidates declined in 1990 over 1988, down sightly from $474.7 million to $471.2 million without any adjustment for inflation. All of this has happened at a time of continuing growth in the American adult population. There were 144.8 million adults age 25 and older in 1984, according to the Census Bureau, but 155.6 million in 1988 and 158.4 million by the preliminary count for 1990. And the number of Americans age 50 and older, the age group most likely to contribute according to all reports, increased from 61.3 million in 1984 to 63.3 million in 1988. So, assuming an unchanging average contribution, the percentage of American adults who are contributors is declining.

Signs abound, moreover, that the size of the average contribution is in fact rising. A group of leadership organizations periodically surveys corporate PACs for information about their fund-raising. In November of 1981 their survey found that the average annual contribution to corporate PACs was $80; by 1990 it had risen modestly, and behind the rate of inflation, to $121 a year.[7] The point simply is that the average rose. In a seminal study of individual contributions to candidates, Richard Conlon, late executive director of the Democratic Study Group in the House of Representatives, documented the decline of small individual contributions under $100. They began to decline almost immediately after the beginning of the post–1974 regime, and the drop continued to 1986, even when Conlon controlled for increases in the consumer price index.[8] No one has repeated Conlon's foray into the reports at the FEC for data after 1986.

The FEC now reports aggregate data only on individual

contributions of at least $500, but recent data on these con-
tributions are certainly consistent with the findings above. In
1978 contributions of $500 or more to congressional candi-
dates were 26 percent of all individual contributions; by 1988
they made up 49 percent of them.[9] It seems probable, in other
words, that the size of the average individual contribution,
whether to PACs or directly to candidates, is increasing. The
broader conclusion is unavoidable: If the average contribution
grows at the same time the adult population increases and the
money supply is roughly stable, not only the percentage of
Americans who are contributors has declined, but so too has
their absolute number.

The softness in the money supply is visible from the vantage
point of solicitation as well. Any fund-raising dependent on
direct-mail solicitation turned volatile in the late 1980s. The
National Republican Congressional Committee (NRCC), the
campaign committee for House Republicans, exemplifies the
volatility; its spending rose from $3.2 million in 1980 to $8.8
million in 1984 and then slid back to $3.7 million in 1990. In
addition, many of the largely ideological PACs fell on even
harder times. The National Conservative PAC (NCPAC, pro-
nounced "Nick-PAC") collapsed from $10.0 million in receipts
in 1982 to $2.2 million in 1988 and then to $366,000 in 1990.
One could pass off the NCPAC failure as a result of special
circumstances—the death of Terry Dolan, its outrageous and
mediagenic leader, and its superfluity after the triumph of
Reagan conservatism—but its failure was not an isolated one.
In fact, the drop in PAC receipts from 1988 to 1990 (from
$384.6 million to $372.4 million) was more than accounted
for by the drop in receipts of the nonconnected PACs from
$106.3 million to $72.4 million. Those nonconnected PACs are
the issue-centered ones without parent organizations that may
solicit any American citizen; of necessity they do so largely by
direct mail or telephone.

Both the medium and the message have troubled direct-
mail soliciting. The medium suffers from the overuse of
computer-based address lists, with a resulting contributor

burnout; a number of PACs, in addition, have encountered problems in the efficiency and reliability of printing and mailing contractors. The message, moreover, is a volatile one. Typified by the four-page letter of apocalyptic warnings, the direct-mail appeal plays on reactions to people and events; it is an invitation to a crusade against the forces of ignorance or destruction. It is by intention sensitive to the causes and events of the hour. So, for example, the nation's newspapers were full of stories in late 1990 about the drop-off in contributions to the National Republican Senatorial Committee after President Bush agreed to tax increases. To contribute via direct mail or telephone is by nature to respond to the stimuli of the day. It is a kind of contributing that does not easily become routine.

Other ways of soliciting contributions are more direct and more personal. They draw on extrapolitical loyalties to a friendly solicitor or to the interests of the PAC's parent organization, and they appeal to specific, well-defined interests rather than to remoter issues and ideologies. They may also be regularized and rooted in periodic events or solicitations— in payroll deduction plans, for example. They appeal to interests and loyalties that are durable and imperturbable, interests not easily shaken by the events and currents of the day.

Most worrisome for confidence in the stability of the money supply is the fragility of the underlying voluntarism itself. Throughout much of the 1980s experts in fund-raising in the private sector worried about the reluctance of younger generations in the United States to join that tradition of voluntarism and, worst of all, about the possibility that they would fail to embrace the tradition as they aged. A study for the Rockefeller Brothers Fund in 1983 reported that the young, upwardly mobile urban professionals, the yuppies, were among "the least generous of all Americans."[10] The same study also found the rich to be ungenerous and their giving to be more sensitive to marginal tax rates and specific tax incentives. After further gloomy news about voluntary generosity in 1987 and 1988, Independent Sector, an organization of major charities and foundations, in 1989 reported an up-turn in giving and volunteering, with special emphasis on the new commitment of the baby boomers. Indeed, it found a 20 percent increase after inflation from 1987 to 1989 in the average charitable contribution of American households. In an accompanying press release, the president of Independent Sector found most of America's "well-to-do" still "not generous"; families with household incomes of $100,000 or more were contributing 2.9 percent of their income on the average.[11] So, in the broader giving community the Reagan years were a time of ups and downs. The most recent word from Independent Sector strikes a note of optimism, but the earlier alarms have not been forgotten.

Great fluctuations in contributions have not yet marked the funding of campaigns. For now, at least, political contributing appears to respond to stimuli somewhat different from those that drive contributions to charities, the arts, and religious organizations. It does not seem to reflect broader social and ethical imperatives, cycles of social conscience or civic virtue, or even the rise and fall of "me" generations. Moreover, level of political contributions in the 1980s seems not to have reflected the current state of the economy, no matter how one measures it: growth of GNP, disposable income, percentage of the workforce unemployed, or per capita income. The entry of individual money into the system was scarcely influenced by the recession of 1982, except perhaps for a slight dip in the smallest individual contributions, and the decline in contributing at the end of the decade began before the economic downturn of 1990 and 1991.

On the whole, then, the decision to contribute appears to stem from an assortment of political considerations. It is affected by the stimuli of political solicitation, and it flourishes among those who display unusual levels of political activity, information, and involvement. It is threatened not by economic or ethical trends but by negative reactions to contemporary campaigns, candidates, and public officials, and by lower individual feelings of political worth or efficacy. In fact, the special willingness of Americans to support voluntarily all manner of political causes and candidates may have reflected an earlier time of confidence in American politics and the individual's place in them.[12]

At the individual level the urge to give reflects some calculus involving the value of giving and the likelihood of achieving political goals. All other things being equal, giving will be greater the more intensely felt the political interest and the greater the perceived benefit of giving. As obvious as it may seem, that point raises a specter as disturbing as the scarcity of money. If in fact the number of individuals contributing to the flow of money is shrinking, the likelihood is that the shrinkage is among less interested contributors seeing fewer benefits from contributing. As they depart the regime of campaign finance, they will increasingly leave the financing of campaigns to those with longer and more explicit political agendas.

Narrowing the explanation of the decision to contribute political money to variables that are largely political does not yield easy explanations, however. And it certainly does not obviate the need for constructive speculation. There was some decline in overall individual giving to candidates, parties, and PACs from 1986 to 1990—from $872.2 million to about $851 million. One wonders if the removal of the tax credit for political contributions in the 1986 revision of the federal income tax laws suppressed some giving. Perhaps it did, but the breakdown of those gross totals into individual giving to PACs, to party committees, and directly to candidates raises the possibility of different political explanations for each of them (fig. 2.2).

The only consistent decline has been in individual giving to candidates. Perhaps this group of donors has on the average shorter political agendas and lower levels of political commitment and thus is more affected by the loss of the tax credit in 1986. Individual contributions to parties appear on the face of it more easily moved by the stimulus of presidential politics. And what of the growing commitment to PACs? Is it merely

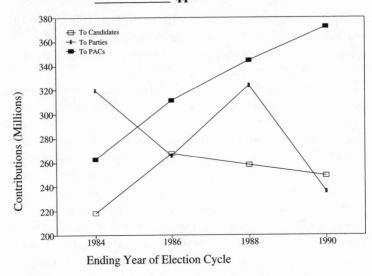

Figure 2.2
Total Individual Contributions to Candidates, Parties, and PACs:
1984–1990

testimony to durability of economic interests and the routin-
ization of political contributions? If it results from considerations of political efficacy, one comes back to Plato's cave and
one of its grand ironies. Is it possible, that is, that the growth
of contributions to PACs is a rush to share new and powerful
political instruments? Has the Progressive worldview, unin-
tentionally and ironically, encouraged the growth of political
money by the exaggerated tales of money's power? Did the
lurid descriptions of PAC power lead individuals to forsake
direct contributions to candidates for contributions through
the new, more powerful political machinery?

Campaigns for national office are only a part, if the best
documented part, of the pursuit of public office in the United
States. Stable receipts and spending in those campaigns do
not guarantee stability in state or local campaigns. It is even
possible that the money that would have fueled continued
growth in national campaigns has been diverted to state and

local campaigns. The data suggest otherwise. The most authoritative estimates of state and local spending rose from $505 million in 1980 to $1.13 billion in 1988, an increase of 124 percent; the increase in spending in congressional elections from 1980 to 1988 ($239 to $459 million) was only 92 percent. If, however one subtracts the referenda campaigns in the state and local data ($40 million in 1980 and $225 million in 1988), since they have no analogue at the national level, the increase in state and local campaigning costs was only 95 percent.[13] The difference between 92 and 95 percent growth is far too small to suggest a movement of money from national to local campaigns.

Yet one does hear stories of PACs, weary with incumbent-driven congressional finance, shifting resources to politics in the states. Whatever the stories, the data speak again. PACs must report total expenditures (disbursements) to the FEC as well as their political contributions to candidates; they do not, however, have to report specific contributions to state or local recipients. Those expenditures, along with the overhead and administrative costs they pay, are buried in the differences between the sum of the total expenditures and the sum of their *political* expenditures (contributions plus independent spending). If PACs were shifting their funds to state and local campaigns, one would expect to find the gap between total spending and political spending in congressional campaigns to be widening. But it is not. Congressional contributions accounted for 45.9 percent of all PAC expenditures in 1980 and for 44.5 percent in 1990.[14]

Any comparison of sources of money within the levels of American federalism cannot overlook basic differences in them. Funds spent in congressional elections originate with individual contributors, whether they come directly from them or via the PACs and parties they finance. Only small amounts come from other sources—chiefly earned interest. In the states and their localities, public funding supports parties and candidates in about a third of the states. In other states corporations, associations, and trade unions are free to contribute directly from their treasuries—without the necessity of having a PAC and its "separate segregated fund." Simply put, state and local campaigns depend less, by some significant but incalculable amount, on the volunteered money of individuals. If individual contributions are the softest spot in a soft outlook for the national supply of campaign money, then the future would appear to be brighter for the flow of money to state and local campaigns.

Shifts in the Distribution of Money

The precarious stability in the supply of money for American campaigning conceals some important internal shifts. The shift in importance from direct individual contributions to candidates to greater PAC funding of their campaigns has already been noted. Individuals increasingly enter their money into the system through organized intermediaries and decreasingly make their own choice of candidates to whom to contribute. Thus, PACs have slowly but inexorably increased their share of the dollars contributed to congressional candidates. While direct individual contributions accounted for about 65 percent of all congressional candidates' receipts in 1978, they accounted for 53 percent in 1990. Political organization triumphs once again.

Accompanying the shift from direct individual contributions to those funneled through PACs has been a shift from the localities to a national market for campaign contributions. In the political idiom it is the shift to out-of-state money, with all the resonances the phrase conjures up of alien interference in what is properly "our" business. The shift is inherent in the growth of PAC contributions because most PACs, the large ones at least, are national organizations operating in a national political arena on behalf of issues and interests that are largely national in scope.

Beyond the PAC factor in generating out-of-state money, however, even direct individual contributions increasingly move across state or congressional district lines. Certain cities have become famous for raising money for out-of-state candidates; New York, Los Angeles, and Washington are the leaders according to an analysis of individual giving by Citizen Action, an advocacy group with close ties to organized labor. Its report on the 1989–90 cycle listed $10,337,000 in individual contributions of more than $200 to congressional candidates, PACs, and party committees from seven zip codes in Manhattan. Of that $10.3 million, $4,056,000 went out of state; from the Citizen Action report one cannot tell what portion went directly to candidates. The entire state of New York provided $10.7 million in individual contributions of more than $200 to candidates in the other 49 states; California followed with $7.9 million.[15] The Citizen Action study captures only one point in time, but others have mapped out the dominant trend toward greater sums of money from out-of-state.[16]

The shift to out-of-district money has been identified a number of times. Janet Grenzke described it in House races from 1977 through 1982. In 1977–78 individual contributions of $500 or more to House incumbents came 52 percent of the time from within their districts and 79 percent of the time from within their state. By 1981–82 those figures had dropped to 39 percent and 67 percent. But when Grenzke added PAC contributions to those large individual contributions, only 11 percent of the total came from within the district and 28 percent from within the state by 1982. Granted that those latter figures represented only somewhat more than half the total receipts and that the study involved incumbents, the trends are nonetheless unmistakable.[17] More recently reporters for the *Washington Post* tracked down the residences of individual contributors of $200 or more and found that 25 percent of them for senatorial candidates in 1988 came from another state; that, they reported, was an increase from the comparable 16 percent in 1984. Their preliminary data for the first 18 months of the 1990 cycle argued that the figure for that cycle would be in the 50 percent range.[18]

The reasons for an increasingly national market in individual contributions are not obscure. Jewish, Greek, Nisei, Chinese, and other ethnic communities, pleased and flattered that one of their own runs for high office, open their checkbooks to help office-seeking sons and daughters regardless of state borders. Similarly, individuals involved in specific industries, environmental causes, and funding for the arts support itinerant members of Congress they view as spokespersons for their cause. Thomas P. (Tip) O'Neill, former Speaker of the House of Representatives, was fond of pointing out that "all politics is local," but some politics are now national. It is not easy to convince the rest of the country that Senator Jesse Helms's impact on American social policy and on federal support for the arts, not to mention American foreign policy, is only an issue between him and North Carolinians. In the most expensive senatorial race of 1990 Senator Helms raised $12.3 million from individual donors, and his Democratic opponent, Harvey Gantt, raised $7.1 million in the cycle; very substantial portions of that $19.4 million came from the other 49 states.[19] The funding of campaigns by a national resource constituency may in fact be the first major inroad into the entrenched localism of congressional politics.

In addition to those two distributional trends—the movement to PAC money and to out-of-state money—both individual and PAC contributions have gotten larger. In the case of individual contributors, the important fact is the escalation in the size of the single contribution. The Conlon study referred to a few pages ago documented the early decline of the contribution smaller than $100,[20] and more recent data make it clear that contributions of $500 and more now account for about a half of all individual contributions to candidates. Systematic data on the average size of contributions to PACs and party committees, especially over time, are impossible to come by. The impressions of insiders are that those sizes are increasing, too, but at a slower rate than individual contributions.

Whatever one's definition of small contributors, it is not clear what happened to them. So charged is the question with the loss of a powerful democratic symbol that the explanations are frequently ex parte and always wistful, for with the loss of the small contributor we have also lost a major goal of the 1974 reforms. All that aside, different reasons explain the departure of different small contributors. Some unquestionably conclude that their small sums make no difference, either because candidates will not respond to them or because candidates, flush with bigger money, really do not need it. The perception in either case is that small potatoes add little to the stew. In addition, candidates do not solicit small gifts as sedulously as they once did; as the money race accelerates, they reduce their fund-raising costs by seeking their funds in larger chunks. Perhaps, too, the small contribution has been the victim of rising affluence and rising expectations, the casualty of keeping up appearances and "going first class."

An annual limit of $25,000 caps the aggregate of individual contributions; it is the total sum an individual may give in a year to all parties, candidates, and PACs. The ultimate sign of concentration in individual contributions, then, would be the number of individuals reaching the limit—"maxing out," as the trade says. The number very probably has risen, especially since the $25,000 limit now has a value of $10,000 in 1974 dollars. Unfortunately, we have no data with which to go beyond speculation. The FEC has never released data on the aggregate contributions of individuals, and it now turns out that it has not been regularly monitoring the aggregate limit of $25,000. Ironically, it has been the new direct-access service the FEC offers, for a fee, to its data base that has provided the raw data; using those data, enterprising investigators have recently surprised the agency and some unsuspecting contributors by publicizing individuals exceeding the $25,000 limit.

No investigators have been more sedulous or enterprising than a duo from the *Los Angeles Times*. In September 1991 Sara Fritz and Dwight Morris identified 62 individuals across the country who had exceeded the $25,000 annual limit, apparently without having been challenged or investigated by the FEC. Only 22 of the 62 contributed more than $35,000, and only three exceeded $50,000; the largest total was $97,750. The 62 generally fell into one of two categories: elderly persons, usually Republicans, who responded to persistent and repeated appeals for money; and "successful business people" with more pragmatic political agendas. The individuals reached for comment pleaded either inadvertent reporting error or ignorance of the $25,000 annual limit. (Since individuals do not report to the FEC, the errors in reporting would not be theirs.) On behalf of the FEC, Commissioner Joan Aitkins explained that the FEC did not have the budget or personnel to pursue what it viewed as a relatively low priority enforcement and compliance problem.[21]

As titillating as the report may be, it suggests a conclusion other than those the reporters may have intended. The number of violations and the size of them are surprisingly small considering the millions of contributors; self-enforced compliance with the FECA would seem to be surprisingly high. And then there are the tantalizing and unanswered questions. If the limit is so widely observed, is there an accelerating number of individual contributors in the $15,000 range and above, and has the number of genuinely "big" contributors in that range been increasing? Moreover, do those nearing the $25,000 limit find other outlets for their political money? Are they, for instance, prime and useful targets in the raising of soft money?

The Citizen Action study again offers the fullest exploration of the concentration of individual giving. As a starting point, it identifies 311,288 individual contributions of more than $200 ("large" contributions) to a federal candidate, PAC, or party in 1989–90. By matching names and zip codes its authors reduce that number to 179,677 individuals accounting for those contributions. Since the large contributions of $200 or more account for 34 percent of those receipts from all sources, Citizen Action assumes that "34% of the money spent by federal candidates was directly contributed by no more than one tenth of one percent of the voting age population."[22] Moreover, Citizen Action's reductive calculations identify 8,579 individuals who made aggregate contributions of more than $5,000 to candidates, PACs, and parties in the 1989–90 cycle. The total largesse of the 8,579 was $95 million, a figure that accounts for 30 percent of the whole 34 percent, or about 10 percent of the total receipts. Citizen Action even pursues extended families: different members of the Gallo family of California presented 20 checks of $1,000 each to Senator Alan Cranston on April 13, 1989. The Gallos, "the largest family PAC in the country . . . contributed at least $294,100 during the cycle."[23]

The work of Citizen Action may overstate the degree of concentration in individual contributions. The reductive procedures it followed for matching names, forced on it by the paucity of reported information, probably overestimates concentration somewhat. It is, however, a pioneering work that offers tantalizing data and ingenious analysis. Even making allowances for overestimation, it argues a degree of concentration greater—far greater perhaps—than the conventionally wise had suspected. Whether the 1989–90 pattern is different from the one in, say, 1983–84 is unknown. It is the most tantalizing question of all, and it remains unanswered.

As for PACs, there is no limit on aggregate contributions in a year or a cycle—none comparable to the $25,000 per annum limit on individuals. The largest PACs can and do give millions in an election cycle to candidates for the Congress. The writers of the FECA amendments in 1974 worried largely about individual fat cats. With no aggregate limits to restrain them, PACs some time ago broke the million-dollar barrier, and in the 1990 campaign 21 different PACs gave a million dollars or more to candidates for the Congress. The Realtors Political Action Committee topped the list with total contributions of $3,094,228. There is concentration, but we have no evidence of a growing concentration of PAC money in the richest PACs. While the 50 largest PAC contributors in 1990 accounted for a total of $55.4 million, or 35 percent of all PAC contributions, the top 50 made 51 percent of PAC contributions in 1978 and 39 percent in 1980.

In a remarkably short time, therefore, the regime post-1974 has begun to show its age, or at least its maturity. Virtually from the very beginning, and well before the slowing down of growth in the sources of money, the campaign money markets began to transform themselves in ways that reflect both the dynamic of a regulatory system and the dominant realities of American politics. In the slow shift from direct individual to PAC contributions, one sees the onward march of political organization. The movement to a national marketplace, to money from other states, testifies to a centralization not unlike the nationalization of American life and culture. The greater power of big contributors suggests the concentration of resources and the declining role of the "little guy" that also marks so much of American life from the mergers and consolidations of American corporations to the decline of the local schoolhouse or regional airline. At the same time all three of these trends bespeak a fading of the hope for a campaign finance of small, local, grass-roots contributors. That hope fades just as hope for reestablishing local, grass-roots political parties also withers.

Stretching the Boundaries of the System

That there should be these four sources of money for congressional campaigns—individuals, PACs, parties, and the candidates themselves—is neither intrinsic to the business of campaigning nor inherent in the ways of American politics. The four of them are simply the creation of the 1974 amendments to the Federal Elections Campaign Act. So too are all the statutory limits to their affluence and generosity. However important and confining, or even wise, they may be, neither the sources of the money nor the limits on them are "natural" or inevitable. They result from congressional decisions.

In defining the system of 1974, Congress created one in harmony with contemporary American politics. It was to be candidate-centered: it dealt with money going to candidates, money spent by candidates, and money spent to support or oppose candidates (note the centrality of candidates in figure 2.1). With the major exception of individuals making contributions, all of the other contributors, recipients, and spenders of money in the campaign were compelled to report their transactions in painful detail to the Federal Election Commission. (FEC records of individual activity are of necessity gathered entirely from the reports of recipients.) Finally, Congress created a regulatory structure to reflect primarily the exchange of cash or of goods and services with assignable cash value. It was a decision reflecting the premise that cash and worldly goods are the most dangerous source of influence generated in the funding of campaigns.

In no sense, however, did the regulatory system of 1974 include all the actors and all the transactions in the funding of national campaigns. Significant sources and their mobilizers remain outside of the FECA. The reasons vary with the particular exclusion. For example, Congress exempted the work of volunteers in the campaign: the stuffing of envelopes for the mails, the putting up of signs, the door-to-door canvassing. Why? Perhaps because assigning a dollar value to such contributions would be difficult and reporting them even more difficult, but more likely because it wished to encourage grassroots participation. Although that exclusion has not yet become a source of contention, others have, as candidates and contributors push harder and harder at the constraints of the FECA on the availability of money.

Largely excluded from the post-1974 system are the increasingly important agents and brokers who facilitate, arrange, or organize the contribution of campaign money. Theirs is not a new role in the process, and it is certainly not insignificant. In the old days of party-controlled finance the brokers were the men of power who groomed and stroked the fat cats. Often they carried official party titles: a party chairman or treasurer, or a chairman of the party finance committee. Their race never really died, and its resurgence in the

1980s has made it a political issue once again. The FECA largely ignored them, unlike the four regulated sources, apparently because they are neither the originators of money nor its final spenders in the campaign. But if obligation to sources of money is the chief concern of the 1974 amendments to the FECA, the broker is no less a source than the contributor. The candidate will certainly be more grateful and indebted to the person who arranges for 100 contributors to stop by for drinks and leave $1,000 checks than to any one, two, or ten of the 100.

Charles Keating, head of a failed savings-and-loan empire and the most celebrated campaign contributor of the late 1980s, knew almost instinctively how to test the constraints of the FECA. A number of times he apparently brokered contributions of friends, family, employees, and associates for senators or their personal PACs. The totals arranged for five senators exceeded $500,000, most of it in the 1985–86 election cycle. It was not a new practice, and it was not illegal; it was only a celebrated case of an increasingly common practice. Keating's name was attached only to any contribution he made personally, and he stayed within the FECA limits on individual contributions. The out-of-state individual contributions are perhaps the most heavily brokered; candidates do not raise the money they do on the upper East side of Manhattan by writing letters or going door to door. A leading industrialist or environmentalist or feminist, or whoever, organizes the occasion, invites the "guests", provides the locale and refreshments, and discreetly suggests the size of the contribution.[24]

While such intermediaries or brokers are the plain, old-fashioned continuations of an old tradition, not quite so plain or old are the brokers who are "bundlers." Bundling goes one step beyond simple fund-raising; it involves taking the separate individual contributions and bundling them together, as it were, with the agent—the bundler—claiming credit for the harvest. The term is not well-defined, and the Charles Keatings may well bundle without being called bundlers. In any event, such words as "bundling" or "bundlers" have no statutory meaning. The popular meaning is clearer, though, if one introduces another distinction: the need to dodge contribution limits. When PACs or parties bundle, they usually do so for that additional purpose. If the PAC or party committee has reached its statutory limit on contributions to candidate Spendmore ($10,000 for primary and general elections together), it may collect the checks of individuals made out to Spendmore, bundle them, and forward them to the candidate, ostentatiously taking credit for mobilizing the individual contributions. The purpose of finding additional money is accomplished without additional sums being added to the PAC or party's total. The spending limit is not breached.

In defining the parameters of the 1974 system, moreover, Congress left out certain activities—and their costs—that bear on the success of campaigns. Chief among them were programs to register voters and get them to the polls to vote. The volunteer labor and contributed cash, goods, and services that support them flow outside of the FECA. In part that exclusion may have reflected another deference to the ethic of participatory democracy; more surely, it resulted from the deference of Democrats in Congress to what had long been a political specialty of organized labor. So long as PACs or groups kept the activities nominally nonpartisan, they were exempt from all the regulation of the FECA. But the Congress created a legal fiction here, for usually the very point was to register and "vote" groups of citizens in which overwhelming support for one party or another, one ideology or another, could be assumed.

For years the mobilization of voters, either in registration or on election day, was the province of organized labor. Labor spending on such programs is "off the books" for the reports filed with the FEC. Enter Charles Keating again, with Senator Alan Cranston, Democrat from California, in pursuit. The senator secured a contribution from Keating of some $850,000 for three tax-exempt voter registration projects, one of which was started by Cranston's son. The projects worked primarily among poor and minority populations, especially Hispanics.

Few members of Congress in 1974 can have anticipated the tie between a single incumbent and voter education foundations. But since the programs fit the exemption, they remain outside the limits of the FECA. Political learning has led to another unanticipated adaptation to the 1974 legislation.

A too-convenient term embraces all of these exceptions and opportunities on the peripheries of the regulatory system: *loopholes*. The word suggests a vulnerability in the regulatory structure which some artful, even unethical person exploits to avoid the broader goals and purposes of regulation. In campaign finance, however, the loopholes are often of Congress's specific devising. In at least one major instance, the exemption of independent spending from statutory limits, the loophole is the result of the Supreme Court's decision in *Buckley* v. *Valeo*. And in another major instance, that of "soft money," the loophole is the result, at least in part, of American federalism and the freedom of the states to regulate the financing of campaigns for their offices. So, in raising soft money, parties, PACs, and candidates raise money that would be in violation of federal law (the FECA) and channel it into states where it is legal; direct union or corporate contributions violate the FECA, but they do not violate the laws of many states. The same goes for individual contributions of $10,000 or $100,000. So, "Charles Keating could contribute about $235,000 to the soft money accounts of the leadership PAC of Senator John Glenn, Democrat from Ohio. Since those accounts were to be spent in the states, the limits of the FECA did not apply."[25]

Beyond the loopholes that Congress and the Supreme Court have fashioned, there is also the predictable ingenuity of the experienced professionals in working the boundaries of the system. A legion of lawyers, bureaucrats, accountants, and campaign specialists have quickly located the ripest opportunities within the 1974 regime, much as their counterparts find the soft spots in the income tax codes for the sophisticated investor or taxpayer. Similarly, newly powerful brokers or intermediaries become secondary sources of money; soft money can be raised by entities governed by the FECA without the money coming under FECA limits; and by shifting money from one set of FECA limits to another, bundling expands the pool of available funds. Even the exemption of registration and "get out the vote" drives from the apparatus of the FECA affords new opportunities for new money. New sources of new money to influence campaigns open along the edges of the regulatory regime but safely outside of its controls.

The first impulse in any assessment of the regulatory fabric is to put a price tag on the monies that escape its control. In one instance, independent spending, it is easy to do because reporting requirements for it remain even since limits on its sums fell in *Buckley*. Independent spending in 1990's congressional elections was about $8 million, a figure less than 2 percent of the direct spending by candidates and parties in the campaigns (see fig. 2.1). In the case of soft money, good estimates are available—$40 to $50 million in the 1988 presidential race—but these figures address the question of money raised, not spent, outside of the FECA. One can also make informed estimates of group attempts to register voters and get them to the polls.[26] But how then does one decide which of the total costs of the campaign to include? What of volunteer activity that the FECA exempts from reporting? What of candidates' forgone income? The hard truth is that arbitrary though they may be, the categories of the FECA and its reporting requirements set the only boundaries one can reasonably employ.

The Surface and Beneath

The pool of available campaign monies is relatively stable for now, but beneath the new stability is a stratum alive with change and instability. That the hidden life and activity might soon disturb the placidity of the surface is always possible.

One set of shifts and undercurrents involves the prime resource of the system itself. The sources of campaign money began to evolve early, and that evolution has progressed apace as the system has matured. Money has shifted from individual discretion to the organized control of PACs and party committees; the source of funds has increasingly been centralized and nationalized as a funding constituency develops quite different from the voting constituency; and the control of money is now more concentrated as fewer contributors control larger sums of money. Furthermore, pressures on the margins—on the regulatory barricades, so to speak—brought ways of raising money and places for finding it that increasingly threaten the system of 1974. Thus the institutionalizing of American campaign finance is surprisingly well advanced less than two decades into the regime of the FECA.

That a regulatory system grows, matures, even develops adaptive mechanisms so quickly and nimbly defies what we think we knew about regulatory processes. Is it possible that political learning proceeds faster than other kinds of social learning? Is it in the nature of politics, and in the nature of political experts, to nurture the skills of adaptation? Perhaps such skills reflect the special nature of national campaign finance in which the actors form a small, specialized, and inbred community and in which the regulated are often the regulators. Whatever the explanation, the sheer rate and extent of change in 15 years testifies to a prodigious amount of successful testing, experimenting, adapting, and innovating.

More unexpected and ultimately more threatening has been a second change: the end of growth in the sources and supply of campaign money. The decline in the number of individuals putting money into the system coupled with growth in the size of their contributions presages erosion in the mass, voluntary base of American campaign finance. Most troubling of all for the reformers of 1974, the nationalizing and concentrating trends have been most marked precisely among the contributors who were the hope of 1974: the individual contributors who gave directly to candidates.

The end to the spiraling amounts of money with which to finance long, wearisome, and expensive campaigns easily becomes a cause for celebration. Like everything about American campaign finance, explanation and justification are not easy to separate. To be sure, the shrinkage in the base of contributors may be an inevitable and necessary part of bringing the growth of the first years of the FECA under control. And a natural slowing down of growth, even at the price of consolidation and concentration, is very probably preferable to an abrupt and arbitrary legislated halt. The slowing down, however, is not without its own consequences, for not all candidate receipts slow down, or slow down at the same pace. Stabilization in the money supply may simply reflect a declining competition for seats in the House and Senate; a drying up of the competitiveness in congressional elections, in other words, may be driving some contributors out of electoral politics and especially out of support for like-minded challengers. Challengers lose, and incumbent candidates do not. The contraction of campaign money, therefore, reflects but reinforces and exacerbates the decline of electoral competitiveness.

Taken as a whole, these changes in the supply of campaign money begin to suggest the status quo ante. The return of the brokers and skillful brokering, the increasing concentration of resources, the declining base of voluntarism—even the cracks in the regulatory structure—all point, distressingly, to the era that culminated in the 1968 and 1972 Nixon campaigns. It is, of course, far too early to proclaim the return of the old regime or a restored reign of the fat cats, but it now seems less remote than it did a decade ago. Moreover, the resonances of the past challenge the ideal that animated the reforms of 1974: a voluntary, citizenly, voter-as-contributor model of campaign finance. It was and is an ideal very close to the American ideal of grass-roots, participatory democracy. Challenges to it threaten far more than a system of campaign finance.

Chapter 3 _____
_____
_____

_____

The Grand Exchange

The belief that purposeful contributors dominate the American campaign finance system is virtually universal. The contributors are seen as the initiators in the exchange of money, even the aggressors, and when violations of law or ethical norms occur, they are the violators. Candidates, by contrast, appear to be passive and dependent, always more sinned against than sinning. It is an assumption that shapes the American view of campaign finance and underlies our explanations of it, however implicit the assumption may be.

No words better capture this governing assumption than the cliché about "the best Congress money can buy."[1] It describes a buyer's market and suggests a compliant, relatively powerless seller. If, however, one abandons the assumption of a unilateral relationship, one begins to challenge much of the conventional wisdom about American campaign finance and to work toward a clearer-eyed analysis of what goes on in it. One also begins at last to give the candidates, especially the incumbent candidates, their proper place in the exchanges of campaign finance.

Since these exchanges all deal at bottom with the winning of elections, the bargains struck in

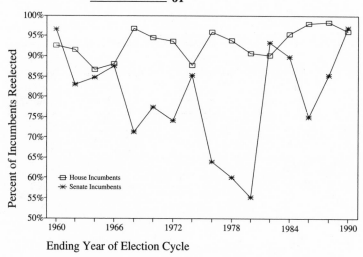

Figure 3.1
Reelection Rates of House and Senate Incumbents: 1960–1990

them are all affected by the candidates' chances of winning those elections—by their competitiveness, that is. In the regime post-1974 that question of competitiveness hinges increasingly on the success incumbents have in winning reelection (fig. 3.1). House incumbents have been virtually invincible since the 1960s. From 1974 through 1990 the percentage of incumbents winning reelection never dropped below the 87.7 figure of 1974; in all subsequent elections their reelection rate topped 90 percent, and it hit a record 98.3 percent in 1988. In the nine Senate elections from 1974 through 1990 incumbent reelection rates varied from a high of 96.9 percent in 1990 to a low of 55.2 percent in 1980, with the median at 85.2, the percentage in both 1974 and 1978.[2]

For what it adds to even such persistent security, the incumbents' growing share of the two-party vote is even more telling. Incumbent candidates for the House won reelection with more than 60 percent of the vote in 73 percent of the 1980 races and 69 percent of the 1982 races; by 1990, 78 percent enjoyed that comfortable margin. Senate incumbents

Table 3.1

Turnover in House Membership: 1974–1990

Year	Number of Open Seats	Incumbents Defeated (Including in Primaries)	Number of Incumbents Reelected	Percentage of House Reelected
1974	44	48	343	78.9
1976	51	16	368	84.6
1978	53	24	358	82.3
1980	37	37	361	83.0
1982	42	39	354	81.4
1984	26	19	390	90.1
1986	42	9	385	88.5
1988	26	7	402	92.4
1990	28	15	392	90.1

Sources: 1974–1988: David C. Huckabee, *Reelection Rates of House Incumbents: 1790–1988* (Washington, D.C.: Congressional Research Service of the Library of Congress, 1989). 1990: *Congressional Quarterly Weekly Report*, November 10, 1990.

won reelection with at least 60 percent of the vote in 41.4 percent of the Senate races from 1974 through 1978, 54.1 percent from 1980 through 1984, and 51.5 percent from 1986 through 1990.[3] The odds against which the challengers battle, in other words, are even worse than the incumbent reelection rates might suggest.

Competitive opportunities do exist in the open seats—those seats for which no incumbent is running. (It says something that we categorize elections and candidates in them by the presence or absence of an incumbent.) Their numbers vary more than one might expect (table 3.1), reflecting incumbents' considerations of health, age, fatigue, and ambition as well as short-term political realities that would force them into difficult reelection races. For a comprehensive measure of competitiveness in a House election, then, the percentage of the House members reelected serves best (table 3.1). It takes into account both the number of open seats and the number of incumbents defeated. No comparable figure exists for the Senate since the entire chamber is not reelected in any one year. In the House, at least, the would-be member knows that the membership now turns over at a very steady and stately rate of 10 percent.

The Alternative of Bilateralism

Belief in the unilateral flow of "pressure" or influence is not limited to campaign finance. It flourishes especially in much of American writing about interest groups and lobbying, which overlooks the purposive, even aggressive behavior of public officials on behalf of their own interests in these dealings. Entrenched as the belief may be, it has had its important critics:

> Nor do we find a linear causal relationship analogous to fluid mechanics—"the pressure is applied here and the results come out there"—as an accurate description of the influence of the public on Congressional decisions. . . . We must stress the transactional nature of the relationship between the congressman and the constituent. Each acts upon the other, and much that appears from a simplistic view to be pressure on the congressman is actually a result of the congressman's actions on the constituency.[4]

Popular and scholarly opinion, however, have not been shaken. Perhaps it is our obsession with money as the dominant source of influence that lies behind the belief in the unilateral relationship. Perhaps it is all of those diagrams of the political system in which the arrows of influence and cause move so relentlessly from individuals to political parties or interest groups and then to governmental institutions and public officials.

Withal, the basic transaction in American campaign finance is a reciprocal, bilateral exchange. It is not only a transferring of goods or services for something of equal value. It is also a mutual relationship in which the actions, goals, and strategies of one participant interact with those of the other. The sum of all the exchanges creates a market in which the exchanges take place, a market that defines alternative options, a range of "prices," and the viable and negotiable terms of individual exchanges.[5]

For exploring these exchanges as efficiently as possible, the one between PACs and incumbent candidates serves best.[6] It is the best known, most commented upon, and most fully documented of the exchanges in American campaign finance. The discussion and data will be limited to campaigns for the House of Representatives. For any kind of analysis, and especially for one across time, the House offers two advantages over the Senate: House districts have approximately the same population, and all House seats are contested in every two-year election cycle.

The goals and strategies behind the PAC contributions are there for the deducing and intuiting, and a substantial and sophisticated scholarship has described them.[7] Although different scholars have developed different categories, the PAC strategies they describe fall into three main groups. There are, first, the pragmatic or legislative strategies, those aimed at maintaining or expanding access to members of the Congress. Then there are the ideological or partisan strategies that reward candidates for their issue positions, their voting records, or their loyalty to a right-thinking political party. And PACs contribute to candidates for organizational reasons peculiar to themselves—to respond to donor preferences, to support local candidates, or to build donor confidence in them by backing winners, for example.

Not unexpectedly, most of these explications of PAC strategies rest on the assumption of a unilateral relationship between PACs and candidates. Nowhere do the candidates, in the pursuit of their own goals and strategies, seem to limit or alter those of the PACs. Never do they shape or even dominate PAC strategies, and never do we entertain the possibility that PAC spending may be determined not by PAC strategy, but by *candidate* strategy or strength in the exchange. We rarely even consider the most likely outcome of bilateral exchanges: that a PAC will be forced into abandoning pure strategies in favor of a mixed or diversified political strategy in making its contributions, at least in part because of the accommodations it must make to incumbents in a bilateral exchange.

For their part, individual incumbents pursue primarily the goal of reelection while seeking also to advance their ongoing political careers. The campaign at hand offers an opportunity to increase name recognition, to augment electoral margins, to assemble vast campaign resources for later races, even to prove a sheer capacity for raising money if for no other reason than to frighten potential challengers away. Some raise money to support a personal organization back in the district, to finance picnics and other festivities for their workers—to do many of the things the parties used to do. Maximizing the sums of money they raise and maximizing the number of votes they get in the election, therefore, are ends in themselves and means to other important ends, both for the current election and for elections to come. In the exchanges with contributors, their interests also require raising the money with as few accompanying demands and as little unfavorable publicity as possible. Laying out such candidate strategies and tactics, however, honors unilateralism by paying no attention to the concessions incumbents may have to make to contributors.

So, there are two separate sets of goals and strategies in the exchange, but the twain seem never to meet. Until we identify PAC or candidate strategies independently of the data of contributions given and received, it seems useful to look simply at the financial exchanges themselves. A PAC may have had one of a number of reasons for giving $2,000 to an incumbent candidate—agreement with the candidate's voting record, approval of the candidate's political party, a desire to get the ear of the chairperson of an important subcommittee. Until we can locate that reason by means other than inferring it from the fact of the contribution, the important point is that the exchange was made, for in the last analysis all PAC strategies come down to the single goal of affecting the outcomes of public policy in one way or another, and all incumbent strategies come down to the ultimate goal of protecting and promoting their political careers.

The Market of Campaign Finance

Since its origin in 1974 the market in PAC-candidate exchanges has developed quickly and dramatically, transforming the fortunes of both PACs and incumbents. During the four election cycles of 1976, 1978, 1980, and 1982 the number of PACs registered with the Federal Election Commission rose from 1,146 to 3,371, an increase of 194 percent. Growth then began to cool, and from the end of 1984 to the end of 1990 the number of PACs increased from 4,009 to just 4,172 (see fig. 1.2). The curve of PAC contributions to congressional candidates has similar contours: enormous growth followed by a tapering off and then a stalling. The growth of just 14 percent between 1986 and 1990 in their contributions to candidates, from $139.8 million to $159.3 million, was only a bit more than the rate of inflation, and the increase of less than a million dollars between 1988 and 1990 was well below it.

In short, we have reached, at least for now, an end to the explosive growth in PACs and PAC spending that marked the late 1970s and early 1980s. Obviously, organizations without PACs, as well as entrepreneurs who might set up PACs without organizational parents, find costs too great for the likely political benefits. The incentives to set up a PAC, for example, appear to be smaller for corporations with interests not threatened by the impact of federal regulation, such as those in the construction or retail industries.[8] Moreover, the persistent criticism of PACs has boosted the organizational costs and public-relations burden of establishing a PAC. Neither of these explanations, however, considers the rising power of the incumbent candidates in exchanges between PACs and incumbents. Greater incumbent power in them can mean only an aggregate decline in the political power of PACs. That decline

Table 3.2
Campaign Finance of House Major-Party General-Election
Incumbents and Challengers: 1978–1990

Year	Mean Spending of Incumbents	Mean Spending of Challengers	Incumbent-to-Challenger Spending Ratio	Mean Beginning Cash-on-Hand of Incumbents
1978	$111,247	$ 75,015	1.5:1	$ 13,142
1980	$164,453	$ 99,633	1.7:1	$ 19,384
1982	$263,434	$128,409	2.1:1	$ 31,542
1984	$280,241	$126,738	2.2:1	$ 45,137
1986	$336,315	$124,950	2.7:1	$ 77,629
1988	$381,878	$119,984	3.2:1	$107,222
1990	$399,309	$109,377	3.7:1	$142,813

Source: Federal Election Commission.

in turn has inevitably affected the cost-benefit analyses of prospective PAC founders.

By the middle and late 1980s precisely those signs of incumbent power were everywhere (table 3.2). Incumbents began electoral cycles with increasing sums of cash on hand—more than five times as much for the average incumbent candidate in 1988 over 1980. The increasingly impoverished challengers begin with very little cash on hand; the average for major party challengers in 1988 was a paltry $167. In average spending, moreover, House incumbents moved from a 1.5:1 ratio to one 3.7:1 over their challengers in the years from 1978 to 1990. The ratio of median candidate spending moved from 3.9:1 in 1980 to 12.3:1 in 1988.

In large part the incumbents' new power in fund-raising results from their increasing certainty of reelection (see fig. 3.1). As the electoral prospects of challengers slowly diminished, PAC money deserted them for the certain-to-win incumbents. Incumbents got 60 percent of PAC money going to House candidates in 1980 and an intimidating 81 percent by

1990. The shift to funding incumbents was "forced" on PACs when it became increasingly difficult for them to influence policy by affecting the outcomes of House elections. In the language of strategies and tactics, PACs abandoned an electoral strategy or electoral tactics for those of legislative access. Whatever the words, the success of incumbents in bolstering their electoral positions encouraged PACs to support them increasingly at the expense of their challengers.

As they became more secure in office, House incumbents became more aggressive in their fund-raising. PAC managers object more and more vocally to their importunings; they use such words as "extortion" and "arm-twisting," and they increasingly complain that fund-raising is an every-day, every-year activity. In the words of one PAC official, "In many of the cases [members of Congress] form committees, have a little breakfast, 'I love you all, appreciate your help.' So you have to go back and make six or ten phone calls to get people to come to this event. It's tiresome, worrisome, difficult, when you're twisted by someone you don't want to give to. It gets worse year by year."[9] Incumbents, that is, learned with a vengeance that their role in the financial exchange need not be passive. They honed their fund-raising skills, hired professional fund-raisers, and seized the initiatives in the exchange. In the absence of other credible competitors for the contributions of PACs, they became oligopolists in the market, able to extract higher prices than they had in a more competitive market. Such were the advantages of being virtually the only game in town.

In short, the position of the PAC movement in congressional elections is vastly different in the 1990s from what it was only 10 or 15 years earlier. Many of the newly formed PACs of the 1970s entered politics believing that they could affect the outcomes of elections. They may well have had the post-Watergate election of 1974 in mind. In that year, only 79 percent of the House members were reelected, the lowest percentage in the entire 1960–90 period. Forty-eight incumbents went down to defeat in either the primary or the general election, and there were 44 open seats; so ripe were the times for change after the fall of Richard Nixon that the average Democratic challenger outspent the average Democratic incumbent.[10] Even the resurgence of the incumbents in 1976 and 1978 did not immediately discourage PACs; almost 19 percent of their contributions to House candidates went to challengers in both 1978 and 1980. Some scholars even predicted that the larger PACs would move increasingly to expand their electoral strategies, beginning to compete more fully with the parties in registering and mobilizing voters.[11]

That prospect soon ended, the victim of greater PAC realism born of greater PAC experience. Early expectations and early enthusiasm faded as the toll of PAC-supported challengers mounted; the difficulty of affecting public policy by electing like-minded candidates slowly bore in on PAC management. The alternative seemed to promise greater benefits. A PAC's support for incumbent candidates would ratify the electoral fait accompli and supplement the lobbying of its parent organization. Its campaign contributions would buy, in the pursuit of legislative access, a more certain service and perhaps even a more valuable one. Constrained to abandon their commitment to winning elections with sympathetic candidates, PACs had little need or incentive to develop into party-like organizations.

In even so brief a history it is clear that although PAC-incumbent exchanges are bilateral, they need not be symmetrical or even stable in their asymmetry. Bolder PACs, more aggressive in their pursuit of electoral strategies, held their own and perhaps even dominated the market briefly in the late 1970s, but incumbents increasingly came to dominate it through the 1980s. Eismeier and Pollock spotted the change early in the 1980s: "The tail may be wagging the dog: The motives and strategies of incumbents, not PACs, appear influential in determining what political action committees do with much of their money."[12] Indeed, the loss of primacy in their exchanges with incumbents has been one reason for the early end to the growth of PACs. Gone now is the optimism of the early days of runaway growth and a heady reputation as the new prodigies of American politics. In its place is the realism and pragmatism of the old legislative politics.

The Incumbent-Led Exchange

Both PACs and incumbents quickly learned the lessons of the new campaign finance. It is not that incumbent reelection rates rose so sharply in the 1970s and 1980s—they did not—but that PACs came to understand those rates and the risks they posed for them. By increasing their support for incumbents they minimized their costs in the exchange: incumbent displeasure for nonsupport and parent-donor displeasure with supporting losers. For their part, incumbents discovered their political muscle and through it their ability to control the sums they raised, the timing of contributions, and the profile of their contributors. While fund-raising might still be an uncongenial task for many of them, its burdens were more easily tolerated with money that came in large sums, that came early enough to reduce the uncertainties in planning a campaign, and that came generously enough to guard against worst-case reelection scenarios.

Where then do the exchanges between House incumbents and PACs stand in the 1990s? Not only do incumbents enjoy increasing PAC support at a time of a stable supply of PAC money, but their PAC receipts account for an increasing portion of their total receipts (table 3.3). The money from PACs accounted for 34 percent of incumbent receipts in 1980 but 48.2 percent in 1990; all House incumbents received $24.6 million from PACs in 1980 and $87.4 million in 1990. The less fortunate challengers took in $7.4 million from PACs in 1980 but only $7.0 million in 1990, a decline from 20 percent of their receipts to 18.7 percent.

Support for incumbents does not, of course, equal support for all incumbents. Access to some members is more valuable than access to others, beginning with the fact of membership in the majority or minority party. The Democrats have con-

The Grand Exchange

Table 3.3

Receipts of House Major-Party General-Election Candidates by
Relative Share from Source

	Receipts from				Total Receipts (Millions)
	Individuals	PACs	Candidates	Parties	
Incumbents:					
1980	n/a	34.0%	n/a	2.4%	$ 72.1
1986	47.5%	44.1%	1.3%	0.9%	$149.3
1990	42.9%	48.2%	1.2%	0.4%	$181.3
Challengers:					
1980	n/a	20.0%	n/a	4.6%	$ 36.8
1986	54.4%	21.1%	18.5%	3.1%	$ 41.4
1990	53.0%	18.7%	22.5%	2.5%	$ 37.6
Open Seats:					
1980	n/a	25.7%	n/a	3.6%	$ 15.4
1986	52.5%	28.5%	13.4%	2.1%	$ 37.6
1990	47.9%	31.7%	15.4%	4.4%	$ 29.9

The percentages do not add to 100 percent because candidates get
revenue from sources other than contributions; by far the most
important of these is the interest they earn on cash invested.
Source: Federal Election Commission.

trolled the House as the majority party ever since 1955, and
even optimistic Republicans concede Democratic control into
the near future. If PACs truly have committed themselves to
seeking legislative access, they should be more generous with
the more powerful incumbents of the majority party. And so
it is: in the 1990 cycle Democratic incumbents received $58.6
million, or 52.6 percent of their aggregate receipts, from PACs.
Republicans netted $28.8 million for 41.1 percent of their total
receipts.

The flow of money from PAC to candidate must be reported
to the FEC and, therefore, to the world, but the flow of access

that PACs say they seek in return is far harder to measure. One approach to the question does establish that the time members of Congress spend with groups is related to each group's campaign contributions. Note, however, that the conclusion speaks to the group rather than its PAC; PAC contributions are related to time spent, apparently, if the PAC's parent group has Washington representation. As an empirical finding it squares with PAC decisions in the 1980s to support the lobbying and representation of their parent groups.[13]

We know nothing about the quality of the access. Is it possible that incumbents actually behave like classic oligopolists and reduce the value of the service they offer the contributing PAC? As incumbents improve their leverage in the exchange, especially as the more senior ones entrench themselves in office, do they yield to the temptation to cheapen the quality of the access? If so, do the incumbents reduce the value by minimizing access or, more likely, by extending the supply of it and thus making it less exclusive? The cost of providing access is low, perhaps limited only by the size and energy of the member's staff and, to a lesser extent, the time and energy of the member. Influence, the ability to affect the shape or direction of public policy, is much more finite. The costs of offering it are also greater for the incumbent; it pits the wishes of the campaign-funding constituency against all of the other demands on the member's vote, with all the conflicts and disappointments such a conflict inevitably entails. Far easier, then, to offer the PAC a "generic" access which is cheaper, less threatening, and in greater supply. The result, as Robert Salisbury has observed, is that interest groups are "virtually awash in access but often subordinate in influence."[14] Unequal footing in the bargaining produces predictably unequal terms in the exchange.[15]

Success in arranging the exchange with PACs does not mean it will be painless for incumbents. In fact they complain almost ostentatiously about the time and energy they spend in raising money and about the demeaning unpleasantness of it. The various complaints are not hard to catalog. Fund-raising takes the incumbents from home, family, and private life; it robs them of time for legislative duties, with inevitable consequences for the ability of the House and Senate to function as deliberative legislative bodies. If it must be done during the campaign, it diverts the candidate's energies and concentration from the campaign itself. Consider, for example, the task of the freshman member of the House from a competitive district. Within two years he or she must raise some $500,000 for the next campaign, or a total of $5,000 a week, allowing two weeks for vacation each year.

The complaints of incumbents, no matter how deeply felt, do not occasion much sympathy in the American public. Like most other ex parte complaints, these mix self-interest with commentary on reality. Even though we have achieved superiority in the exchange, the incumbents seem to be saying, fund-raising is a dirty and compromising business, and we are among its major victims. Having raised more and more money with which to dominate their challengers and reduce the competitiveness of congressional elections, the incumbents plead for sympathy. It is a plea no more likely to succeed than that of the millionaire athletes and rock stars who lament their loss of privacy while enriching themselves on the proceeds of publicity. Most Americans freely concede that one pays a price for success.

The question of fund-raising effort, however, raises a serious issue about the exchange itself. The complaints from members of Congress suggest that they spend more and more time raising money, and a good many observers support their claim. But House incumbents raised only 8.6 percent more money in 1990 over 1988, $111.35 million against $102.53 million, and they are also raising it in larger sums than ever. Are members now working harder to raise a unit of $100 or $1,000? If so, it is another kernel of evidence that the supply of money is not so plentiful as it once was or, alternatively, that contributors grow more unwilling to contribute. However one frames the problem, money may indeed be harder for incumbents to come by, with all the implications such a change has for the incumbent-PAC exchanges. The specter again is one of increasing scarcity and the transformations it will work.

All of this is not to suggest that PAC managers are craven and submissive before the power of the House incumbents. Many PACs do preserve options and maneuverability for themselves. At the pole of greatest freedom are the labor PACs, committed as always to supporting candidates loyal to their liberal-labor ideology; their special case gets attention in the next chapter. Business and corporate PACs with more general goals of support for a pro-business or conservative philosophy may also resist complete pragmatism, especially if their specific interest is less subject to threats of congressional action.

More frequent by far—and the most common form of PAC mixed strategy—is the making of ideological or partisan distinctions among incumbents. Agricultural PACs collectively gave only 5 percent of their money to House and Senate challengers in 1988, but they differed sharply in their support of Democrats and Republicans. More than 64 percent of the money from dairy production PACs went to Democrats, wereas only 29 percent of the funds from forest products PACs did. Dairy farmers come from more Democratic parts of the country than do wood and lumber companies. Even more important, policy issues cut along party lines for them, Democrats tending to favor both the price support programs dear to dairy farmers and the environmental concerns so troubling to much of commercial forestry. Similarly, PACs representing interests in energy and natural resources gave only 7 percent of their money to challengers. But again, specific interests broke very differently between the two parties. PACs of the natural-gas distributing industry gave 59 percent of their funds to Democrats, but the PACs of oil and gas producers and marketers gave them only 31 percent.[16]

As interesting as those attempts by PACs to adjust to incumbent power are the adjustments not made. PACs might have begun to give larger sums to fewer candidates as a way of increasing their bargaining power. By and large they have not done so. The average PAC contribution to a House incumbent was $554 in 1978 and $1,131 in 1988, an increase of 104 percent. Keep in mind, however, that the total sum of PAC money going to House incumbents increased from $14.7 million in 1978 to $82.2 million in 1988, an increase of 459 percent. Even leaving inflation aside, the size of the average contribution in no way kept pace with the rising sums. In part the PAC reluctance to concentrate funds reflects a fear of publicity and notoriety, a concern about the conclusions some local reporter will draw. If the PAC has a parent organization, the parent's lobbyist will pressure for a policy of widely dispersed contributions, just enough to open as many House and Senate office doors as possible. Large contributions also create organizational problems for a PAC: difficult decisions about which incumbents to shower with the concentrated riches, more donor unhappiness over favorite candidates rejected, more anxiety on the part of the Washington representative over incumbents angered and access restricted or denied. Attention to all of these interests and concerns leads most PACs to disperse their funds widely. At the same time, incumbents may well prefer the smaller sums; they are innocuous and even invisible, and they make lesser claims on the recipient. If incumbents can lure PAC money from many sources to their campaign treasuries, they may even try to develop a diversified "portfolio" of contributors.

In contrast to their exchanges with 4,000 PACs, incumbents collectively deal with millions of individual contributors. The transaction is perforce much more impersonal and distant, the terms of the exchange much more implicit. Moreover, the expectations of the contributing individuals are unquestionably more varied, running the gamut of possible expectations from access for a personal interest or enthusiasm to the pleasure or gratitude of an old acquaintance. And yet the movement of individuals' money has developed PAC-like characteristics. While individual contributions account for a gradually diminishing part of incumbent resources, they have drifted away from challengers and to incumbents over the 1980s, although more gradually than PAC funds. Of all the

PAC money going to House major-party candidates in the 1984 general elections, 78 percent went to incumbents; by 1990 the incumbent share had risen to 84 percent. The share of individual contributions going to incumbents rose between 1984 and 1990 from 63 to 69 percent.[17]

Challengers, therefore, do better with individual contributors than they do with PACs. In 1990 the House challengers got 18 percent of all the money individuals gave major-party candidates for the House in the general election; they received only 7 percent of comparable PAC money. Thus a two-sided question: why so much individual money to incumbents, and why not more? Why do individuals contribute like PACs and yet shrink from contributing as overwhelmingly as PACs?

Probably the largest number of individuals, the ones whose contributions are mimicking the access strategy of PACs, give to incumbents simply because they know or know of them. They respond, as they often do with their votes, to the incumbent's name and face, to the incumbent's mailings and appearances in the media, to the incumbent's professionalism and persistence in fund-raising. And if they are constituents, as many small individual contributors are, they may be grateful, too, for the incumbent's attention to their problems and requests. Moreover, the individuals organized by brokers and intermediaries—many of them disposed to make large contributions to candidates from distant places—behave like PACs because they are PAC-like. Theirs is organized giving on behalf of some uniting interest or interests like Charles Keating's concern for the well-being of the savings-and-loan industry (see chapter 2).

Whence, then, comes the individuals' money for the challengers? It is money taking electoral risks, supporting a challenger because rightness is more important than competitiveness. One thinks of the extensive national fund-raising by all manner of interests, the arts community and gay groups most visibly, to support Harvey Gantt's race against Senator Jesse Helms in 1990. Individual contributors have far less at stake politically to inhibit risk-taking—no Washington lobbying effort to support, no organizational interests to protect, often no constraining structure of political priorities. Nonpolitical considerations are also freer to affect their contribution decisions. Most intriguing of all is the possibility that some of the organized and brokered individuals representing those well-articulated interests are in fact hedging the bets of those interests. While their PACs may be pursuing the less risky route by supporting incumbents, can they individually be putting money into old-fashioned ideological and electoral politics?

Challengers and Open-Seat Candidates

The exchanges between challengers and their contributors are the obverse of those of the affluent incumbents. Challengers are the losers in the zero-sum game that brings resources into incumbent-challenger races. Winning far fewer than 10 percent of their House races in recent years, they are the candidates whom waning competitiveness left behind. By 1990 they were getting only about 10 percent of all PAC contributions to House and Senate candidates and 23 percent of the money given directly by individuals. Consequently their campaigns depend heavily on loans and investment by the candidates themselves, always the campaign finance of last resort and an "exchange" in a class by itself. Simply put, challengers do not raise very much money. Even the major-party challengers for a House seat who made it to the 1990 general election raised only $111,131 on the average, an average that includes what they gave or lent themselves from personal funds.

In the past challengers could be optimistic when short-term political forces threatened incumbents, especially those from marginal seats. With the country in a significant recession and a Republican in the White House in 1982, Democrats and their sympathizers saw an opportunity to win House seats in the November elections. The opportunities were underscored by the large number of insecure Republican incumbents, insecure both because they had won in normally Democratic districts in the Reagan landslide of 1980 and because they had had so few months to exploit the advantages of incumbency. Both the National Republican Campaign Committee and business PACs rushed to shore up Republican incumbents; corporate PACs, which had given 47 percent of their incumbent-bound contributions to Republicans in 1980, raised that to 58 percent in 1982. Even though the Democrats failed to recruit and fund a first-rate cohort of challengers, they defeated 22 Republican incumbents in the House. (In the four elections of 1984 through 1990 Democratic challengers beat Republican incumbents only a *total* of 20 times.) As House incumbents increasingly protect themselves from political events and trends outside of their districts, challengers may well wonder if 1982 will ever happen again. In campaign finance the question is whether challengers will ever be able to woo contributors on the argument that national political trends materially enhance their chances of winning.[18]

With meager prospects of victory and often little visibility or name recognition, what can challengers offer in the contributor-candidate exchange? They may get party money for reasons having to do with the goals of the party; it is important for the party not to forfeit an office by default, if only to maximize voter appeal for the whole ticket of party candidates. Alternatively, the party may be investing in a promising new candidate, increasing his or her name recognition and experience for later assaults against the House incumbent. The chief asset the challenger may bring to the exchange with party committees, then, may be a position on the general-election ballot under the party's label. It is a curious but substantial asset, for it ties the fortunes of the party to those of the challenger.

Challengers are in even weaker positions with PACs and individual contributors. Some of them contribute out of misguided optimism or a false assessment of the challenger's chances of winning. More, however, contribute out of personal friendship or group loyalty: lawyers for a lawyer, teachers for a teacher, Irish Americans for an Irish American. Labor PACs contribute to Democratic challengers to publicize their issues, to give their interests a voice; while winning may be the major electoral goal, under unfavorable political conditions especially, it may not be the only one. For the politically motivated contributor the challenger may at best offer a modestly effective sacrificial victim, one likely to go down to defeat while chipping away at the support of the incumbent and waving the banner of truth and virtue. For the purposes of raising money, however, it is not a strong—and certainly not an enviable—position to be in.

The plight of the challengers is perhaps best illustrated by the maxim that challengers do not win elections as much as incumbents lose them. In 1988 six challengers beat House incumbents in the general election, and five beat incumbents seriously or mortally wounded by their own ethical-legal problems. The chairman of the House Banking Committee, Fernand St Germain, Democrat from Rhode Island, lost after a campaign focused on the finding by the House Committee on Standards of Official Conduct that he had violated laws and House rules on financial disclosure. Democrat Bill Chappell, Jr., of Florida, chair of the Subcommittee on Defense of the House Appropriations Committee, was linked to a Pentagon procurement scandal. Republican Pat Swindell of Georgia was under indictment for allegedly lying to a grand jury about an illegal money-laundering operation. Fellow Republicans Jack Davis of Illinois and Joseph DioGuardi of New York were hobbled by charges, respectively, of ties to local corruption and of impropriety in campaign fund-raising.[19] Contributors to the campaigns of their five victorious challengers read the signs of incumbent vulnerability clearly and in a timely way. The five winners raised an average of $474,855 for the 1988 campaign against the average of $111,131 for all major-party House challengers.

Offering little hope of victory for potential contributors, challengers fall hopelessly behind incumbents and open-seat candidates in the race for money. They are classic victims of a downward spiral of electoral expectations, casualties of the three-way interaction of money, chances of winning, and quality of candidate. Without a reasonable chance of winning, high-quality candidates do not appear; the quality of challengers, one study finds, depends more on the past partisan history of the district than on anything else.[20] And with neither a good chance of winning nor a promising candidate, contributors do not come forward. How then to break the three-way dynamic of despair? If a party could raise money early, both to recruit a quality candidate and to turn around the political history of the district, money might come. The early "seed" money would testify that "others" saw a chance of victory, and it would also bring professional campaign management and fund-raising. Money and candidate would beget optimism, which begets more money and, ultimately, a thriving campaign and a visible candidate, which in turn make it easier to raise more money. But increasingly there is no party or other agent to make the original investment, perhaps because the odds in the battle against the incumbent and past vote margins look so hopeless. In the long run, contributors can be wooed only by a sharp improvement in the challenger's chances of winning. It is the only fuel the upward dynamic burns.

The open-seat races, by contrast, are the great competitive scramble, the one field of genuine opportunity for both candidates and contributors in House election politics. And a scramble it is—four out of five candidates for open-seats who file reports with the FEC never reach the general election, most of them having failed in the primary. The sums of money spent in open-seat campaigns testify to their competitiveness. In 1989–1990 the major party general election candidates in House open-seat elections spent an average of $483,729; the average House incumbent in that cycle spent a good deal less: $399,309.[21] That relationship, furthermore, was constant through the 1980s; incumbents spent $164,453 on the average in 1980, major party open-seat candidates $208,198. So, the stakes are high in open-seat elections, and understandably so.

Approximately two-thirds of all House members in the 1980s entered the Congress by winning an open-seat election.

Of all campaigns, those for open seats most nearly approach the textbook model of competitiveness. Absent an incumbent, the two major-party candidates more closely approach financial equality than does the usual incumbent-challenger pair. While the incumbent-challenger funding ratio was on the average 3.7:1 in 1990, in 14 of the 29 open-seat campaigns in the 1990 cycle the two candidates were within a 2:1 ratio. Without incumbents, open-seat elections are also more vulnerable to national political currents, more responsive to party voting, more reflective of the events of the campaign—more sensitive, that is, to all the influences that incumbency tends to suppress. In short, they provide the electoral opportunities that encourage contributors to pursue their goals in and through the election contest itself.

Republicans especially have felt the attraction of the open-seat opportunities, disadvantaged as they are by the power of entrenched Democratic incumbents and the futility of their own challengers. In fact, their open-seat candidates outspent Democrats throughout the 1980s; Republicans in the 1988 general election outspent Democrats by an average of $484,684 to $446,959. Yet Democrats outspent their Republican opponents in 1990 by an average of $520,296 to $443,377, even though more Democrats had opponents who spent no funds.[22] It is not easy to say why, especially since 17 of the 27 seats open in 1990 had been most recently held by a Republican. One election does not a trend make, but for the moment it is one more straw in the wind that suggests increasing Republican problems in funding challengers and open-seat candidates—and thus in escaping permanent minority status in the House.[23] In an era of divided government combined with decreasing electoral competitiveness, futility is bearing in on Republicans in the House as surely as it is on Democrats contesting for the presidency.

Even though there is no incumbent House member running in the open-seat race, there is nonetheless a silent or proxy incumbent: the dominant political party of the district. Contributors easily assess the "normal" two-party vote in the district against which they can gauge the impacts of the two candidates, their campaigns, and short-run political trends. In fact, it is the presence of party disposition in the district of an open seat that most often distances it from the classic model of competitiveness. However, a party as a proxy incumbent is not as powerful as a real, flesh-and-blood incumbent. In 1986 only 35 percent of open-seat winners won with 60 percent or more of the vote; only 39 percent won so comfortably in 1988. Those percentages are less than half the comparable figures for incumbent victors in the same years. Moreover, in the 1980s party control of a congressional district changed hands in 25 percent (43 of 173 cases) of the open-seat elections.

There is of course one partial exception to the silent incumbency of party: the election after post-census redistricting has upset and recast old district lines. And 1992 is such an election year. The wiliest of political operatives may analyze the new districts ward by ward or precinct by precinct for old party trends, but most contributors will start their figuring with a much lower level of information and a much higher level of uncertainty. Furthermore, redistricting by itself creates uncertainty by creating open seats; a state's gain of House seats creates them automatically, and any state's redistricting necessitates them if incumbents must be forced to run against each other either in order to construct districts with equal populations or to absorb the loss of a seat.

So, speculation is rife that 1992 may be a year of tremendous open-seat opportunity. The census count of 1990 has given eight states a total of 19 additional seats in the House;[24] redistricting will also create a few more open seats by throwing two incumbents into the same district. In addition, the number of open seats created by voluntary resignations will be greater than usual. Some members, having been thrust into new or uncongenial districts, always retire for political reasons in a reapportionment year. As average tenure in the Congress lengthens, furthermore, the number of members over 70 creeps up and with it a certain backlog of possible retirements; in the 97th Congress (1981–83) there were 13 members of the House over 70; by the 101st (1989–91) there were 22.[25] Finally, 1992 marks the last opportunity for members of Congress to convert their political surpluses—the cash on hand of their personal campaign committee—to personal use; if they wish to do so, they cannot run in 1992.[26] The possibility that these factors will combine to create a record or near-record number of open seats—estimates have run as high as 40 to 50—had some regular contributors salivating. There were in fact reports as early as 1990 that some PACs were socking money away for the 1992 races, and the total cash on hand that PACs reported at the end of 1990 was the largest total ever.

Since open-seat campaigns most closely approximate our ideals of major-party competitiveness, the exchanges in campaign finance are as close to the classic funding ideal as one comes. Candidates are not certain of winning, but they are not merely good soldiers or sacrificial lambs either. Nor are they often raising money to build a subsequent political career or to indulge in the other non-electoral goals that the safe incumbents do. They raise money to win the election at hand, and in the exchange most of them offer potential contributors all the fruits of a first electoral victory: the heady sensation of victory itself, the gain of a seat in Congress for the preferred party or ideology, and eventual access heightened by genuine gratitude.

Contributors seize the opportunity. In the open-seat races they do not abandon electoral strategy as they do in the incumbent-challenger campaigns. Most telling, the percentage of money contributed in open-seat elections to candidates polling in the 40–60 percent range did not diminish in the 1980s. The percentages of PAC funds given to candidates in that range also remained remarkably constant; of PAC contributions to House open-seat candidates, 74 percent in 1980, 74 percent in 1984, 75 percent in 1988, and

Table 3.4

Corporate PAC Contributions to Republican House Incumbent and Open-Seat Candidates: 1978–1990

Year	Incumbents		Open Seats	
	Contributions	% of Total*	Contributions	% of Total*
1978	$ 1,719,593	46.4%	$ 705,693	69.6%
1980	$ 3,771,461	47.2%	$1,046,743	87.6%
1982	$ 8,219,187	58.4%	$1,687,038	77.5%
1984	$ 8,943,829	47.7%	$1,489,626	88.1%
1986	$11,142,091	48.6%	$1,891,582	75.2%
1988	$13,114,723	45.9%	$1,114,797	69.2%
1990**	$13,720,497	43.6%	$2,148,320	66.1%

* Total is the sum of all corporate PAC contibutions to major-party general-election candidates.
**Data for 1990 include primary and general-election candidates.
Source: Federal Election Commission.

then 73 percent in 1990 went to candidates getting between 40 and 60 percent of the vote.[27] Had the push for legislative access reached open-seat campaigns, one would have seen money drift from these most competitive candidates to the sure winners, the winners eventually polling above 60 percent of the vote.

There is, finally, another sign that electoral strategies are still alive in open-seat campaigns. Corporate PACs play pragmatic legislative politics by contributing heavily to Democratic incumbents. Their commitment to an ideological electoral politics in the open seats, by contrast, is evident in their overwhelming support of Republicans (table 3.4). For the seven cycles from 1978 through 1990, 76 percent of corporate PAC contributions in open-seat campaigns went to Republican candidates. While those aggregate data conceal a large number of mixed strategies by individual corporate PACs, they speak clearly to the point that PACs will still take electoral risks—when those risks are worth taking.

The Special Case of the Senate

If the power of House incumbents in their exchanges with contributors is rooted in their phenomenal reelection rates— above 90 percent—the lesser dominance of Senate incumbents mirrors their considerably lower reelection percentages. As was the case in House elections, the first and formative years of the post–1974 regime were some of the worst in American history for sitting senators. After a middling level of success in 1974 (an 85.2 percent reelection rate), incumbents won reelection only 64.0, 60.0, and 55.2 percent of the time in 1976, 1978, and 1980. Senatorial reelection in that three-election period, with its aggregate 59.5 percent incumbent success, was at the lowest level for any three consecutive elections in all of Senate history.[28]

Even though Senate incumbents improved their performance in the 1980s and actually exceeded that of the House in 1990—Republican Rudy Boschwitz's loss to Paul Wellstone in Minnesota being the only loss among 32 incumbents seeking reelection—their rate of reelection for the decade remained well below the rates of House incumbents (see fig. 3.1). Similarly, their funding advantage over their challengers remained smaller. Especially after the slaughter of the incumbents in 1976 and 1978, and with expectations of a substantial Reagan victory in 1980, challengers actually lowered the incumbent advantage ratio from 1.9:1 in 1978 to 1.6:1 in 1980 and then 1.5:1 in 1982 (table 3.5). Senate incumbents began to reach a 2:1 funding margin only in the mid-1980s, settling into a 2.1:1 margin in both 1988 and 1990. (In 1990 House incumbents outspent their challengers 3.7:1.) Moreover, senators began to build intimidating cash balances, if later than their House counterparts did; by 1988 the average senator's cash on hand at the beginning of the cycle was $406,756. The Senate thus appears to fit the House reelection and funding patterns, though somewhat less dramatically. Lower levels of incumbent entrenchment seem to lead to lower levels of incumbent funding superiority.

Table 3.5
Campaign Finance of Senate Major-Party General-Election
Incumbents and Challengers: 1978–1990

Year	Mean Spending of Incumbents	Mean Spending of Challengers	Incumbent-to-Challenger Spending Ratio	Mean Beginning Cash-on-Hand of Incumbents
1978	$1,341,942	$ 705,437	1.9:1	$ 29,344
1980	$1,357,232	$ 845,570	1.6:1	$ 20,148
1982	$1,796,054	$1,189,012	1.5:1	$ 64,608
1984	$2,484,715	$1,041,577	2.4:1	$106,863
1986	$3,488,380	$1,781,380	2.0:1	$286,757
1988	$3,772,389	$1,825,713	2.1:1	$406,756
1990	$3,547,194	$1,703,505	2.1:1	$391,514

Source: Federal Election Commission.

Yet generalizations about the electoral politics of the Senate, especially any plotting of changes over time, are a risky business. The Senate seats up for election in 1980 were not the seats contested in 1976 or 1978, and one must look at three consecutive elections to get an approximation of a full Senate election, hoping always that the different political contexts at three different times will not distort the view. The very nature of the Senate thwarts easy analysis in other ways, too. The Senate constituencies, the states, have vastly different areas and populations; senators from California represent 30 million people spread over 159,000 square miles, while senators from Delaware represent less than a million people living on fewer than 2,000 square miles. Analysis of Senate races also involves too few cases to support generalization; there has been, for instance, an average of only 4.4 Senate open-seat races a cycle since 1980. The six-year term even raises hob with calculations of cash on hand; since senators spend much of the money they raise in the first four years in the ongoing campaign, their cash balances as they approach reelection campaigns underestimate the money they raised and spent long before their challengers even surfaced.

Those caveats notwithstanding, it is obvious that incumbent senators come to the funding exchange with many advantages. By the beginning of the 1990s they were outspending their opponents by two to one. Whatever their leverage, however, they have never been able to extract as large a percentage of their total receipts from PACs as have the House incumbents; only 24.6 percent of their receipts came from PACs in 1990 against 48.2 percent for House incumbents. Conversely, other Senate candidates got a larger share of their receipts from PACs in 1990; PACs provided 16.3 percent of challenger funds and 33.1 percent of the funds of open-seat candidates (table 3.6). The importance of PAC money in Senate campaigns, therefore, differs from its importance in House races in two important ways: it accounts for a smaller overall part of the total receipts of all candidates, and it is a relatively more important part of challenger and open-seat candidate funding than it is in the House of Representatives (see table 3.3).

Those data reflect the receipts of senatorial candidates. The picture differs if one looks at the PAC money as PAC contributions. In the 1980s PACs significantly increased the share of their Senate contributions going to incumbents. In 1980, 50 percent of the money PACs gave to candidates for the Senate went to incumbents; by 1990 that same figure was at 71 percent. In the intervening years the percentage had never risen higher than the 63 percent in 1982. So, PACs pursue electoral strategies more often in Senate races, surely because of the greater competitiveness of challengers and open-seat candidates, but perhaps also because of the lesser power of Senate committees and thus the lesser value of on-the-scene access for PACs pursuing narrow and well-defined interests. At the same time PACs have lately been shifting resources to incumbents. That shift in some part also reflects the number of incumbents seeking reelection; the class of 1990 was 32, the largest number in the post-1974 regime.[29] But the shift to incumbents probably also reflects their increasing electoral

Table 3.6
Receipts of Senate Major-Party General-Election Candidates by
Relative Share from Source

	Individuals	PACs	Candidates	Parties	Total Receipts (Millions)
Incumbents:					
1980	n/a	21.6%	n/a	1.0%	$ 36.6
1986	67.6%	26.2%	0.5%	0.5%	$ 90.3
1990	68.6%	24.6%	0.0%	0.6%	$118.8
Challengers:					
1980	n/a	19.9%	n/a	2.0%	$ 30.1
1986	61.9%	18.0%	7.8%	0.5%	$ 54.0
1990	59.9%	16.3%	8.2%	0.7%	$ 49.3
Open Seats:					
1980	n/a	17.8%	n/a	1.7%	$ 11.4
1986	64.7%	23.5%	1.7%	0.3%	$ 47.6
1990	48.5%	33.1%	0.6%	0.1%	$ 10.3

The percentages do not add to 100 percent because candidates get
revenue from sources other than contributions; by far the most
important of these is the interest they earn on cash invested.
Source: Federal Election Commission.

security: higher reelection rates, more cash reserves, and
greater national name and fame.

As for the lower overall level of PAC support for senatorial
candidates, it may result from the parsimony of the PACs themselves. The numbers make the argument. The average campaign of a Senate incumbent cost $3.7 million in 1990, or
between eight and nine times the average incumbent's campaign for the House ($443,500). But the average PAC contri-
bution to Senate candidates in 1988 was only $2,067 compared
to an average contribution of $1,193 to House candidates in
the same cycle. The same number of active PACs is available

for House and Senate exchanges, and more important, the same contribution limit, $5,000 per candidate per election, applies to House and Senate races.[30] Thus the average House incumbent can raise half of his or her funds ($225,000) in about 150 PAC contributions of about $1,500. The Senate incumbent on average raises one-quarter of total receipts ($925,000) in 420 PAC contributions of about $2200.

Those averages conceal a great deal of variation, to be sure. There are PACs that make substantial contributions to Senate candidates; in 1988, in fact, more than half of the PAC money going to senatorial candidates came in contributions of $5,000 or more ($23.4 million of $45.7 million). But there simply are not enough of them to raise the level of PAC funding for Senate candidates. Why aren't PACs willing to contribute in ways that reflect the cost and magnitude of Senate campaigns? The FECA limits are clearly no overt barrier; the $2,067 average contribution to Senate incumbents is far below the effective legal limit of $10,000 per election cycle. In part, contributions to Senate candidates suffer in the implicit comparison PACs make to contributions they give to House candidates. They suffer also from the competition of sheer numbers; in 1990 there were 807 major party candidates running in the general election for the House but only 67 running for the Senate. PACs, for their part, want low-risk contribution policies—policies that broadly disperse funds to avoid the embarrassment of journalistic finger-pointing that large contributions can occasion, the anger of the spurned or bypassed seeker of funds, or the unhappiness of their own donors. But paramount is an access-oriented psychology among the PACs, an inclination to "invest" fixed sums in large numbers of candidates, to pay the sum the candidate seeks at a fund-raising event rather than to think in terms of the total costs of a winning campaign. In short, it is the psychology of a "one-size-fits-all" contribution.

Given the lower level of PAC support for them and given the fact that the level is not rising, Senate incumbents rely much more on individual contributions than do their House counterparts. Unlike most House incumbents, they can and do raise large sums from individuals in other states. They offer much greater eminence than do House members, and some even cultivate the well-tailored, photogenic manner of celebrities. Their campaigns are the classic locus of the well-brokered reception in which the senator flies in for cocktails, smiles, handshakes, a few words, and a covey of $1,000 checks. Often the policy concern of the guests is within the policy ambit of the senator's chief committee responsibility. Crucial to the whole transaction, of course, is an intermediary—perhaps an industry leader, an officer of a membership association, or the Washington representative for the interest that unites the guests.

Senator Tim Wirth, Democrat from Colorado, has attracted some attention by tabbing these intermediaries "Tommy Tycoons."[31] The media usually call them and their recruitees "wealthy contributors," reflecting perhaps a populist definition of wealth in the 1990s. Because the Federal Election Commission has never systematically reported contribution data by the in-state/out-of-state distinction, one relies on the anecdotal evidence and the scattered stories about senators' forays into distant urban centers to see fellow religionists, fellow members of an ethnic or national heritage, fellow professionals, and the well-organized contributors from a single industry or a single policy enthusiasm. They doubtless account for many of the out-of-state makers of large contributions that Citizen Action identified.[32] What part of the contributions which the FEC simply labels as from "individuals" are from the out-of-staters is unknown.

Whatever the portion, they have most of the characteristics of PAC contributions. They express an interest or set of interests the contributors share, and they come usually as part of a desire to affect the outcome of public policy, however indirectly or implicitly. Even the contributions of ethnic, racial, and religious groups, based in part on shared pride and solidarity, are not without policy interests. Jewish communities are involved with the future of Israel, Irish communities with the future of Northern Ireland, and virtually all communities with immigration and naturalization policy. In short, these brokered contributions are often as "interested" or "special-interested" as PAC money; the difference and the problem is that we have a far harder time discerning the interest. Those members of the Congress who accept these funds while ostentatiously spurning PAC money would seem to be making a distinction without much of a difference.

Senate incumbents, then, do not have quite the bargaining power of House incumbents. The rates at which Senate incumbents were reelected from 1980 through 1988 were on the average 15 percentage points below those of House incumbents. PACs, and even many individuals, do pursue access strategies in funding them, yet they are able to preserve electoral opportunities for themselves. In fact, the viability of electoral politics in some Senate races—the support for challengers and higher levels of support for open-seat candidates—suggests that the pragmatic politics of access one sees in House campaigns is a fallback strategy of self-protection. Support for incumbents in the hope of achieving access to them may be a default strategy, a way of making the best of an otherwise unpromising set of electoral opportunities.

Contributors are also lured into electoral politics in the Senate by the bigger stakes in Senate elections. If one elects, or helps elect, a senator, one has elected about 2 percent (1/51) of a majority; elect a member of the House and you elect only half of 1 percent (1/218) of a majority. Given the turnover rate and the small margin of party majorities in the Senate, the election of a senator in a given year may amount to 20 or 30 percent of the seats needed to recapture control of the Senate. The prize is greater and the chances of winning it better. The cost-benefit ratio in competitive Senate races is therefore more favorable for contributors than it is in House elections.

Nowhere is the difference between House and Senate campaign finance clearer than in the funding of a close campaign for a Senate seat at a time when the majority's edge in the Senate is not invulnerable. Those campaigns have been lavishly funded by any standard in American campaign finance. The 1990 race between Senator Jesse Helms and his challenger, Harvey Gantt, is illustrative. In a state with only about 7 million people, the two candidates spent a total of $21.2 million. It is in such races that the greatest opportunity for political gain, the winning or holding of control of the Senate, and the probabilities of achieving it come together. And it is here that the politics of a Senate election—visible beyond a single state, supported by sources from all over the country, and turning on issues of ideology that resonate nationally— become most national. That some Senate elections hinge on nationally visible battles between great nationally held ideologies or political positions may, of course, be the greatest stimulus of all for the continued pursuit of electoral strategies by contributors to those campaigns.

The Rationalities

The contributors and candidates in the great exchanges of American campaign finance spend money in order to reach very tangible goals. In that sense they behave rationally. But rationality implies not only the goals but also an efficient pursuit of them. Change the goals and you change the imperatives and thus the standards of what is an efficient and effective way to achieve them. Nothing better illustrates the dangers of misspecifying goals and misassessing effectiveness in reaching them than the failure of the "need" model to explain the exchanges of campaign finance.

Why do House incumbents raise so much more money than they "need," and why do PACs and individuals contribute to their campaigns with so little regard for what candidates "need"? Some of the affluent incumbents—about 60 in a usual election year—have little or no opposition. Why do they need campaign contributions? The need in question, of course, is electoral: the money the candidate needs to stage a winning campaign. But winning by what margin? Does need permit a victory margin of 5 percentage points, or 10, or 20, or more?

Clearly, the exchanges of campaign finance are made without much reckoning of electoral need. But why?

In the first place, electoral need is hard to measure a year or 18 months before an election. The challenger may not even have emerged, much less any hints of the challenger's resources or campaign skills and tactics. Even when such essentials are clear, the incumbent cannot know what sum of resources will be needed for victory, for no candidate controls all of the events and twists of the campaign. It is not like saving to buy an automobile, the approximate price of which one knows a year or two before the purchase. Moreover, even experienced candidates know very imperfectly which campaign expenditures will achieve their electoral goals; it is as Lord Leverholme, the British merchandising giant, once said about another art of persuasion: "I know I waste half my advertising budget; the only problem is that I do not know which half." So, under conditions of great uncertainty, incumbents react with fear and insecurity to worst-case scenarios. Not even 95 percent reelection rates reassure them. Their political memory banks contain personal histories or those of colleagues to document the most pessimistic projections, those of the failed 5 percent. Furthermore, their imaginations easily conjure up visions of a last-minute, well-financed, mediagenic challenger. The best way to deal with that scenario, they believe, is to discourage it from ever happening by establishing an early superiority in campaign funding.

Second, the need model fails because incumbents, especially well-established ones, have goals for financing their campaign that go beyond winning the election at hand. What may appear to be unneeded money may be the funds necessary to accumulate an overwhelming electoral margin, even a landslide, in order to establish credentials of electability for higher office or discourage attractive challengers in the next election. The surpluses may also demonstrate the necessary fund-raising prowess for a race for that office—the governorship of the state or a seat in the Senate, most usually. Ten members of the House of Representatives ran for the Senate in 1990, and nine of them either used their existing committee and its cash balances or transferred cash balances to new committees for the Senate race. The existing or transferred cash-on-hand totaled $1,313,400, with the median at $123,620 and the average at $145,930. The sums ranged from the $374,808 transferred by Lynn Martin, the Republican senatorial candidate in Illinois, to the $9,748 used by Larry Craig, Republican from Idaho.

The contributors' goals do not quite fit the need model either. For one thing, the risk averse among them do not seek close or competitive elections; they want a reasonably certain victory. If they can assume a safe electoral outcome, they contribute to achieve a legislative goal rather than an electoral one. The contribution is really intended to open legislative doors or to keep them open, or it may simply be given to avoid the anger of an incumbent. Contributors may give money for many of the same reasons that candidates take it, especially to establish their political importance, their financial means, even their political machismo. In some instances the big contribution becomes a kind of political potlatching.

Once again it is in those competitive open-seat races that the assumption of a need-based rationality best applies. Here both candidates and contributors are pursuing their ultimate political goals in the campaign; the benefits they seek hinge on who wins the election. Other non-electoral, longer-term political goals have been pushed into the background. This is clearly the exchange that countless Americans have in mind when they criticize the use of campaign money for purposes other than those of the election—for giving and accepting money beyond electoral need for all manner of non-electoral purposes. The electoral definition of need is integral to the pursuit of electoral strategies, and both define the classic exchange in campaign finance. This classic exchange, alas, has been less and less common since the mid-1980s.

So, for better or for worse, the participants in many of the exchanges in campaign finance go beyond the classic electoral goals and rationality the public would prefer. Millions of dollars are being given and spent for purposes beyond the campaign per se. Because of the increasing power of the incumbents in the exchange, the share of those millions going to non-electoral purposes is increasing. It is a bedrock rule of politics that political actors bring their own very personal and very diverse purposes to political activity. Regulation may limit the activity but does not easily reshape the purposes behind it.

Multiple goals lead logically and rationally to multiple strategies. That is the "metarationality" of the mixed, delicately tuned, strategy. Candidates, even incumbents, do factor in some idea, however generously padded, of what they will need for a winning campaign. They may also, as I have argued, pursue extra-electoral goals of a diversity and complexity beyond confident cataloging. Contributors, too, mix strategies to respond to complex pressures and expectations. A typical corporate PAC has to satisfy the desires of the parent organization's Washington representative for contributions to key incumbents while meeting the demands of its donors to support some favorite local candidates and of its management to support Republicans attuned to a pro-business philosophy. In a few cases the strategy is crassly mixed by contributing both to the incumbent and the challenger; more often the mixture is concocted more subtly by pursuing different goals in different campaigns.

Even so brief a discussion of political rationality cannot pass without a word about risk-taking. If the essence of rationality is in the selection of means likely to reach specified goals, the word *likely* defines the risk-taking. Means are rarely absolutely certain to achieve ends; so, at what level of probability of success does the rational man or woman pursue them? And—hardest question of all—what separates the risk-takers from the risk-averse? In terms of American campaign finance, why do some PACs take on the risks of supporting challengers and open-seat long shots while others opt for a lower-risk policy of supporting incumbents? This is one of the questions that I explore in chapter 4. Suffice it to note here that risk aversion is a matter of degree. The mixing of strategies by contributors and candidates, in addition to addressing the problem of conflicting goals, also responds to conflicting or shifting willingness to incur risks in campaign politics.

No matter what millions of American adults may think, the campaign finance system is not a simple case of paying the piper and calling the tune. American campaigns are funded by a series of varied and complex exchanges in which different actors seek different goals in different modes of rationality. One cannot easily identify aggressors or exploiters in such a marketplace, for the relationships between contributors and candidates are bilateral and unstable, dependent always on very specific but shifting calculations of cost and benefit. Those calculations and the people who make them ultimately yield to the single consideration that more than any other defines both the risks and the stakes in the exchange: the candidate's chances of winning the election.

The time of slowed growth in campaign funding in the 1980s saw the rising importance of incumbent candidates in the funding exchanges. Confident of reelection, many of them assumed an ever more aggressive posture in fund-raising. Many in fact succeeded in raising sums that would achieve goals far beyond reelection. Incumbents increasingly governed the exchanges by limiting the options of contributors; collectively they created the low-risk, low-benefit option that many contributors seized as a feasible alternative to electoral politics. The pipers had begun to call their own tunes.

In terms of the system of campaign finance, incumbents seized the initiative from PACs, probably contributed to the end of PAC proliferation, and certainly ended PAC plans to make an unprecedented impact on American electoral politics. By the 1990s PACs to a considerable degree had retreated to a resumption of the historic role of groups in American politics. They increasingly reverted to securing access and influence in the legislative process. Without important options in many congressional elections, their funding efforts often became means to other ends, mere ancillaries to their longtime involvement in legislative representation.

As it entered the decade of the 1990s, the regime of American campaign finance featured a great variety of exchanges spread along an electoral continuum, the poles of which were defined by the presence and the absence of electoral competitiveness. At one pole were the exchanges of the incumbents certain of reelection, exchanges in which the candidates defined the stakes and the costs. At the other were the exchanges in the elections for open seats that most approached full or perfect competition, exchanges in which contributors enjoyed their greatest leverage and which offered the richest opportunities for achieving goals in the election itself. Much of conventional wisdom about American campaign finance reflects assumptions close to the latter pole, the one of competitiveness. Much of the divergence of realities about the funding system since 1974 reflects the hard fact that it is the exchanges negotiated nearer the pole of noncompetitiveness that are now the more common.

Chapter 4

The Organizational Factor

Nothing symbolizes the post-1974 regime in campaign finance more vividly than political action committees. They dominate the media-born images of campaign funding and embody most of the public fears about a campaign finance that relies on voluntary private largesse. For some political activists they represent both the opportunities and the fruits of collective action under the new regime. They are, in short, its most conspicuous icons.

In passing the critical amendments to the FECA in 1974 the Congress did not intend to empower organized giving or fund-raising. It wanted primarily to end the power of the individual fat cats in presidential and congressional politics. In their place the reformers clearly hoped for, perhaps even anticipated, a system of campaign finance of almost naive simplicity and pristine motives: a flood of small individual contributions surging up from the political grass roots of the nation. That hope died quickly, a victim of the unplanned incentives for collective action in the new FECA and an irresistible move to group-based organization in all of American politics. The number of PACs multiplied; and less visibly, candidates, especially the incumbents, also discovered the power of organization, most notably in the revival of legislative party organizations. Brokers emerged anew to organize individual contributions in an increasingly national marketplace. So, more or less simultaneously, both contributors and candidates rediscovered one of the immutable laws of political action: organized, aggregated activity achieves more political goals more effectively.

With the instruments of political organization increasingly available, American politics entered an age of concerted action—whether in neighborhood action groups, in a flourishing Washington representation, or in the funding of campaigns. A heightened pluralism came to all of American politics, but it came to campaign finance almost for the first time in the 1970s and 1980s. With it came all the questions of the consequences of organized politics. At least as long ago as James Madison's authorship of the 10th and 51st papers of *The Federalist,* the notion of organized factions and their ability to exert countervailing limits on each other has been central to the American political tradition. Madison and his followers introduce a great paradox: that in organization there is both strength and weakness. Organization leads to a flourishing, if somewhat disorderly, representation of interests, but in the strivings of these organizations to affect the making of policy, they check, oppose, and offset, however fortuitously, the aims and influence of each other. The ultimate result, the pluralists maintain, is to prevent dangerous concentrations of political influence. The paradox within the paradox is that the greater the number of organizations and the greater their particular strength, the greater the limiting and countervailing consequences of their political activity.

Those paradoxes set the major theme for this chapter: the effects, both in marshaling influence and in offsetting it, of the new organizations in American campaign finance. The architecture of the chapter is simple: first the introduction of the organized contributor, the PACs especially, and then the emerging attempts to organize both candidates and contributors in the marketplace of campaign finance. The structure, that is, reflects the two levels on which organization works: the level of the actor per se and the level of the alliance, collaboration, and coalition among actors. That order, in turn, assures a progression from the best known and documented case of organization, the PACs, to those about which we know far less.

Political Action Committees

The term *political action committees,* one that does not appear anywhere in the FECA, denotes a loose category of all the committees in federal campaigns other than political party committees and the official campaign committees of candidates. The lack of a statutory name has not, however, impeded their growth; there were 608 registered with the Federal Election Commission (FEC) at the end of 1974 and 4,123 in the middle of 1991. A large majority (3,027) of the 4,123 has a sponsoring parent organization—a labor union, a corporation, a membership association, a cooperative—but a substantial minority (1,096) does not. These latter PACs are created as an act of political entrepreneurship by individuals. A corporation or labor union that sponsors a PAC cannot transfer its assets to the PAC for any political use, but it is free to pay the PAC's indirect overhead expenses. That is to say, their PACs must raise the money they spend politically by voluntary gifts, and they must keep those funds for political use in what the statutes call "a separate segregated fund."

The money PACs spend politically from those separate funds come from an uncounted number of individual contributors. In the 1989–90 cycle PACs reported receipts of $372.4 million from individual donors. If we assume that the average donor to a PAC gave $50, we assume a total of almost seven and a half million contributors to PACs in the two-year cycle.[1] If we discount arbitrarily for repeaters, there are safely between 5 million and 7 million contributing individuals. Those individual donors do not, however, generally enjoy participatory rights in the governance of the PAC. The management of PACs, usually defined and selected by the parent organization, may listen to the wishes of donors as a matter of comity or organizational harmony, but very few PACs are governed democratically. That fact may ironically be one of their attractions: PACs offer an opportunity for political involvement without a commitment of the contributor's time or energy. The limited commitment and involvement of their donors is one of the distinguishing marks of PACs as political organizations.

PACs that operate in federal elections—campaigns for the two houses of the Congress and campaigns for president— are closely regulated by the Federal Election Campaign Act of 1974. It requires that all PACs register with the FEC and report their finances and political activity to it periodically. PACs that meet the statute's standards for a "multicandidate committee"—raising money from at least 50 donors and spending it on at least five candidates for federal office—may contribute $5,000 per candidate per election. Virtually all PACs so qualify, else they would be bound to the individual contribution limit of $1,000. The statutes also decide from whom PACs may solicit funds. Corporate PACs, for example, are free to solicit stockholders and management personnel, and labor PACs may solicit only their members; each may solicit the other's clientele under limited circumstances, but they rarely do.[2]

Early in its record-keeping the FEC began to separate PACs into simple categories that reflected the different ways the FECA regulated them. Since those differences reflected largely the nature of the parent organization, so did the FEC categories. The corporate and labor PACs were the most self-evident—and homogeneous—of the groups; far less numerous and important were the PACs of cooperatives and corporations without stock. The category the FEC named, somewhat ambiguously, "trade, health, membership" is in fact a collection of all PACs of membership organizations other than labor unions; it will be more simply labeled the membership category here. Finally, there is the category of PACs without any parent organization: the nonconnected PACs. Since the

FEC collects, aggregates, and publishes its data about PACs in these categories, they define much of the analysis one can undertake with them. To reaggregate the data into other categories is a bit like unscrambling eggs. But what began as categories growing out of regulatory imperatives have, surprisingly, become useful analytical categories, because from their legal and structural differences the various kinds of PACs have developed important organizational and behavioral differences.

PACs had existed since 1943 with the founding of the CIO's Political Action Committee; the parent of all PACs then gave its name to all of its offspring. Its successor, the AFL-CIO's COPE, became something of an exemplar for PACs in the early years.[3] The friendlier legal climate of the FECA lured more groups and entrepreneurs into organizing PACs in the 1970s. The rapid takeoff and the rapid leveling of that growth—the S-shaped curve of the number of registered PACs—suggests that the normal distribution of the learning curve was present (see fig. 1.2). The pattern of growth suggests the normal diffusion of innovation, that is, one driven by a powerful dynamic of social learning.[4] The availability of the new avenue to political influence was widely chronicled by the mass media; *Time* magazine devoted a cover to the new "PAC Men" in late 1982, boldly proclaimed, "Turning Cash into Votes."[5] Business and professional organizations energetically promoted the PAC movement. The Public Affairs Council, an organization of corporate officers for public or governmental affairs, became an important clearinghouse of information on how to set up and manage a PAC. For political activists, weary of the failures and weakness of the parties, PACs seemed to be a major breakthrough in the mobilizing of political influence.

The growth curves for various types of PACs (fig. 4.1) suggest, however, that the diffusion of innovation was in fact a number of processes. Labor unions had pioneered the PAC movement and had largely achieved their organizational potential before 1976. The absence of labor PAC growth after 1974 is therefore a sign of early strength, not weakness; the

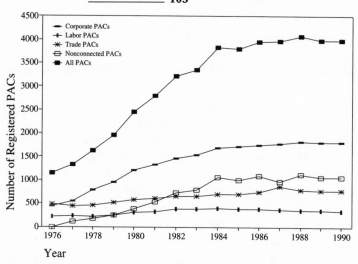

Figure 4.1
Number of PACs Registered with the FEC by Type: 1976–1990

relatively small numbers of labor PACs are also a sign of organizational centralization and consolidation within the American labor movement. The earlier takeoff in growth of corporate PACs reflects their homogeneity and the extensive network of contacts that joins especially the largest American corporations. Membership PACs follow only a bit behind; the world of membership associations is similarly cohesive and informed. Nonconnected PACs develop last, spurred perhaps by the celebrity of the National Conservative Political Action Committee in the 1980 Senate campaigns, but spurred also by the founding of countervailing liberal PACs and by the later development of leadership PACs.[6]

As Figure 4.1 also indicates, the period of PAC expansion was surprisingly brief, another exercise in accelerated political learning. The "diffusion of innovation" cycle begins in an optimism born of the post-1974 uncertainties. The newly attractive organizational form, the political action committee, offers possible (if somewhat vague) political advantages. Some groups are attracted because they foresee advantage in it;

others do not see likely gains, but they are not confident enough to ignore an option that their competitors are seizing. The certification of PAC power by the mass media in the early 1980s, greatly stimulated by NCPAC's perceived success in the 1980 senatorial campaigns, adds to the optimism. Eventually, though, PAC managers discover—as many did by the middle 1980s—that the political payoffs are less clear and less important than promised, and indeed that entrenched congressional incumbents have begun to dominate the contributor-candidate exchange to their advantage.[7] At that point the number of new PACs dwindles to a level barely able to sustain the total population. That such unwarranted optimism should fade is not surprising, for the leaders of political organizations are realists above all.

Significantly, the total number of PACs does not decline. Since the mid-1980s the number of PACs choosing to disband has just about equaled the number of new ones. An average of more than 500 PACs exited in the two-year cycles of 1984, 1986, and 1988. An even greater number became inactive; only 3,044 of the 4,172 PACs registered at the end of 1990 were active in the 1990 federal campaigns. Even though the number of PACs registered with the FEC at the end 1990 declined only 2 percent from the end of 1988, the number of active PACs—those making contributions to candidates in the cycle—declined 8 percent from 3,308 to 3,044. Those exiting and inactive PACs are chiefly small ones, and their defections have not greatly altered the face of the PAC movement. But their departure is one more indicator of the increasing concentration of campaign funds in the post-1974 system.

The major departures among the PACs have been among the nonconnected PACs with short-term purposes, such as supporting a specific presidential candidate or bill before the Congress. Not having the long-term interests of a parent organization to consider and not enjoying the continuing support of a parent group, they are freer to cease activity. Throughout the 1980s the nonconnected PACs have also displayed a much greater degree of inactivity than other PACs.

In the 1989–90 cycle, for instance, 46 percent of them were active, compared with 80 percent of all the other PACs registered with the FEC.[8] The lack of an organizational base beneath the organization of the PAC itself indeed sets the nonconnected PACs apart from the other PACs on a great many points. They must, to take another example, bear two other burdens special to themselves as a result of not having a parent: they must raise and pay their own overhead costs, and they must raise money largely through volatile direct-mail and telephone solicitations.

PACs with organizational parents have largely chosen options other than inactivity or disbandment. Most of them simply submit to incumbents by channeling more of their money to them, often regardless of the incumbent's issue, ideological position, or need for campaign funds. Most PACs with parents, that is, prefer continued activity, even redirected activity, to disbandment. And that is the case for very predictable organizational reasons. PACs become ends in themselves; their managers and boards see them as tokens of good citizenship, and their convictions about the value of PACs make them resist pessimistic conclusions. Moreover, their parent organizations, parents also to lobbying programs, embrace the logic of putting the siblings to work in tandem. Above all, political fear and uncertainty raise a great barrier to dissolution. Even though PAC managers may doubt the efficacy of their activities, they are not sure enough about that assessment or its consequences for the parent to risk acting on it. There is always the fear that exit will surrender some hard-to-define political edge to one's competitor PACs. Finally, both PAC and parent fear that exit will also anger incumbents grown accustomed to its largesse; the parent's lobbying operation would reap the resentment.

If there are organizational reasons impelling PACs to stay the course, there are also organizational imperatives limiting their political options. The PACs with parents must weigh the impact of their contributions on the public image of the parent, especially if the parent, a fast food chain perhaps, is vulnerable to public reaction. They also must attend to the parent's Washington lobbyist or representative who is anxious not to ruffle any incumbent feathers. Simultaneously they cannot ignore the wishes of donors to the PAC, whether those donors want a purer pursuit of party or ideology or support for local candidates they know and admire. The conventional wisdom among PACs is that there are three useful strategies in placating the donors to the PAC: support their favorite candidates, offer at least some support for the ideologues, and maintain a record of backing winners. The required skill is more than a high-wire act—it places the PAC on three crossing wires simultaneously.[9]

In fact, one theme recurs in the organizational studies of PACs: the localism of their political decisions. Analyzing the 1984 contributions of corporate PACs to House candidates, Eismeier and Pollock found that 26 percent of their money went to candidates from the home state of the PAC.[10] Addressing different data but a similar localism, John Wright concludes: "Paradoxically, the organizational arrangement that allows PACs to raise and allocate large sums of money also restricts their ability to influence roll calls. Because money must be raised at a local, grassroots level, local PAC officials, not Washington lobbyists, are primarily responsible for making allocation decisions. Consequently, congressmen who desire contributions must cultivate favorable relationships with local officials, and this arrangement tends to undercut the value of contributions as a bargaining tool for professional lobbyists."[11] Divided between the national and the local, and between the pragmatic and the ideological, most PAC managers face imposing assignments in political diplomacy. They find success in it only by crafting their own mix of PAC strategies.

The Special Case of the Labor PACs

Viewing the traditional separation of functions in which parties dominated American electoral politics and groups dominated the politics of representation before government, scholars concluded that the groups were, as political organizations, poorly suited for electoral politics. They were too narrow in scope of interests and issues, too unaccustomed to the risk-taking and hurley-burley of election campaigns, and too unsuccessful in becoming reference symbols for their members or adherents to function successfully in the electoral arena. PACs have attempted to transcend those weaknesses with the one great strength at their command: mountains of cash. Whether or not they have succeeded is precisely the question of the efficacy of PACs as a form of political organization.

Evaluations of PACs usually proceed, however, from the misimpression that a PAC is a PAC and that they are all one kind of political animal. In truth PACs range from those that give a few thousand to those who give a few million, from those promoting a single policy alternative to those with a burning commitment to an all-encompassing ideology, from those led by a single driving force to those encouraging donor democracy. The trick is to find both the great similarities and the main axes of difference beneath all of the diversity.

If one looks at political activity and political choices rather than organizational traits, one set of PACs, those of organized labor, stands out from the rest. Table 4.1 illustrates with economy the ways in which the labor PACs active in 1988 differed from the corporate, membership, and nonconnected PACs active in the same cycle. In brief, labor PACs have greater average assets than other PACs, they give a significantly higher percentage of their contributions to non-incumbent candidates, and they make their contributions to candidates in much larger sums. Moreover, they are much more "unipartisan" in their contributions; more than 92 percent of their 1988 contributions to House candidates went to Democrats. By contrast, the PACs of corporations—the only other group of PACs that compares in issue or ideological homogeneity with the labor PACs—split their 1988 House contributions evenly, 51 percent to Democrats and 49 percent to Republicans.

Table 4.1
Political Spending of Corporate, Labor, Membership, and
Nonconnected PACS: 1988

	Corp.	Labor	Member	Noncon.
Percent of Contributions to Democrats*	47.1	92.3	55.2	63.3
Percentage of Contributions to Incumbents*	80.1	64.1	81.2	59.0
Average Contribution to Candidates*+	$1,034	$2,466	$1,454	$1,693
Average Total PAC Contributions*+	$34,750	$138,655	$65,108	$32,269
Percentage of PACS in category Active (contributing)	89.0	72.3	80.5	56.5
Total Independent Expenditures by PACS*	$0.1m	$0.2m	$3.9m	$16.2m

*Contributions and independent expenditures are to or for all
candidates, both primary- and general-election, for all federal
offices (House, Senate, and presidency).
+The base includes only those PACS active in the 1987–88 cycle.
Source: Federal Election Commission.

To a far greater extent than other PACS, in other words,
labor PACS have escaped the new power of incumbents and
retained a viable place for themselves in electoral politics.
They give substantially larger sums to challengers and open-
seat candidates than do other PACS, and they focus their contributions on the candidates of the party closest to their issue
positions (that is, the Democrats). Moreover, their greater support of challengers suggests a greater capacity for taking political risks and for working toward longer-term political goals.
Better than other PACS, they have been able to achieve a viable
mix of legislative and electoral strategies.

Embedded in other categories of PACS there are, to be sure,
PACS with labor-like patterns of political activity. A search
through the data on the 1988 cycle reveals 275 corporate and

membership PACs that met two labor-like criteria: they gave 80 percent or more of their contributions to candidates of one party, and they gave no more than 75 percent of them to incumbents.[12] But they were small PACs with a median receipt total of less than $15,000 and an average of about $58,000; only 11 of them (4 percent) had receipts greater than $250,000. Their average total in contributions to candidates in 1988 was just a shade over $32,000. Apparently an electoral strategy is far easier for the smaller PACs with fewer and more homogeneous pressures on them. The secret, which only labor PACs seem to have found, is to be both large and electorally venturesome.

In explaining the special case of labor PACs, one looks first to the broader labor movement. Labor PACs are clearly national and centralized; major labor unions are, too. On the average labor PACs amass far greater political assets (cash receipts), and they are far fewer in number; in 1987–88, 401 labor PACs had an average of $195,783 in receipts, while 2,008 corporate PACs had an average of $48,265. Furthermore, for whatever reasons—greater homogeneity of interests, perhaps—labor has been able to build an influential peak organization, the AFL-CIO and its "peak PAC," the Committee on Political Education (COPE). By 1988 only about 15 percent of all union members in the United States were outside of the AFL-CIO, a reflection of the homogeneity of ideology and goals binding labor unions together politically.

More important, perhaps, is tradition and commitment. Labor PACs substantially predate the period of the FECA—one third of the PACs in existence in 1974 were labor PAC. These PACs developed out of labor commitment to electoral politics, a context typified by labor's endorsements of candidates and its long-standing programs of registering voters and getting them to the polls on election day. Finally, labor has the inestimable advantage of traditions of collective action and militancy, traditions embodied in its anthem, "Solidarity Forever." Collective action is the basic premise of trade unionism, for all depends on solidarity behind shared goals and on collective bargaining and the collective strike. As other PACs were leaving electoral commitment for legislative pragmatism in the 1980s, labor PACs intensified their commitment to electoral politics even in a time of troubles. Millions of union members voted for Ronald Reagan in 1980 and 1984, and union membership declined from 21 million in 1980 to 17 million in 1988. In that span of time, however, labor PACs increased their contributions to federal candidates from $14.2 million in 1980 to $35.5 million in 1988 before sliding to $34.8 million in 1990.

Labor's PAC strategy grows from labor's commitment to the Democratic party, a commitment reflected in its overwhelming support for Democratic candidates (table 4.1). It is also reflected in the substantial sums that labor PACs give directly to the Democratic campaign committees in the House and Senate; labor support for those committees totaled $1.5 million in 1988, 27 percent of all the PAC funds they received. Moreover, access for labor PACs is access to a majority legislative party, and that fact makes the closeness of their alliance with the Democrats possible. If labor PACs were to face the likelihood or the certainty of Republican majorities in the Congress, the goals of access and of support for an ideologically congenial Democratic party would diverge. Labor PACs would have to make the hard choices corporate PACs now do, the choices inherent in supporting one party while seeking access to the other.

It is in the nonlabor PACs that the weaknesses of PACs as electoral organizations are most apparent. Unlike labor PACs they do not mobilize large numbers of voters, for they have not become reference groups or symbols for their donors (that is, their "members"). The donors' affiliation with the nonlabor PAC is often tenuous and passive, often secondary to other political affiliations or loyalties; political activity via the PAC is for many of them a not very intense or demanding form of political activity.[13] Second, the parents of nonlabor PACs also have limited political goals and commitments. Their political agendas often are very short—a significant contrast to those of the AFL-CIO—and they often act hesitantly, fearing the negative reactions of broader publics such as stockholders, members, or customers. Consequently, in a large number of cases the political action committee becomes a risk-averse organization far more comfortable in achieving focused policy goals through lobbying than through the public contesting of elections.

In that dichotomy among traditional PACs there is a conspicuous in-between case: ideological PACs without parent organizations. They do not have the members and loyalists tied to the broader goals of a parent that labor PACs do, nor do they have labor's wider commitment to voter mobilization. But many of them do recruit political risk-takers around an issue or ideology; and many have long supported challengers. In short, many of them remain committed to electoral politics. Among them, too, are new and evolving organizational forms that go beyond the stereotypical PAC. Emily's List, for example, is registered as a PAC and makes contributions in the usual ways, but in its pursuit of its feminist agenda it is also a donor network in which membership requires dues of $100 per election and a pledge to contribute at least $100 to at least two candidates endorsed by Emily's List. It is an organizational form that suits especially the autonomous, politicized contributor, and it may well be a PAC variant with a future. Its future would probably be assured if Congress were to drop the PAC contribution limit to $1,000 or $2,000.

Thus, if one arrays PACs along a continuum from the most party-like to the least party-like, from the most adapted to electoral politics to the least adapted, the labor PACs are much nearer the party pole than other PACs. They are the most inclusive, the most electoral of the PACs; only they are allied with a parent organization's other electoral activities, endorsing candidates and mobilizing voters, and only they approach a party's capacity for organizing large numbers of individuals under comprehensive programs or ideologies. At times they see their loyalists desert to support a candidate of the other party, but so do political parties. With their exception, and the exception of some nonconnected PACs of ideology, PACs generally are overmatched by the incumbents and their legislative parties, the parties in government, in the contesting of elections. It was perhaps inevitable that they should eventually shift to using their participation in campaigns as an adjunct to the legislative politics that had always been the arena of their group success.

The political parties have also been contributors, though relatively insignificant ones, to candidates for the Congress. Although their contributions to all congressional candidates in 1990 ($4.3 million) accounted for only 0.9 percent of candidate receipts, they did spend more than four times that sum, a total of $19.3 million, in coordinated (so-called "on behalf of") expenditures to support their partisans' campaigns. Those totals would appear to entitle the parties to a place with PACs as organized contributors. But appearances are deceiving. It is not the political party spending the money; it is, increasingly, the legislative campaign committee of the party in the House or Senate. The party's incumbents control those committees, and they make sure that they will pursue the individual and collective interests of the incumbents. Moreover, the committees do not necessarily speak for the national party. The financial activities of the Senate and House campaign committees will, therefore, be considered later as a part of the attempts of candidates to organize their side of the exchange.

The Candidates Organize

The advantages of incumbency breed new advantages. Incumbent success in reelection races and thus in campaign finance reflects another comparatively new asset: their ability to organize in the grand marketplace of campaign finance. The most important and the most institutionalized of these organizational mechanisms are the four campaign committees in the U.S. Congress: the Democratic Congressional Campaign Committee (DCCC), the Democratic Senatorial Campaign Committee (DSCC), the National Republican

Congressional Committee (NRCC), and the National Republican Senatorial Committee (NRSC).[14] Similar committees exist in many state legislatures, and in still other states either the legislative caucuses of the parties or the party leaders function similarly. Whatever form the organizations take, they express the collective interest of a legislative party in the campaigns for legislative seats.

Whereas individual incumbents have a number of personal political goals in campaign finance, most of them having to do with reelection and a personal career, their legislative parties have two related collective goals: maximizing the number of seats they hold in the legislative chamber and achieving a majority within it. Members of Congress seek the power and perquisites of majority status in the House or Senate just as surely as they seek their own reelection. As a number of House Republicans have recently observed, always being in the minority is just not as much fun. The problem, though, is not in defining the collective interests but in finding ways of pursuing them, especially in balancing the interests of the collective and individuals within it.

Incumbents have not easily accommodated the collective goals. Commenting on the 1982 campaigns, Jacobson pointed to the decisions of individual House Democrats, in their quest for certain reelection, to compete with the committees of their own party for a limited pool of campaign contributions—even in a year when the state of the economy promised success for well-financed Democratic challengers.[15] Nonetheless, the incumbents and their parties have slowly worked out some arrangements. First of all, the Democratic and Republican national committees have largely withdrawn from congressional finance, reducing what had been three-sided negotiations to two sides: the individual incumbents and their appropriate legislative campaign committee. In 1990 the DNC spent only $51,000 in total contributions and coordinated expenditures on all of the congressional campaigns; the more affluent RNC spent a total of $302,000. All but $1,393 of the two-party total went to races for the House.

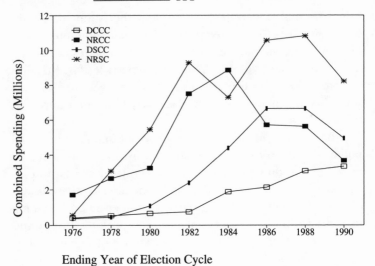

Figure 4.2
House and Senate Campaign Committee Spending on
Congressional Campaigns: 1976–1990

More important, the House campaign committees, the
DCCC and the NRCC, sharply increased their receipts, thus reducing competition for funds between individual incumbents
and individual non-incumbent candidates (fig. 4.2). The steep,
if volatile, rise in the resources of the party committees in the
mid–1980s permitted them to take a much greater role in
funding the party's challengers and open-seat candidates—
making up, ironically, for some of the PAC funds increasingly
being diverted to incumbents. The fact that the rebirth of the
DCCC and NRCC came precisely in the period in which incumbents gained control of their market for campaign resources
also eased the competition. Newly affluent, the incumbents
could share the pool of available funds with greater grace.

With greater affluence, the campaign committees also began to develop greater efficiency in spending. For one thing,
they began to spend an increasing percentage of their money
in coordinated expenditures rather than direct contributions

Table 4.2

Characteristics of House Incumbents Receiving Contributions
from the DCCC or NRCC: 1988

	DCCC		NRCC	
Amount of Contribution	Beginning Cash-on-Hand	General Election%	Beginning Cash-on-Hand	General Election%
$ 0	$122,484	76.83	(none)	(none)
$ 0–250	$128,010	76.45	(none)	(none)
$ 250–1000	$ 93,424	76.20	$ 71,707	65.00
$1000–2000	$427,257	63.00	$203,367	76.22
$2000–3000	(none)	(none)	$130,361	74.34
$3000–4000	$ 25,698	69.00	$ 84,612	74.35
$4000–8000	$ 35,586	62.44	$ 61,311	65.77
$ 8000+	$ 11,734	56.80	$ 48,982	58.59

Source: Federal Election Commission.

to candidates, thus ensuring for themselves a more direct role
in individual campaigns.[16] In 1980 the DCCC and NRCC devoted
only 5.3 percent and 38.0 percent of their funding, respectively, to coordinated expenditures; by 1988 those percentages
had risen to 61.6 and 73.1. At the same time they began to
support only those incumbents in certifiable need—incumbents with relatively limited cash on hand and facing a strong
challenge for reelection. By 1988 their support for incumbents
was selective to an extent unimaginable six or eight years earlier (table 4.2).

Most crucial to the efficiency, the party committees began
to target their funds into those campaigns—both of incumbents and non-incumbents—where it would most likely be apt
to affect the election outcome.[17] In 1988, for example, the
DCCC spent an average of $27,246 in contributions and "on
behalf of" activities on their candidates getting between 43
percent and 50 percent of the general-election vote, the NRCC
an average of $66,617 on theirs. For candidates who won only
between 31 percent and 43 percent of the vote, however, the

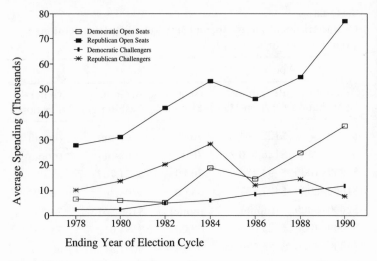

Figure 4.3
Major-Party Spending on General-Election Challengers and Open-Seat Candidates: 1978–1990

DCCC spent an average of $13,896, the NRCC an average of $23,007. By these measures the party campaign committees now spend more effectively, more rationally, to achieve the party's collective goals.

Perhaps, therefore, it was inevitable that the rationality of the campaign committees should lead them to recognize the futility of financing their party challengers. Increasingly through 1990, the DCCC and the NRCC shifted resources to open-seat candidates (fig. 4.3). The trend is especially clear in the NRCC expenditures. The Democrats as the party with a substantial majority in the House may well be able to indulge itself in the longer-range goals inherent in the support of most challengers. In any event, the trends indicate that the spell of winning grips the parties as firmly as it does the PACs. They also say that the legislative parties, as parties of incumbents, pursue their own narrow and well-defined goals for their segment of the party. Supporting almost certain losers, party label or no, is not one of them.

No one better symbolizes the new importance of the party campaign committees than Rep. Tony Coelho, a California Democrat. Coelho took over a disheartened DCCC in January 1981 after 27 Democratic incumbents had lost their seats in the Reagan landslide. Under Coelho's direction the DCCC improved its outlook, its staff, and its fund-raising techniques; its total receipts, which had been $1.2 million in the 1980 cycle, soared to $15 million in 1985–86. Coelho also sharpened the committee's political strategies and instincts; its resources increasingly were targeted on Democratic incumbents in trouble and on challengers with a chance of unseating a Republican. Perhaps because of his involvement in competitive House districts, Coelho was one of the loudest voices within the party urging it closer to the political center and to a middle-class agenda. He relinquished the chair of the DCCC to be his party's whip in 1986, leaving the DCCC an enduring and effective instrument for maintaining the Democratic majority in the House.[18]

Beyond reviving and redirecting the campaign committees, congressional incumbents have other ways of supporting their collective interests. Two deserve special mention. Those with ample campaign funds simply make contributions to other needier candidates for the House. In the absence of FEC aggregation of totals, we depend on anecdotes and investigative enterprise to assess their importance. The anecdotal evidence is typified by the report in 1990 that 66 House Democratic incumbents had contributed $54,700 to their beleaguered colleague, Rep. Sidney Yates of Illinois, from the funds of their own campaign committees.[19] In the leading investigative enterprise, one focused on the 1983–84 cycle, Clyde Wilcox identified 197 incumbent House members who transferred $900,037 to other House candidates. (Senators transferred only $111,765 in those two years.) Their funds went to both incumbents (only 52 percent, however) and non-incumbents—heavily to marginal candidates in both instances, often to candidates from the same state, and to a more limited extent to candidates of similar policy views.[20] To what extent are such transfers organized by party leadership, senior members, or the candidates themselves? We do not know. The results do, however, bespeak an efficiency that suggests something more than isolated individual decisions.

Second, the PACs of senators and representatives, the so-called leadership PACs or personal PACs, have transferred increasing sums to other candidates for the Congress.[21] In the 1985–86 cycle these PACs of House incumbents were overwhelmingly Democratic; 89 percent of their contributions went to Democrats. More to the point, 54 percent of their money went either to challengers or to open-seat candidates. In serving the personal interests of the PAC founders—support for their leadership positions or aspirations—the leadership PACs also serve the collective partisan interests of incumbent members.

For the progress of the new accommodation between incumbents' individual and collective interests, one need look no further than the daily newspaper. A story in the *Washington Post* in mid-1991 reported the success Rep. Vic Fazio of California, chair of the DCCC, was having in reducing the committee's post-1990 debt by tapping the cash-on-hand of the campaign committees of the individual Democratic incumbents: "More than 100 of the House's 266 Democrats have ponied up their $5,000, and the $525,000 Fazio has collected from members is a key factor in drawing down the DCCC's debt to about $1.5 million. Less than five months into the two-year election cycle, Fazio already has easily surpassed the record for member fund-raising." The story pointed out that Fazio's success reflected concern in the party about its collective fate in the redrawn districts of the 1992 election.[22] It could also have noted that the incumbents' generosity reflected their prosperity. In various ways, incumbent power and its consequent affluence permits incumbents more easily to resolve the conflicts between their collective and their individual interests.

All of this evidence of increasing attention to the interests of the party collectivity comes from the U.S. Congress. Similar developments are afoot in the state legislatures. While the reelection rates of incumbents (at least in 14 states) appear not to have risen since 1968—the rates then were already well above those in the Congress—the vote margins and the numbers of incumbents winning without contest have risen.[23] Another study of 20 states finds, similarly, that marginality in elections to the lower house of the state legislature has declined in 14 of them from 1950 to 1986, with a perceptible rise in competitiveness in only two.[24] As always there are the isolated nuggets of illustrative data: races for the lower house of the New York legislature in the combined years of 1986 and 1988 were won by vote percentages of 65 and greater about 78 percent of the time.[25] The conditions are right, in other words, for incumbents in the state legislatures to move into supremacy in the exchanges of campaign finance.

More relevant to the argument here, organizations of incumbents are alive and very well in the state legislatures. California is not necessarily representative of the 50 states, but as the most populous and as a political trendsetter it attracts more than ordinary attention. The legendary Speaker of the Assembly, Democrat Willie Brown of San Francisco, raises sums in seven figures for worthy Democratic candidates; he gave $1.6 million in 1986 and $2.7 million in 1988 to various party and individual campaign committees. In 1986, indeed, the Democratic campaign committee, called Assembly Democrats, spent $2.5 million in the general elections for the Assembly, and the Assembly Republican PAC spent $1.4 million. Although generosity may be more tempered elsewhere, the story of California incumbents channeling funds into collective support for needy fellow partisans can be repeated in other states.[26]

Moreover, those party or leadership bodies in the states use their money increasingly to support non-incumbents or incumbents engaged in close races.[27] To resume the California illustration, the Assembly Democrats in 1986 gave only $249,000 of their $2.5 million to incumbents; $1.9 million of it went to eight Democrats running in open seats. Of the $1.4 million the Assembly Republicans gave, only one incumbent got a modest $15,750 from it. Indeed, those are records of freedom from incumbent demands far beyond any yet posted by the DCCC or the NRCC in Washington.

Legislative incumbents have widely struck an informal bargain in reconciling their individual and their collective electoral interests. It is a bargain made possible by their ability to win reelection almost at will and by their consequent ability to raise substantial sums of money. Not only do safe and powerful incumbents raise large sums for themselves; they also help the party committees to raise funds for the collectivity at newly augmented levels. Moreover, they have built the campaign committees as major sources of expertise and support, even of surprisingly inexpensive services, in party campaigns.[28] And they have moderated their own claims on the resources of the campaign committees, freeing them to attend to the party's challengers and open-seat candidates.

Ultimately, the strengthened party campaign committees become useful in the pursuit of a collective interest beyond winning elections and majorities: the creation of a separate and autonomous legislative party. Listen to Tom Loftus, who in 1984 was the Speaker of the Wisconsin Assembly and the chairman of the Assembly Campaign Committee: "We raised about $150,000 this year to help Democrats running in marginal seats. In most cases we recruited the candidate. We provide training through campaign schools. We provide personnel and logistic support, issue papers, press releases, speakers for fund-raisers, fund-raisers themselves, and phone banks; we pay for the recount if it's a close race; we pay for the lawyer if it goes to court; if they have kids, we pay for the babysitter. In other words, we do everything a political party is supposed to do."[29] With their campaign committees, the incumbents build political parties that serve only the agendas and priorities of the legislative partisans and that insulate them from the pressures of other parts of their party. Collective action has helped to bring the legislative parties freedom from the agendas of the presidential or gubernatorial parties.

The Contributors Counterorganize

Contributors find it much harder to organize the marketplace of campaign contributions. Aside from the special case of labor PACs, the ability of PACs to organize is severely limited by the specificity of their interests, by the constraints of parent organizations, by their deeply rooted localism, by their responsiveness to their donors. Even old and respected peak organizations find it difficult to break the entrenched individualism of their member PACs.

Despite its considerable efforts, the Business-Industry PAC (BI-PAC), for instance, has only partly succeeded in weaning business PACs away from pragmatic, access-oriented decisions and toward ways more ideological and pro-business. In 1988 all corporate PACs gave 48.7 percent of their contributions to House candidates to Republicans and 90.2 percent to incumbents. The 54 PACs that made contributions to BI-PAC in that cycle (and presumably, therefore, PACs receptive to BI-PAC's views) gave 62.6 percent of their direct contributions to Republicans and only 80.3 percent to incumbents—a shift in BI-PAC's "direction," but a modest shift nonetheless.[30] The PACs of corporations and business associations who were members of the Public Affairs Council—a promoter of business PACs but less evangelical than BI-PAC in urging a pro-business ideology on PACs—deviate considerably less from the average of all corporate PACs. In 1988 they gave Republicans 51.6 percent of their contributions to House candidates, incumbents 86.1 percent.

If two comparatively cohesive groups of corporate and business PACs cannot organize more effectively behind a strategy that reflects some joint interests, might they nonetheless at least pool their resources behind competitive candidates in fairly close races? . The contributions of the 54 BI-PAC loyalists in 1988 to House candidates do show some signs of a pattern, of an organized contribution strategy, or even of collective risk-taking. Rep. Thomas J. Bliley, an unopposed Virginia Republican, topped the list of their favorites, getting contributions from 23 of the 54 (43 percent), one of only five House candidates on more than a third of the contribution lists. Of the 24 most preferred recipients, all were incumbents, and only seven of them polled less than 60 percent in the general election. There were, however, only two Democrats among the 24, the single most impressive indicator of BI-PAC success. The contributions of the 54 to candidates for the Senate were more focused and risky. The top 24 among Senate candidates included five Democrats, all from the South or Southwest, but many more challengers and open-seat candidates. The top five (from 29 to 34 contributions from the 54) were all Republicans and included two successful open-seat candidates (Trent Lott of Mississippi and Connie Mack of Florida) and two unsuccessful challengers (George Voinovich of Ohio and Peter Dawkins of New Jersey). Voinovich tied for first place at 34 donations with the one incumbent, Pete Wilson of California.

The conclusion is inescapable: Corporate and business PACs find it more difficult than incumbents and labor PACs to organize effectively behind their collective interests in elections. The problem may indeed be in the very notion of collective interests. Labor unions and their PACs share a loose but commonly held political ideology, and they share as well an interest in sustaining the instruments of collective bargaining in an unfriendly world. Corporations pursue narrower and more diverse political interests, often those of a single policy issue or a single economic sector. They are more decentralized (there are more than 3 million of them in the United States), and local interests weigh more heavily in their political decisions. They are also far less accustomed to electoral politics and thus less committed to the need for political coalitions. The very idea of collective action among PACs suggests more focused, rational electoral strategies to defeat or elect specific candidates. But it is precisely that kind of action that incumbent reelection rates have made futile. Nonlabor PACs increasingly seek legislative access, and the pursuit of access is inherently individual. One does not seek it by collective action.

Formal organizations and networks aside, are there less formal, less institutionalized, and less visible leadership structures among the PACs? Over the last decade a new class of very large PACs has emerged, growing in receipts more rapidly than have other PACs. In 1980 the corporate PACs with receipts of $500,000 or more accounted for 2 percent of the receipts of all corporate PACs; in 1988 they accounted for 13 percent. The share of similarly large membership PACs rose from 43 to 58 percent. Is it possible that these big PACs, these new major players in PACdom, have had a role in defining the agendas and strategies of PACs? Have they, by reason of their sheer financial bulk, become their de facto leaders?

Both logic and the reports of observers agree that the large PACs are the best informed and the most sophisticated of all PACs. In the late 1970s they appeared ready to lead the PAC movement in a transformation in which PACs would become rational actors in electoral politics—organizations that would allocate their resources efficiently in campaigns largely to elect or reelect candidates reflecting their ideological or issue positions. Some observers even thought that PACs would begin to become, like labor, more party-like as political organizations, more willing, for instance, to endorse candidates and mobilize voters.[31]

Quite the opposite happened, again with the exception of the labor PACs. The PAC movement was in fact transformed in the 1980s, but in quite a different way and by two unanticipated decisions: the decision of major PACs to remain operating as PACs despite their feelings of reduced efficacy, and their decision to shift from electoral strategies to those of legislative pragmatism. Were those decisions that hundreds of PACs arrived at separately and independently, or were they led by major actors or networks in the PAC movement? It is true that the organized networks—BI-PAC and the Public Affairs Council are only two examples—continue to preach the value of PACs and in that obvious way to discourage PACs from disbanding. BI-PAC, at least, also steadfastly continues to preach against the increasing legislative pragmatism of PACs, especially when it ignores the issue positions or partisan affiliations of the incumbents they assist. In no sense have they led or encouraged the development of a legislative strategy among PACs in the 1980s.

What then of the leadership of the largest PACs? Have *they* led the collective shift of PACs to incumbent support in the last decade? The evidence does not indicate that they have. If one compares the 25 largest PACs with all the PACs in the labor, corporate, nonconnected, and membership categories, there are no significant differences in their treatment of incumbents in any given year. The largest PACs seem not to have led the move away from electoral strategies and to incumbents, and more important, they show no signs of having resisted it. In brief, they appear collectively to have acted very much as did their smaller confreres. Their failure to exert much leadership offers another bit of evidence about the constraining cross-pressures the larger PACs operate under—as always, with the exception of labor PACs.

Individual PACs adapt as best they can to conditions within them and external to them. In the 1980s they responded quickly—too quickly—to the more aggressive solicitation of incumbents and their intimidating rates of reelection. Had they been able to organize, or had they been able to alter their practice of dispersing their contributions so widely, they might have resisted the dominance of the incumbents in the marketplace of campaign finance. But most of them are fragmented, risk-averse, and relatively unorganized, and that is the root of the political weakness of PACs as players in electoral politics.

The Brokers and Bundlers

PACs and candidates have organized with differing success, but what about individual contributors? Enter the brokers and bundlers once again. Whether it is garden-variety brokering or the more artful bundling, the aggregation of individual contributors is on the surface of it an organizing of them and their contributions. In campaign finance, though, things are not as simple or straightforward as they seem. When PACs and incumbents organize, they do so to serve their interests better. But whose goals are served when individual contributors are organized? For the answer, one must ask another question: Who organizes them? An agent, a broker, enters the exchange by the act of organizing the individual contributors, and often the brokered exchange serves primarily the interests of the brokering intermediary. The broker's goals are certainly their own, but those goals may also be the goals of candidates, they may be the goals of contributors, they may be the goals of both, or they may be the goals of neither.

Take, for example, the most celebrated of the Washington bundlers: the National Republican Senatorial Committee. Long a source of imaginative conduit schemes, the NRSC created the Inner Circle in the late 1980s as an elite fund-raising club offering proximity to prominent Republicans as an incentive for an individual contribution of at least $1,000. In the 1990 cycle the NRSC reorganized it as an independent fund-raising committee; contributors gave to a specified group of candidates, and the extent of their receipts was determined by the estimated closeness of the 1990 race they faced. The contributions counted against the $1,000 limits on individual contributors and not against the limits on the NRSC.[32] However one may estimate the proximity of the Inner Circle to the NRSC and thus to the boundaries of legality, the organizational advantage clearly accrues to Republican candidates for the Senate through their instrument, the NRSC. Yet the contributors gain as well. If they share electoral goals with the Republicans, they help to elect Republicans in their concerted action. At the same time they earn the gratitude, and surely the access, of individual Republicans as well as the Republican collectivity in the Senate.

Or take, as another illustration, the brokering of a well-known Washington law firm specializing in lobbying for clients.[33] The firm arranges a fund-raiser for an incumbent uncertain of reelection, locates contributors for her, or, alternatively, raises money through the firm's PAC. At the least the broker enhances access to the grateful incumbent; that heightened access can be transferred to a client and is therefore a very marketable commodity. In this case, too, the goals of the Washington law firm are quite separate from those of both the candidate and the contributor. The relationship is three-sided with advantages for all—but with the greater advantages, probably, for the mediating broker. With the introduction of a broker, the struggle for influence through exchanges of campaign funds ceases to be a zero-sum game and often becomes genuinely three-sided.

Charles Keating's much-chronicled brokering on behalf of the savings-and-loan industry provides a third illustration. The broker in such cases is again the big gainer; even though his cash contribution may be no greater than that of his fellow contributors, the candidate's gratitude, and whatever flows from it, is disproportionately his. If there is a modal or average case in brokering, this is it; it probably describes much of the out-of-state fund-raising in venues such as Manhattan and Beverly Hills. The brokers' interests are those of the contributor writ large, and their many brokerings make themselves into an influential elite that some have called the new fat cats of American campaign finance.

The variety of cases, the configuration of interests, the enhancement of political goals—the possibilities are virtually endless in the universe of brokered contributions. By all informal accounts and alarms, the role of the broker grows with each passing electoral cycle. The growth of out-of-state money and of large individual contributions over $500, both documented in the second chapter, offer powerful indirect evidence of the rise of brokering. Until we have more reported data on such exchanges, however, we engage only in informed speculation. Even with firmer data, it will never be easy to sort out the aggregate effect of the brokering on the contributor-candidate marketplace. Which interests and whose interests profit from brokered exchanges remains an elusive question.

Brokered money is the last frontier—at least for now—in

the regime of campaign finance, and the brokers, the conduits, are the new frontiersmen. Their ability to organize donors yields sums far beyond the $10,000 PACs can give. Senators, especially those from the largest and most competitive states, face prospects of $15 million campaigns. That prospect produces fund-raisers like Senator Alan Cranston, Democrat from California, whose talents were documented in the hearings about Charles Keating's dealings with five senators:

> Records and testimony show that when Cranston met a potential donor, he immediately broached the subject of contributions, took down the prospective contributor's name and telephone number on a 3-by–5-inch card and then telephoned his fund-raiser to pass the information along for a follow-up call. . . .
>
> The California lawmaker, who has a reputation as a master fund-raiser, says he adheres to three principles in soliciting contributions: People who give once are likely to give again. Rich people *like* to be asked for large sums. And people who have given to other causes frequently are willing to contribute to Senate campaigns.[34]

Other senators and those House members relying on brokers may seek the big money for reasons other than electoral vulnerability. Whatever the reasons that drive them, the brokered exchange is a classic match of the aggressive power of incumbency with the willing power of wealth.

The Organizational Factor

Since not all political activists find it equally easy to organize, organization becomes a source of selective advantage and thus of political inequality, whether in mobilizing voters or in negotiating the exchanges of campaign finance. Furthermore, as the stories here suggest again, in American politics it seems harder to organize organizations than individuals. The imperatives and conditions that bring political organizations into being make them reluctant, inward-looking members of alliances. As their size increases, so does their political inflexibility and indecisiveness, and perforce their incapacity for organized action. For many PACs their localism, their narrowly defined political goals and interests, and their intra-organizational problems work against even the most diligent efforts to organize them. So their ability to organize works to buttress the already strong position of incumbents in the PAC-incumbent exchanges.

Its selective impact aside, the fact of increasing organization testifies to the maturing of the post–1974 regime. Organization is a major adaptation to its practices and its regulatory limits by its most experienced and politically sophisticated players. Organization reflects their initiatives, even their imagination, in realizing their ambitions both by building aggregates of political resources and by using them more rationally and efficiently. Skills at doing those things unite the raiser of money in the Southwest and the campaign committees on Capitol Hill.

In some instances, organization in the exchanges of campaign finance achieves little more than the usual alliance or coalition: greater aggregates of support for a given interest. In others, though, it elevates the exchanges to a more rational, more purposeful level. Organization reduces the buffering of less political, more diffuse giving or soliciting in favor of the more focused pursuit of goals. The evolution of the legislative campaign committees is a case in point. Organization provides a safety in numbers, and that safety helps to reduce risk aversion; it lures the ordinarily timid into chancy electoral strategies, such as in the party-mediated support for marginal candidates. The effect of organization, then, is to increase the political impact per thousand dollars, to create more purposeful dollars that will achieve more political goals than other dollars. Learning, adaptation, organization, and rationality in campaign finance ultimately are all intended to maximize some actors' political influence.

The reborn legislative committees provide incumbents with one great advantage. They permit them to divide the pursuit of their own goals and the pursuit of the collective goals of their legislative party. Incumbent organization—the legislative campaign committees—promotes the goal of maximizing the number of party seats by providing funds for the less skillful or less advantaged of their partisans in the exchanges of campaign finance: namely, the threatened incumbents, virtually all viable challengers, and many open-seat candidates. PACs face the same problem of specific interests and more general, collective interests, and yet they enjoy less success in organizing the collective interests. Perhaps they are hampered by the pressures within them for confining themselves to the narrow interests that bind the PAC together. Perhaps the law of numbers, and the inevitable diversity and cross-pressures that numbers bring, works against organization. Perhaps, indeed, they lack the easily articulated collective interest—increase the number of party seats—that unites the incumbents.

Organization on the side of candidates features primarily the resurgence of the legislative parties both in the Congress and in the states. At the same time, the organs of the mass party—the Democratic and Republican national committees—increasingly restrict themselves to funding executive campaigns and state party operations. The legislative parties insure their own reelections and their majority status, but they also win their independence from the wider, popularly based party and the party of the executive. Their ability to raise more money for their legislative candidates is therefore hardly a sign of general party strength or revival. It is instead a sign of the inability of the major parties to hold their legislators accountable to any wider constituency in the party.[35]

Looked at in the longer perspectives of American campaign finance, the increasing importance of organization harks back to the status quo ante. The brokers of today are the descendants of the fat cats, the old party treasurers, the campaign managers, and the finance committees and their chairpeople who raised the money in the old days. And just as then, they bring a third set of interests to the contributor-candidate exchanges. The newly powerful party campaign committees and their analogues in the states are today's paler versions of the old political party asserting its dominance of those exchanges in the name of the party's collective interests. The new element in all of this is the context of the post–1974 regulation of contributions and party spending. Organization now serves both for advantage in the exchanges of campaign finance and as a device for minimizing the various constraints of the FECA.

The repeated resonances of the status quo ante, of campaign finance before the 1970s, underscore again the growing distance between the status quo and the ideal of an unorganized, atomized campaign finance dominated by the free-will offerings of people down at the political grass roots. The searches for aggregated, organized advantage—and for offsetting organized advantage—carry us further from the hopes of the last great wave of reform. The goal of a campaign finance of disinterested and innocent individualism seems less attainable than ever.

Chapter 5 _____

The Fifth Source

In the sea of eager judgment about American campaign finance, there is an island of ambivalence. Americans are puzzled and uncertain about the use of public funds to finance campaigns. The other four sources—individuals, PACs, parties, and the candidates themselves—do not enjoy extravagant public support, but they have at least won a grudging acceptance as the instruments of voluntarism and more recently as exercises of First Amendment freedoms. Indeed, the fact that public funding is a departure from voluntarism and privatization, no matter how one dresses it up, stands as its greatest liability.

The ambivalence about the use of public money permeates all levels of American politics. Candidates accept public funding while giving it little or no support as public policy. Mass public opinion, usually so decisively one-sided on issues of campaign funding, is so closely and uncertainly divided about the fifth source that it tilts one way or the other depending on the clauses or the rhetoric of the pollster's question. No one has better exemplified the American ambivalence than Ronald Reagan. In his presidential campaigns of 1976, 1980, and 1984 Reagan accepted more money in public funding—a total of $90 million—than any other seeker after any public office, and yet he apparently never checked the box on his income tax returns authorizing a contribution to the fund providing the money.

As things go in campaign finance, public funding is a simple concept: providing candidates with funds from a governmental treasury to pay the costs of campaigning. Simple though the notion may be, it came onto the American political scene at a time, the mid-1970s, when the public sector was beginning to contract. The number of public-funding programs and experience with them are therefore limited. There are two public-funding programs at the national level: one for the pre-convention (presidential-primary) part of the campaign for the presidency, and the other for the post-convention (general-election) part. Then there are public-financing programs in nine states. Four of them, the major programs, disperse more than a million dollars an election to candidates (Michigan, Minnesota, New Jersey, and Wisconsin); five range from the modest to the negligible (Florida, Hawaii, Massachusetts, Montana, and Rhode Island).[1] There are also public-funding programs in the nation's two largest cities, Los Angeles and New York, in Seattle and Tucson, and in scattered other localities.[2] In sum, public funding covers fully the most important election campaign in the United States but only a small minority of all the others. And in no case does the experience predate 1974.

Within these relatively few programs there is a riotous variety of philosophy and practice. Only the one for the presidential general-election campaign provides 100 percent funding for eligible candidates—that is, funding equal to the spending limits the candidates accept to get the public funds. The rest cover only a smaller sum, often about one-third, of the permissible expenditures. Some of the public money comes to candidates by entitlement, usually as a result of their party's recent vote-getting record; in other programs candidates qualify by raising a specified sum from other sources or by raising money for matching with public funds. But whatever the variations, they all have two related features in common. They are all voluntary—candidates must choose to accept the public funding—and in all of them there is a connection between the public funds and legislative attempts to limit candidate spending.[3] Therein are the nubs of the matter.

The Presidential Funding Systems

The financing of American presidential campaigns encapsulates much of the diversity within the public-funding option. What may seem superficially to be a single plan for public funding is in fact two very different plans, one a partial-funding program for the pre-nomination period and the other a full-funding option for the autumn general-election campaign. Yet both are products of post-Watergate shock and reformism, and both run with funds released by the checkoff of funds on the income tax returns of millions of Americans. They are, moreover, the programs of public funding about which Americans know the most. What problems they see in using this fifth source and what instruction they derive about public funding comes in the main from the presidential experience.

The general-election system, the one for the campaign culminating in November, is by far the simpler of the two presidential-campaign systems. The Democratic and Republican candidates are automatically eligible for public funds unless their party's popular vote has slipped below an unthinkable 25 percent at the last presidential election. Whatever their personal feelings and motives, the major-party candidates in 1976, 1980, 1984, and 1988 all accepted the funding.[4] The sum of the allotment from the U.S. treasury is the current indexed value of $20 million in 1974 dollars; that sum is also the candidate's spending limit, with the exception of a $50,000 allowance for the spending of personal resources. In 1988 George Bush and Michael Dukakis each received $46.1 million in federal funds. Their respective national political parties also raised and spent $8.3 million on behalf of their campaigns, the full sum permitted by the public-funding statute.[5] If a candidate were to choose not to accept public funding, none of these spending limits would apply, and contributors would be bound by the usual limits on contributions for a single election: $1,000 for individuals and $5,000 for PACs.

Aside from its position as the only American program of full public funding, the presidential plan has been special in another important way. It is one of a very small subset of public funding programs to gain voluntary acceptance from all major-party candidates from its inception through 1990. Thus, in the presidential campaigns we have not faced the scenario of a publicly funded candidate, constrained by spending limits, campaigning against a privately funded candidate uninhibited by those limits. Parity has been established, the candidates freed from money-raising exertions and distractions, and the sources of their direct funding removed as a campaign issue. And so the plan of 1974—simple, direct, predictable, almost comprehensive, and relatively easy to administer—has operated much as its advocates planned. The sums have not been negligible, but they have grown only at the pace of inflation: $92.2 million for the two major party candidates in 1988, a sum equal in constant dollars to the $43.6 spent in 1976. The 1988 total was only four to five times greater than the expenditures of the major-party candidates in the California race for a Senate seat in the same year.

Public funding of the races for the presidential nominations of the two major parties is, by contrast, both more complicated and less predictable. The number of candidates receiving public funds is not fixed; one establishes eligibility for them rather easily by raising $5,000 in sums of $250 or less in at least 20 different states. In view of the fact that the eligibility threshold is not indexed, it was more than twice as easy in real dollars to qualify in 1988 than it was in 1976. For the eligible candidates, the U.S. treasury then matches all individual contributions of $250 and less up to an aggregate limit of $5 million in 1974 dollars (in 1988: $11.6 million). A total of 48 Democratic and Republican seekers after a presidential nomination

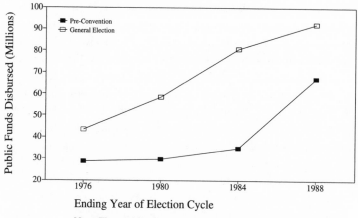

Ending Year of Election Cycle

Note: The total for the 1980 general election includes $4.2 million for John Anderson, an independent candidate.

Figure 5.1
Public Funding of Pre-Convention and General-Election Campaigns for President: 1976–1988

have received public funds in the four cycles from 1976 through 1988.[6] In addition, two minor-party candidates have earned public funding: Sonia Johnson, the candidate of the Citizens party in 1984, and Lenora Fulani of the New Alliance party in 1988. Only one serious major-party candidate—Republican John Connally of Texas in 1980—has chosen not to accept the public money. The total sums spent in each of the four presidential years have reflected both the general rate of inflation and the varying numbers of seekers after the party nominations (fig. 5.1). The major cause of the fluctuations in the number of funded candidates in a given year was the absence or presence of an incumbent president seeking reelection. The sharp jump in 1988 resulted from unrestrained races in both parties, it being the first election since 1968 in which an incumbent president was not running for reelection.

Spending limits, as always, accompany the acceptance of public money. In this case they are of an almost sadistic complexity. Candidates may spend no more than $10 million in

1974 dollars (in 1988: $23.1 million) in the entire process of rounding up convention delegates in the 50 states; it is a figure exactly twice the maximum sum they can earn in public funds.[7] At the same time they are bound by spending limits for each of the 50 states, the limit being based on population: the larger of $200,000 or 16 cents for each voting-age citizen in 1974 dollars. In 1988, spending in the smallest states, including crucial New Hampshire, was limited to $461,000; the largest limit, that for California, was $7.5 million. To ease the pressures on those limits and to end evasions of them such as housing staffs in neighboring states, the FEC in late 1991 adopted rules that exempted certain expenses from the totals. Candidates no longer had to include many of their expenditures on advertising, travel, and political consultants.

In no other American election campaign are electoral and financial considerations so closely interwoven. In presidential cycle after presidential cycle the states elbow each other to move into the early months of the presidential-primary season, especially into February, March, and April, in order to maximize their impact. The first federal checks are not paid out until January 1 of election year, although certificates of eligibility for the funds issued earlier have in the past stood, good as gold, as collateral for loans to needy candidates. Once into the crucial season of the first caucuses and presidential primaries in January through March, candidates must decide how to allocate their funds and spending limits among the states.

For every kind of participant in the process there is a special set of problems in this compressed campaign for convention delegates. For the front-runners trying to sustain momentum for an early win, there is the danger that an all-out early campaign will fail and exhaust too much of the total spending limit, leaving the candidate short of spending authority in April and May. Walter Mondale in 1984 had spent about two-thirds of the limit by the end of March, forcing him to cut staffs in Washington and on the road in order to spend the final one-third largely on his media campaign.[8] The candidates starting back in the pack—Gary Hart, Mondale's main competitor, for example—invariably are short of funds and need to raise additional money on the basis of good showings in the early state processes and national polls. The constraints of the state-by-state limits, especially those on such states as Iowa and New Hampshire, work an especial hardship on their bootstrapping.

In brief, the restrictions and limitations that surround the public financing before the nominating conventions add up to the most intrusive aspect of the entire FECA. Public funding here impacts the politics of the process as well as its financing. It is perhaps the best example in public funding in the United States of legislators yielding to the temptation to try to accomplish too much with public funding—in this case to encourage small individual contributions, to allocate spending by state, to limit expenditures overall, and, unwittingly perhaps, to force an earlier start to the campaign in order to qualify for public funds. And then there is its administrative impact. Aside from the accounting nightmare candidates face to comply with the limits and deadlines, virtually all of them centralize authority in their campaigns to facilitate compliance; the result is to limit the initiatives of their people in the various states. The administrative imperatives of the program do not adjust easily to the traditions of grass-roots politics.

Taken together, the two presidential plans greatly simplify one aspect of presidential campaign finance: the sources of the money used. In the pre-convention period the sources are chiefly the public funds and the contributions of individuals that earn the matching public funds up to a maximum of $250 (table 5.1). For the 1984 and 1988 runs the candidates for both the Democratic and Republican nominations raised approximately one-third of their funds in public money, with almost all of the rest coming from individual contributors. The very small percentage coming from PACs is easy to explain: PACs generally do not give money in any elections or processes prior to the selection of major-party candidates, and lack of matching money for PAC contributions adds one more disincentive for their contributions. For the general campaign,

Table 5.1
1988 Presidential Campaigns: Pre-nomination Campaign Receipts and Federal Matching Funds (in Dollars)

Candidate	Adjusted Campaign Receipts	Federal Matching Funds	PAC Contributions	Individual Contributions
Democrats				
Babbitt	3,378,374	1,078,939	1,276	2,253,379
Biden	3,738,022	0	2,700	3,978,720
Dukakis	28,504,017	9,040,027	27,135	19,322,815
Gephardt	10,307,718	2,896,398	1,047,365	6,271,817
Gore	12,338,971	3,853,402	544,155	7,868,976
Hart	3,432,762	1,084,066	0	2,291,846
Jackson	19,958,545	7,701,169	88,127	12,259,663
LaRouche	3,856,187	825,577	5,000	3,025,438
Simon	10,092,892	3,603,919	333,842	6,077,225
Dem. Subtotal	95,607,488	30,083,497	2,049,600	63,089,843

Republicans			
Bush	31,798,284	8,393,099	686,243	22,322,141
Dole	26,533,924	7,618,116	1,997,475	16,907,969
Du Pont	8,061,570	2,550,954	0	5,419,250
Haig	2,046,392	538,539	19,820	1,369,090
Kemp	16,693,501	5,877,341	623,360	10,177,365
Robertson	30,907,283	9,691,019	0	20,584,883
Rep. Subtotal	116,040,954	34,669,068	3,326,898	76,780,698
Fulani (New Alliance party)	2,149,432	938,798	0	1,210,638
Total	213,797,874	65,691,363	5,376,498	141,081,179

Source: Federal Election Commission.

of course, the sources are quite simple: the public funds and the party spending. (I will address the sources of money that flow outside of the public-funding system—the soft money—shortly.)

Simplified though the sources may be, the early individual contributions are amassed in some of the most intense fund-raising in all of American politics. The task is formidable. Most campaigns are trying to make national figures out of candidates who are local figures, a governor of a state perhaps, while also raising the money that will assure a substantial matching sum from the U.S. treasury. Moreover, they are trying to do so in a remarkably short time, often in no more than the six months between autumn of the year before the presidential election and April of the presidential-primary season. Lining up a fund-raising wizard thus becomes the major early decision for a budding president. The need is for more than brokering—it is for metabrokering, since a wizard in essence functions as a broker of the brokers, the person with access to the intermediaries whose ability to raise money is locally or regionally based.

Although the public money comes from the U.S. Treasury, it gets there by a special route: the checkoff option on individual income tax returns. The taxpayer confronts two lines headed "Presidential Election Campaign" on the first page of his or her return. "Do you want $1 to go to this fund?" asks the form; a second question similarly addresses "your spouse." To the side of the yes and no boxes for each response the IRS adds this reassuring statement (in somewhat smaller type): "Checking 'yes' will not change your tax or reduce your refund." From the taxes of the willing, money is diverted in one- and two-dollar sums to the Presidential Election Campaign Fund, from which eligible candidates receive their money. The same kind of checkoff system also provides the money in most state programs.[9] Florida, not having an income tax, initially committed itself to use general tax revenues, but in 1991 it shifted some of the costs of its infant program to taxes on political contributions by PACs and parties.

Federal and state funds fed by the income tax checkoff now suffer from declining percentages of yes-checkers. For the first time since 1974 the percentage of U.S. taxpayers authorizing use of "their" money dipped below 20 percent to 19.8 percent in 1989. That percentage is the most tangible and most threatening sign of the American ambivalence about funding campaigns from the public treasury. Indeed, the size of the percentage suggests not ambivalence but opposition.

Public Funding and Mass Opinion

Public funding never was the darling of the taxpaying public. Even in its earliest years, with the reverberations of Watergate still audible, it never received the support of even 30 percent of the filers of income tax returns (table 5.2).[10] From that point the participating percentage has slowly but inexorably slid below the 20 percent mark. So, even though the base of taxpayers has broadened, the sums of money designated for the Fund have slowly declined, too. By 1991 it appeared that there would be barely enough money in the Fund to pay the commitments to all claimants in the presidential campaigns of 1992. The shortfall, in the absence of some changes, will be far worse in 1996.

It would be a mistake, however, to rush on and leave the impression that the decline in citizen participation had chiefly or solely created the shortage in the Presidential Election Campaign Fund. The root of the problem is really in partial indexing; the payments out of the Fund to candidates and the parties (to support their national nominating conventions) all increase with changes in the consumer price index, but the sums going into the Fund do not. They are still the same $1 and $2 amounts Congress authorized two decades ago. Secondarily, the eligibility formula in the pre-convention portion ($5,000 in sums no larger than $250 from 20 different states) is not indexed either; it is thus now easier than ever to qualify for public money. The system always has been a disaster wait-

Table 5.2
Presidential Election Campaign Fund: 1976–1990

Year	Checkoff Rate (%)	Total $ Checked off	Total Disbursements ($)	Fund Balance ($)
1976	27.5	33,731,945	69,467,521	23,805,659
1977	28.6	36,606,008	521,124	60,927,571
1978	25.4	39,246,689	6,000	100,331,986
1979	27.4	35,941,347	1,050,000	135,246,807
1980	28.7	38,838,417	101,427,116	73,752,205
1981	27.0	41,049,052	630,256	114,373,289
1982	24.2	39,023,882	1,070	153,454,501
1983	23.7	35,631,068	11,786,486	177,320,982
1984	23.0	35,036,761	120,149,768	92,713,782
1985	23.0	34,712,761	1,617,842	125,870,541
1986	21.7	35,753,837	5,596	161,680,423
1987	21.0	33,651,947	17,784,000	177,905,677
1988	20.1	33,013,987	158,560,805	52,462,359
1989	19.8	32,285,646	1,843,017	82,927,013
1990	n/a	32,462,979	2,426	115,426,713

Source: Federal Election Commission.

ing to happen. The only question has been when, and the declining participation has merely hastened the date.

So, the Fund is running dry. The Federal Election Commission estimated in the fall of 1991 that it would be short approximately $3.5 million for 1992. The public-funding statute actually addresses such an eventuality; in a time of shortfall the first claim on the Fund is the commitment to finance the parties' national conventions, the second is the general-election campaign, and the third (and lowest) is the presidential-primary season. Thus in 1992 the candidates in the pre-convention scramble were to be paid only part ("on a pro rata basis") of the funds to which they were entitled under the statutory formula, and under new Treasury rules they would be paid only once a month.[11] Furthermore, a policy of first-come, first-served would prevail; candidates' claims in January 1992 would be matched fully, even if that meant depleting the balance in the Fund for February or March matching claims. Were the Fund depleted in January, those latter claims would have to be met with money flowing into the Fund from current tax returns, and the FEC estimated that they would not cover the candidates' claims against them.

The political implications of those Treasury decisions kicked up a mighty ruckus in the latter half of 1991. George Bush, an incumbent president facing little or no competition for renomination, was raising sums that would constitute a major claim against the funds available in January, leaving the cupboard almost bare in subsequent months for the late-starting and relatively unknown Democratic aspirants. The Treasury Department, denying any partisan motivation, turned aside a request from the FEC to factor into its allocation of funds for the three priorities the millions that taxpayers will contribute (that is, check off) to the Fund after the primary-season claims abate. At the last minute—early 1992—the FEC announced that the Fund would indeed cover claims on it for 1992, largely because of the modest fund-raising by the Democratic contenders. The FEC did, however, predict a serious shortfall in 1996.

The problems in the federal Fund are the problems of the states writ large. Minnesota's checkoff percentage on its income tax returns dropped from a high of 27.1 percent in 1977 to 18.8 percent in 1989. But Minnesota has twice done what supporters of public funding have long pleaded with the Congress to do: it has raised the amount of the checkoff from $1 to $2 in 1980 and then to $5 in 1987. Minnesota supports campaigns for the governorship and other statewide offices as well as those for both houses of the state legislature, and in addition it makes grants to the political parties. So, how is it that support has eroded not only nationally but in a state with one of the highest voter turnouts and one of the best-funded public sectors in the nation?

Spurred by the falling balance in the Presidential Election Campaign Fund, the FEC in 1990 commissioned a private "focus-group" study of American taxpayers to better understand the checkoff decisions. Two separate sessions in three American cities, one each for supporters and nonsupporters of the Fund, documented both the strong feelings people have about the checkoff, especially the negative feelings, and the low levels of information they have about it. The dominant impression one gets from the study is of an opposition to public funding rooted in unhappiness with candidates, campaigns, electoral politics, even governmental waste and folly. In the words of the summary of the report's findings, "It was often difficult to keep the group focused on the subject at hand because of their anger at politicians and a perception of wasteful spending by government. Their anger associated with those concerns contaminated their consideration of Presidential campaign funding and expenditure."[12] After warning that the "position of nearly all the non-contributors appears to be immovable," the authors recommended, somewhat anticlimacticly, that the public-funding program, because of its size and obscurity, "deserves to have promotional activity directed to the public."[13]

Actually, there are as many explanations of the falling checkoff rate as there are observers, and most of them are probably right. It does reflect a growing disapproval of all campaigning and partisan politics, and it does reflect ignorance about public funding, an ignorance bound to increase as time distances most Americans from the founding debate over the program and the Nixon campaigns that led to it. The impression that there is too much money in American campaigns already and that it is too influential cannot work in favor of checking off. Many Americans, furthermore, simply do not believe the words on the 1040 form that checking the box will not increase their tax liability or decrease their refund. Then, there are the philosophical objections, ranging from an absolutist conservative opposition to most government action to a more selective view that public funds ought not to be

used to subsidize partisan activity or political speech. Speculation centers also on tax accountants who do not check off
for their clients, whether out of oversight, personal opposition,
or a desire to avoid troublesome explanations or a client's
indecision. Yet saying that all of these explanations—and others, too—are valid does not tell in what strengths and proportions they operate.

Public-opinion polls offer additional insights, and public
funding is the one policy-centered topic in campaign finance
for which there are plenty of data. Unlike the FEC's focus-
group study, the polls report the responses of carefully drawn
samples of American adults. The dimensions and volatility of
opinion about public funding, including presidential public
funding, becomes apparent just by looking at recent questions
and opinions, all of them from 1990:

- Question: "Would you favor or oppose public financing of
  congressional elections?" Responses: 38 percent in favor
  and 55 percent opposed.[14]

- Question: "It has been suggested that the federal government provide a fixed amount of money for campaigns of
  candidates for Congress and that all private contributions
  be prohibited. Do you think this is a good idea or a poor
  idea?" Responses: 58 percent think it a good idea, and 33
  percent think it a poor idea.[15]

- Question: "Earlier I asked you whether you favored or opposed providing public financing for congressional campaigns and barring all other contributions, including money
  from PACs. Now, some people say, if campaigns are publicly
  funded, taxpayers will end up paying for all the negative
  campaigning and mudslinging on TV today. Do you strongly
  favor, favor, oppose, or strongly oppose that proposal for
  public financing of campaigns?" Responses: 29 percent
  opted for one of the favorable replies, and 60 percent for
  one of the negative replies.[16]

- Question: "Would you favor or oppose public financing of
  congressional elections, or don't you have an opinion on

this?" Responses: 20 percent favor, 31 percent oppose, and 49 percent do not know or have no opinion.[17]

The pattern to the volatility is predictable. Millions of American adults have an uncertain opinion or none at all, but there is probably a plurality opposed to public funding per se. When one introduces other considerations into the question, however, opinion fluctuates with those considerations—perhaps another indication of the shallowness of opinion about public funding by itself. All in all, there is probably a plurality, perhaps even a majority, for public financing combined with spending limits and/or the exclusion of private contributions—a majority, that is, for something like the public funding of presidential elections which less than 20 percent of the income tax filers support with a check mark. *Ambivalence* is perhaps too timid a word.[18]

In another sense, the checkoff rate has declined because opposition to it has been vocal and vigorous and because support has been so muted as to be inaudible. Most of the hostility has come from the Republican party, notwithstanding its presidential candidates' sharing from the proceeds of the Fund. Ronald Reagan's relationship with it has already been noted, but Gerald Ford and George Bush also drew from it. One more point from the Reagan years is relevant; the proposal for revising the income tax code that came from the Reagan administration in 1985 had in it a proposal dropping the checkoff entirely. Moreover, George Bush did not address the problem of the 1992 shortfall in the Fund in his campaign finance message of mid–1991. A few Democrats have spoken out in favor of maintaining the Fund, and so have a few newspaper editorialists, but it has hardly been a high-profile defense. The politics of public funding have changed greatly since 1971 and 1974—the best indication of all about public support for it.

Soft Money

Of all of the attempts to breach the regulatory structures in post-1974 campaign finance, none has been more publicized, even more notorious, than the raising of soft money. A term of epic imprecision, it most usefully refers to money raised outside of the restrictions of federal law (and often to circumvent those restrictions) with the intention, nonetheless, of influencing the outcome of a federal election, directly or indirectly. That definition, however, omits the agent or actor, and it is often the agent, the recruiter of the soft money, who is the point of contention. The agents are candidates, even presidential candidates, or PACs or party committees, themselves subject to the limits and requirements of the FECA. Hard money, on the contrary, is money that meets all of the litmus tests of the FECA and is thus available for spending in the campaigns governed by the FECA.[19]

It is a capacious definition—the jargon of campaign finance is no more exact than that of the rest of American politics—and one most easily grasps it by illustration. Suppose that the officers of a large corporation, knowing that direct corporate contributions violate federal law, give $50,000 to the Republican state committee in California, where such contributions are legal, with the hope that by strengthening the party they may help the Republican candidate for the U.S. Senate to victory. Soft money? Perhaps, but probably not: both a purposeful agent and a plan for the money's federal impact are missing. But had the money been steered to California by the National Republican Senatorial Committee, even kept in its soft-money accounts, and then allocated to California as a part of a soft-money campaign to build party organization and improve Republican chances of recapturing the Senate, the case is classic. The difference, of course, is an agent with a purpose, and so we return once more to the issue of intermediaries and brokers, if in a somewhat altered guise.

The presidential campaigns of the 1980s made soft money a national issue and put it high on the reformers' agendas. Since soft money did not need to be reported to the FEC—it moves outside of the FECA's aegis—public knowledge is sketchy.[20] The major parties did, after considerable chivvying, make a partial accounting of it in 1988, and Alexander and

Bauer estimate that $45 million was raised by participants in the presidential election, $23 million by the Democrats and $22 million by the Republicans.[21] Much of it was indeed raised by the presidential candidates, Michael Dukakis and George Bush, and all of it was channeled to state and local party committees where it was spent for party building programs, for general campaigning for the party ticket (such items as bumper stickers, sample ballots, lawn signs), and for registration and voter turnout programs—all of which would create some benefit, however indirect, for the party's presidential ticket. The contributions, the soft money per se, did not qualify as hard money for two reasons: Bush and Dukakis, having accepted public funds were prohibited from accepting private funds, and many of the contributions would also have violated federal law in any event for being a contribution from a prohibited source (for example, a union or corporation) or of a prohibited size (most of the individual contributions were well over the $1,000 limit, some as large as $100,000).

Soft money as a funding strategy springs from three very American institutions or conditions. It is, first, a creature of American federalism, possible because both the national government and the states regulate campaign finance and because most of the states choose to regulate it far less rigorously. Safe havens for money not legal under the FECA are therefore not hard to find. Second, it reflects the indivisibility of national and local party politics. Any assistance to the state or local party or to state or local candidates will help, in some measure, a party candidate for national office in the same election. In fact, money spent by a state party on voter turnout may relieve a national party or presidential candidate of having to make those very expenditures. And third, the phenomenon of soft money reflects some overt and intentional concessions by the Congress in 1979 to American grass-roots politics. Those legislated exceptions to the FECA require some extended explanation.

From the beginning Congress excluded from the coverage of the FECA all programs of voter registration, education, and mobilization run by nonparty groups as long as they were not politically selective. It intended the FECA to deal with the flow of cash and not with volunteered labor or the fulfilling of civic duty. If organizations began to urge their members or employees to vote for specific parties or candidates, those political "communications" were only partially "excluded"; they had to be reported to the FEC but suffered no other restrictions.[22] Then in 1979, in the last significant amendment to the FECA, Congress excluded from the FECA's contribution and spending limits various party-building activities of state and local parties—activities such as providing sample ballots, recruiting volunteers, and turning out voters on election day. The purpose was ostensibly to help those parties find a role in an increasingly national and centralized campaign politics.

These exclusions, particularly the first and third, have entered the debate over soft money precisely because they are funded by money spent outside of FECA regulatory boundaries. Critics of the presidential system increasingly point to the labor programs (that is, the first exclusion) as an example of a loophole through which money flows outside the system primarily to help Democrats. Some of them cast their definitions of soft money broadly enough to include it. Those criticisms reflect a certain lack of candor in two respects: they expand the concept of soft money for ad hoc purposes, and they gloss over the fact of congressional intent by references to loopholes. The third exclusion, the one dealing with party committees, *is* central to the consensus concept of soft money. Under the exclusion, state and local party committees may raise and spend money for sample ballots, bumper stickers, registration drives, and the other business of grass-roots politics without concern for the FECA's limits. Any part of those expenditures that can be allocated to the campaigns of candidates for the Congress or the presidency, however, must be paid with hard money raised within the limitations of the FECA.

For all of these reasons—federalism, the indivisibility of partisan politics, and the 1979 exclusions—and for the reason of a good deal of political ingenuity, soft-money expenditures in the 1988 presidential campaigns increased resources raised in it by almost a third ($45 million) over the statutory limits of $108.8 million ($46.1 million for each candidate and $8.3 for each national party). The breaking of the barriers is only the first of the sources of unhappiness with soft money, though. The $45 million also marks the reentry of new fat cats into presidential campaigns; at least 397 individuals, including Charles H. Keating, gave $100,000 or more to one of the parties. Further, much of the fund-raising was done by George Bush and Michael Dukakis, involving them in the distractions of raising money during the campaign and in the creation of obligations to large contributors. Finally, such soft-money sums raise broader questions of the integrity of the public-funding system, of the meaning of 100 percent public funding, of candidates' pledges to limit expenditures, and of the intent to exclude the raising and giving of private funds. Journalists and other reformers surely exaggerate when they proclaim, for example, the "demolition" of the public-funding program.[23] And yet, those sums of soft money bring us closer in one more way to the status quo ante 1974 or 1976.

Increasing sums of soft money, especially in presidential campaigns, have also sorely tested the FEC. Common Cause, for instance, takes the position that the solicitation of soft money is illegal because it violates the twin pledges of presidential candidates not to spend beyond the statutory limits and not to raise money from private contributors.[24] It also has waged a campaign of some years to force the FEC to put a stop to it. The position of the FEC is, at least in part, that soft money involves policy matters that are properly in the province of the Congress, especially since the exclusions of 1979 are a part of the problem. Common Cause went to federal district court, and in a limited victory for Common Cause the judge ordered the FEC to revise its rules to make sure the use of soft money by state parties did not violate federal law.[25] The FEC eventually responded by adopting new rules that went into effect January 1, 1991. They defined more clearly the excluded ("exempt") party activities, required reporting by

PACs and party committees maintaining hard- and soft-money accounts, and provided intricate ways of allocating hard- and soft-money costs in joint activities (such as administration and voter registration drives) on behalf of both state and federal candidates.[26] The FEC released the first results of the new reporting in August 1991, and there matters stand, except for attempts to deal with soft money in reform packages before the Congress.

The major break in the regulatory structures Congress mandated in 1974 thus occurs in the main showcase of public funding in all of American campaigns. Is the conjunction merely fortuitous? Or is soft money a result of some quality inherent in public funding? Before rushing to such a conclusion, one needs to consider the alternative explanation. These regulatory structures are like great hydraulic systems: there is constant pressure on the system from the liquid it contains— money flows as well as talks—and leaks or ruptures occur as a result of both weakness in the wall and pressure in the fluid. The regulatory wall is weak at the presidential point because of the national-local nature of the campaign and the parties and because of Congress's inability to regulate the state-local portion. As for pressure, it is greatest here not primarily because of public funding but because of spending limits pegged too low for the magnitudes of both the office sought and the campaigns for it. Expenditures in virtually all other campaigns increased at a rate considerably above the rate of inflation between 1976 and 1988.

Yet the suspicion nags that there is a connection between soft money and the exclusion of private funding from the country's most important election campaign. But is the problem with public funding per se, or is it with *full* public funding in a broader context of campaign finance that encourages private funding and the play of private interests in every other electoral campaign in the United States? Whatever the answer to those questions, full public funding does indisputably exert a confining control on campaign funding that is qualitatively different from the devices of contribution limits and reporting requirements. With it the Congress seeks to control the flow of all money into the campaign and to regulate the sum of all expenditures in it. Inevitably, the greater the degree or kind of control, the greater the incentive to find a way around it. Both the incentives and the challenges to the adaptability of experienced and inventive movers of political money are enormous in presidential campaigns.

Public Funding as Carrot and Stick

Originally the main justification for public financing was as a replacement of interested, even predatory private funding and its providers. But the Supreme Court displaced that rationale in *Buckley* v. *Valeo* in 1976.[27] By holding that spending limits per se were unconstitutional restrictions on political activities protected by the First Amendment and that they were permissible only if voluntarily accepted, the Court created the need for an incentive to induce voluntary acceptance. The availability of public funds became that incentive, the big carrot for controlling the costs of campaigning.

After *Buckley,* therefore, the use of public funding as a policy option in campaign finance systems changed in important ways. There was now a link between public funding and limits on spending; for the first time one now had to have acceptance of the former to impose the latter.[28] Public funding increasingly became not an end in itself but a means to the goal of limiting campaign spending. Even legislators once doubtful about public funding now embraced it, however chastely, as the only way to get to the desired goal of spending limits. The logic of these post-*Buckley* calculations, interestingly, indicates that in the 1980s the policy goal of limiting expenditures ranked higher than the goal of replacing interested private money.

When public funding became the means to two important policy goals instead of one, its viability as a policy option increasingly hinged on enticing candidates to choose it. Discussion of acceptance ratios began to surface in the public-funding debate, especially in the states. Two empirical conclusions emerged about the rates at which candidates accepted public funding. First, Democrats were more likely to accept it than Republicans, whether the office was statewide executive office or a seat in the state legislature. Democrats have historically been the party favoring governmental, public solutions to problems, and Republicans have always expressed greater philosophical objections to public funding, much as they do to public solutions for providing affordable health care. At the same time, of course, Republicans in the states generally find it easier to raise money than Democrats, especially in the states in which campaign contributions are less severely regulated. With the Democrats controlling 69 of the 98 legislative chambers in the states,[29] Republicans feel the need to raise larger sums of money to overcome the advantages of incumbent Democrats. Beyond the partisan division on acceptance, however, a second set of considerations affects the rate of acceptance: the mix of incentives and constraints in the public-funding program.

The attractiveness of the incentives largely has to do with the stake from public funds, its size, the ease of acquiring it (that is, the severity of matching requirements), and its size as a percentage of spending limits. The chief constraint is the penury or generosity of the limit on expenditures. In addition, many candidates regard the "hassles" attendant on public funding—the record keeping on eligibility, on matching funds, and on expenditures, with the consequent reporting and accounting—as a strong disincentive to acceptance. Almost as central to the acceptance decision is the availability of alternative sources of funding, a complex calculation turning on more detailed questions of party, constituency, statutory regulations, and candidate fund-raising skills.

Leaving aside the questions of alternative funding as virtually unmeasurable, a simple calculus of the relative weight of incentives and disincentives remains. To simplify even further: the greater the amount of public funding and the higher the expenditure limit, the greater the probability that the can-

Table 5.3
Participation Rate of State Legislative Candidates in Minnesota
Public Funding Program: 1976–1990

Year	House		Senate	
	Democrats	Republicans	Democrats	Republicans
1976	96.9%	85.4%	96.9%	93.3%
1978	98.4%	75.6%	—	—
1980	85.1%	48.7%	79.1%	45.0%
1982	95.5%	82.1%	100.0%	83.9%
1984	96.9%	75.8%	—	—
1986	94.6%	68.3%	91.0%	67.7%
1988	92.2%	84.1%	—	—
1990	97.5%	91.0%	98.5%	100.0%

Source: Minnesota Ethical Practices Board.

didate will accept the public-funding package. Data from Minnesota legislative elections confirms the proposition (table 5.3). The initial acceptance rates declined slowly, if irregularly, until the legislature (before the 1982 elections) linked the spending limits to the consumer price index, thus raising them and the payment limits. Acceptance rates jumped. The increase was greatest among the Republicans if only because they had the greatest room for increase. But their remarkable conversion to public funding suggests two conclusions, both limited only by evidence from a single state. First, Republican philosophical objections to public funding apparently were not governing many of the earlier decisions not to accept. Second, and more generally, cost-benefit analyses will cut differently for the two parties. Republicans, with greater abilities to raise private funds, will not respond to the less lavish mix of funds and spending limits that will entice most Democrats.

Initially the proponents of public funding counted on one additional incentive: voter displeasure with a candidate who refused public funds in order to harvest unlimited private money and to spend unlimited sums. It has turned out to be far less potent a threat than the reformers wanted. There may have been a few instances of voter wrath somewhere in the country, but they have not been documented; moreover, two Republican governors, one each from Minnesota and Wisconsin, states with substantial public-funding programs for gubernatorial candidates, won election while spurning public funding.[30] In elections to the Minnesota lower house, a total of 225 Republican candidates have spurned public funding between 1976 and 1990; 128 of them (57 percent) won their elections. In fact, candidates do not often succeed in making acceptance a useful campaign issue, much less a winning one; Democrat Tom Loftus tried in Wisconsin in 1990 but lost badly to the privately funded Republican, Tommy Thompson. Indeed, if the public pressure were great, one would not have to arrange substantial incentives for candidates to accept spending limits.

In the recent years of fiscal austerity, public funding has encountered a new obstacle: the shortage of public funds for any new government programs. Its advocates now face hard questions about using public funds for election campaigns when medicaid payments, library hours, and school budgets are being cut. In keeping with the times, public funding has been transformed from a carrot to a stick. Once a positive inducement to accept spending limits, it now increasingly becomes a punishment for not accepting them. Minnesota's new attempt to regulate spending in the state's senatorial and congressional elections waives the spending limits for the candidate whose opponent does not agree to observe them; in addition, the candidate receives state funds for his campaign. In a race in which both candidates accept the spending limits, there is no public funding. In such plans, therefore, there would be no public funding if all candidates accepted spending limits; public funding, having served its purpose as a threat, benignly disappears.[31]

Consider, then, the three incarnations of public funding as public policy in less than two decades. It began and succeeded in the early 1970s as a way of replacing interested private funds and funders. After *Buckley* it was reincarnated to serve double duty: incentive for spending limits as well as replacement of suspect private money. And it is now coming increasingly to be the threat by which candidates are cajoled into agreeing to spending limits. If it succeeds as well as its proponents hope, there will be no public funds spent, and we will, in the name of public funding, be back to a campaign finance of private and interested money. Among the ironies of campaign finance in the United States, few are as arresting as this one. The transformation of public funding in less than 20 years may be the ultimate reflection of public ambivalence about it.

The Outlook for Public Funding

Like every other policy issue in campaign finance, public funding is a partisan issue. Overwhelmingly Democrats support it and Republicans oppose it. Those party lines are most sharply drawn in the Congress, but it is present, too, in the states in which the question has been debated. The Senate took a test vote on the issue in the spring of 1991, the occasion being a Republican amendment to the campaign finance bill that would have eliminated all public financing and spending limits for presidential campaigns. All 56 Democratic votes opposed it, and 38 of the 42 Republicans voted in favor. Whatever the differing party fondnesses for governmental solutions, the facts of party fund-raising capacities cannot ever be out of mind either. It was a key issue in the debates of the early 1970s, and it remains one today.

That deep partisan split is only one reason for the slowed progress of public funding. A number of state programs have fared badly because of funding problems. Too many were underfunded either with an inadequate checkoff or with a plan of income tax add-ons, a plan in which the taxpayer voluntarily adds a sum to net tax liability. Several states have entered upon public funding recently, but neither Florida nor North Carolina, for example, has yet provided funds equal to their plans. In fact, the list of public-funding programs in viable financial condition in 1992 is short: the presidential general election plan and those in four states (Michigan, Minnesota, New Jersey, and Wisconsin) and a handful of localities.

Even the healthy programs have not escaped the pressures of a shrinking public sector, resistance to taxes, recessionary drops in revenues, and greater programmatic competition for scarce public funds. And then there are the perils of a widespread commitment to the checkoff. It was born of political expediency as a way of securing support for public funding under the fiction that only supporters of the idea would be paying for it. It was an approach that the Congress had always rejected for Social Security taxes, for it was a denial of the collective, public nature of public policy. In its way the checkoff was a public-policy innovation within the greater innovation of public funding, and once having made a commitment to it, legislatures find it hard to back away from it.

So in the very mechanism for providing the money, public funding began with a compromise born of ambivalence. Having been invited to vote with their pens, or their accountants' pens, millions of Americans have done so. They act out of a confused amalgam of reasons, some of them touching public funding marginally if at all. But if the framers of the public-funding legislation ever expected the average voter to make the checkoff decision after weighing the pros and cons of experience with public funding, they were deluded by their populist hopes. The complexity of the subject defeats all but the experts, and even they do not easily come to consensus judgments.

The minuses in public funding are more conspicuous than the pluses. Leaving the arguments of principle and partisan advantage aside, and taking the presidential programs as the best-known examples, we come down to the operational issues. The administrative problems are considerable, and features such as the matching program and the state-by-state spending limits raise them to staggering proportions; the FEC was still auditing some of the pre-convention campaign reports from

1988 well into autumn of 1991. Furthermore, pressures on the spending limits—evasions of state limits before the conventions and the soft-money binge after them—compromise the integrity of the plan and invite cynicism about the pledges of candidates and, by extension, about a good deal more of American politics. Then there are the compliance costs in accounting, bookkeeping, administrative oversight, reporting, and legal work. Finally, the presidential programs attract criticism from all sides for their treatment of third-party and non-mainstream candidates. Whereas the public tends to be unhappy with funding the "kooks" in the pre-convention period—Lyndon LaRouche's three dips into the treasury stick in many craws—many scholars and some activists have been unhappy that third parties are not funded more forthcomingly in the post-convention period.

It is a lengthy bill of particulars, and a committed critic could probably extend it. There is a problem with it, however; many of those problems are with spending limits, not with public funding per se. The Supreme Court has joined the funding and the limits into a single plan, but they are separable components. Much of the administrative burden and much of the evasion result from attempts to limit expenditures—misadvised attempts, largely, as in the state-by-state limits and in general-election spending limits that were from the beginning too low. If one imagines a "purer" case of public funding, public funding without spending limits simply to provide adequate funds for competitive campaigns, one imagines away a good many of the problems with the status quo.

Even without separating the problems with public funding and the problems with spending limits, public-funding programs, again typified by the presidential programs, have achieved much of what they were intended to achieve. Their spending limits have tempered the growth of campaign spending. Even including the $45 million in soft money in 1988, the rate of growth since 1976 is well below that of congressional campaigns. Congressional spending increased from $99 million in 1976 to $403 million in 1990, a rise of 307 percent.

Direct presidential campaign spending for both the pre-convention and general-election periods totaled $106.5 million in 1976 and $328.9 million in 1990, an increase of 209 percent. Even if one adds to the 1990 sum the $45 million in soft money, whose impact on the presidential campaign was well below the $45 million level, the increase over the 1976 total is 251 percent. Moreover, public funding by its nature has replaced interested private money. Observers will differ on how great a gain that is, but the legislative goal has been won. Public funding has also reduced the distractions and disruptions occasioned by the money chase during a campaign, and its early availability has permitted longer-range campaign planning. Finally, public funding has provided money for the candidate without access to major private funds. In the pre-convention period it permitted an energetic outsider such as Jimmy Carter to finance his way to a party nomination. In the general-election campaigns it achieved a parity of resources between the major-party candidates simply by legislating it.

Accomplishments can be argued, even documented, but there is little public recognition of them, much less any satisfaction or celebration. The 19.8 percent checkoff rate seems unmistakably to document that point. The presidential soft money, so well publicized, casts a pall with its intimations of the ancien régime and its seeming betrayal of the public-funding bargain. The changing fortunes of the public sector, furthermore, diminish any optimism about public funding as anything but a stick with which to beat recalcitrant mega-spenders. For the advocates of public funding, it has understandably become a time for hunkering down and defending old victories in new times.

Even though public financing slips slowly down the reformers' agenda, the problem that placed it high on the agenda in the first place—the dangers of interested private money—remains as salient as ever. Alternative attacks on the problem, chiefly the outlawing or crippling of PACs, are doomed to failure for both constitutional and practical reasons. (That argument is developed more fully in the next two chapters.) No matter how daunting the fiscal realities or the politics of campaign finance, direct public funding in important sums remains the viable policy alternative to private funding and the baggage that donors carry. American legislatures have not been able to reinvent the wheel or to find a replacement for it.

Ultimately, Americans are caught up in the greatest ambivalence of all in our collective response to public funding in the late 1980s and early 1990s. We seem to prefer private to public funding, but we reject the consequences of private funding. We are not happy either with money that supports private interests or with unlimited campaign spending. We want the consequences of public funding without the public funding itself. It is a perplexing riddle for which we have not yet found the solution.

Chapter 6 _____
_____
_____

_____

If It's Not Broken... Or Is It?

On a Sunday edition of the *NBC Nightly News* in April 1991, Garrick Utley, the anchor, segued from a report on the state of banking to the next topic: "And while we're on the subject of money, how about politics. Money buys influence. How do you stop it? We'll find out next. Our focus this evening, money and politics, efforts to curb widespread corruption in state politics. Consider this. During the past 20 years, convictions of state officeholders on federal corruption charges have increased sevenfold. What kind of corruption is there? How can it be stopped?"[1] Andrea Mitchell, reporting from Washington, continued the story: "It's becoming a bigger and bigger problem in state government: the corrupting influence of special interests using their money to grease the wheels of politics." She then reported on the alleged bribing of legislators in South Carolina and Arizona. "In state governments around the country, corruption is rampant. At a minimum, lobbyests' *[sic]* money buys access and clout. In the worst cases, state legislators are bought and sold like trading cards." Mitchell finished the essay on money and politics with an exploration of public funding and opposition to it by Republicans and incumbents. The final Utley-

Mitchell colloquy amounted to an enthusiastic endorsement of public funding.

It was only a few minutes of network television on a slow news day—an inordinate proportion of stories on campaign finance appear on Sunday television or in Monday morning newspapers—but the story linked two allegations of bribery of state legislators to perfectly legal campaign finance practices and then tied the two together with a single solution: public funding of campaigns. One might pass it by if it were an isolated linking of campaign finance to bribery and other kinds of illegality, but it is not. In 1986 *Newsweek,* commenting on the indictment of the Wall Street broker Ivan Boesky for illegalities in the financing of corporate takeovers, observed that the Boesky case "follows what seems a chronic scandal in the defense industry, where virtually all of the top contractors have been found cheating the government. Washington is awash in PAC money, and presidential crony Michael Deaver is only the most conspicuous of the capital's influence peddlers."[2] From that passage, it would not be easy for even an informed citizen to conclude that PAC contributions were legal political activity protected by the First Amendment.

Such an opinion-shaping environment does not encourage much dispassionate analysis of the eight election cycles held under the FECA. Campaign finance becomes an indistinguishable part of broader political and social pathologies. The judgment is clear and in a sense simple: most or all campaign contributions are bribes. If contributions are some form of bribery, it follows that the raising of those contributions by public officials is a form of extortion. The judgment is not only negative, it is absolute as well; there are no hard distinctions to make, no need to separate the positive from the negative, the useful from the destructive, the legal from the illegal in campaign finance.

A parallel, if more systematic, point of view exists within academia. One legal scholar, Daniel H. Lowenstein, argues that all transactions in campaign finance are bribes: "It is a significant and politically relevant fact that under our present system of campaign finance, politicians and interest groups engage routinely not in "legalized" bribery, as is commonly supposed, but in felonious bribery that goes unprosecuted primarily because the crime is so pervasive."[3] Amitai Etzioni in his survey of the ills and wrongs of American politics refers repeatedly to campaign contributions as "legalized corruption."[4]

Such absolute judgments, if unwarranted, will eventually fall of their own weight. They are certainly at variance with American political tradition and both the norms and the words of the FECA. However much one may disagree with the verdicts of corruption, they and the other unflattering assessments of voluntary campaign finance are an unavoidable part of the politics of reform. Indeed, the conventional wisdom sets the agenda of debate over campaign finance, both among the public and in legislatures. The diverse and even diffuse complaints about the post-Watergate regime can be reduced to a relatively small number of core concerns. Heading the agenda are the twin fears that campaign money buys excessive influence in legislatures and that it determines who wins or will win public office. Less well articulated but just as passionately held are two other convictions: that the smart and savvy are evading the regulatory system and that candidates are spending too much money in their campaigns. This chapter is devoted to an examination of those four claims.

Progressive-populist myths about the monied interests have been a century in the making. They cannot and should not lightly be ignored, as versions of reality or as shapers of political opinion, or as critiques of the FECA. All of that, however, does not relieve one of the responsibility to treat them with a measured skepticism.

The Purchase of Legislatures

The question of motive haunts every campaign finance system relying on voluntary contributions. *Why* do they give? When a disclosure system discloses as much as the American one does about a visible set of organized givers representing society's major interests, the question rises to a salience that campaign finance rarely achieves. The answer to it is beyond dispute; they give to influence governmental decisions. The hard questions come next: the nature of the influence the contributors seek, the ways they go about seeking it, and the extent to which they achieve it.

The debate over the purchase of legislatures is not about generic contributors. It is about PAC contributors, whether they appear explicitly or are merely implied in such phrases as "the best Congress money can buy." Their splendid visibility as the organizations of the "special interests" links them and their contributions to the ongoing, century-long debates over the three-way alliance of money, organization, and interest in American politics. Now that PACs increasingly give to secure legislative access, a strategy in which their ties both to incumbents and to lobbyists are closer, they underscore all of the old concerns. We no longer talk of PAC attempts to penetrate electoral politics but of their part in the traditional struggle of interests in American legislatures. Almost imperceptibly, but fundamentally, the debate has shifted from influence in election outcomes to influence over legislative outcomes.

Thanks to the reporting and publicity the FECA forced on candidates, PACs, and parties, the FEC oversees the largest data archive on any system of campaign finance anywhere in the world. Its data are easily accessible, and the "law of available data" has led to a flowering of research on them, both by the scholarly community and by journalists and public-interest organizations. Their industriousness has produced works of many genres, but one of the most common—a veritable industry in itself—is the exploration of the PAC-Congress nexus. The variants on the theme, too, are recognizable: the largest PAC contributors to congressional candidates over a cycle or a decade, the major recipients of PAC money in the Congress, the contributions from PACs of one industry to the members of one committee or to supporters of a particular bill or cause, the mounting flow of PAC money from one sector of the economy as its interests are threatened or challenged. Often the investigations have a current stimulus; they are the campaign finance angle on the broader story, say, of the savings-and-loan crisis, the rewriting of the federal tax code, or the attempt to pass the Brady bill's restrictions on the sale of handguns.

Such reports share one limiting defect: they establish correlation, not cause. Yes, PACs do largely give money to candidates who will vote the way they want them to; it would be surprising if that were not the case. Contributors contribute to like-minded candidates, just as voters vote for like-minded candidates. That relationship is easy to document, but the harder question remains: do PACs contribute to candidates because they know how they will vote, or do legislators conform to the wishes of PACs that gave money to their campaigns? Does the money follow the votes, or do the votes follow the money? It is a problem in simultaneous cause, cause that seems to move both ways between one act and another. Any analysis of campaign finance is repeatedly bedeviled by such problems.

If that were not enough, the journalistic evidence suffers because it is anecdotal, focusing on the limited, often dramatic event. Furthermore, the event and the evidence are often chosen to show a relationship, not because they are representative of the full universe of PAC-incumbent exchanges. So, the anecdotes are almost invariably of PAC successes in the legislative process. But what of PACs representing interests on "the losing side"? PACs and their parent organizations suffer frequent, even monumental loses. Many of the savings-and-loan victories were won over the opposition of the banking industry, and the real estate interests absorbed big losses (for instance, the limiting of real estate investments as tax shelters) in the 1986 revision of the income tax laws, sometimes even at the hands of legislators who had received contributions from the Realtors PAC.

Beyond these failures of design and method are problems of explanatory assumption. Many of the PAC-Congress studies use money and the whole apparatus of campaign finance to the exclusion of other explanations of legislative behavior. If the PACs do "buy" the Congress, if we are to conclude they are major shapers of legislative decisions, what then of the ability of the parties, the president, the voters, the lobbyists, and Washington representatives to shape those same outcomes? And what of the impact of the personal beliefs and attitudes of the members themselves? The PAC of the National Rifle Association, called the Victory Fund, disburses about $4 million each cycle ($4.2 million in 1988) to candidates for the Congress; the NRA budget for Washington lobbying probably exceeds that figure. The NRA also commands the loyal support of 2.8 million members, who focus intently, even solely, on NRA issues in their voting and grass-roots lobbying. Some Western members of the House believe that the NRA vote in their districts can shift vote totals by close to 5 percent. One does not easily separate out the effects of the NRA in these various systems of influence, but it should at least be evident that its PAC contributions have not made its other political activities superfluous.

Academic scholars, for their part, attack the same questions in more systematic ways. They cannot, however, escape the need to establish correlations and to infer cause from them, nor can they escape the problem of simultaneity in doing so. Using larger bodies of data—large numbers of roll-call votes, for instance—and more sophisticated measures of correlation, they generally find little if any relationship between the money and the votes. In research typifying the best of academic analysis, Janet Grenzke studied the contributions of 10 of the largest PACs to 172 long-term members of the House in the 1970s and early 1980s. The PACs were involved in a wide range of policy issues, and all had specified earlier a list of House votes they were interested in during the period. Using a two-stage least-squares regression to control for the effect of factors other than the contributions—the political composition of the member's district, for example—she specified the hypothesized direction of cause in the simultaneous correlation: from money to votes. In the subsequent analysis Grenzke found little support for the hypothesis that PAC contributions influence the roll-call votes of House members.[5]

How does one explain the gap between popular knowledge and academic conclusion? In part it results from the usual popular overestimation of PAC will and capacity. PACs themselves are more realistic about their bargaining position with incumbents than is the general public. They say over and over that they want to support like-minded men and women in public office and that they seek only "access" to legislators, an opportunity to persuade or make a case. Organizationally they are not adapted to greater political ambitions than that, and they have come slowly to realize it. As John Wright concluded in his study of the contributions of five of the country's most affluent PACs, "The ability of PACs to use their campaign contributions to influence congressional voting is severely constrained by the organizational arrangements through which money is raised.... Because money must be raised at a local, grassroots level, local PAC officials, not Washington lobbyists, are primarily responsible for making allocation decisions. Consequently, congressmen who desire contributions must cultivate favorable relationships with local officials, and this arrangement tends to undercut the value of contributions as a bargaining tool for professional lobbyists."[6] Behind that conclusion lies Wright's finding that contributions from the five PACs increased only marginally the probability that the recipient House members would vote the position of the contributing PAC—would shift, that is, from an expected vote as measured by the liberal-conservative scale of the Americans for Democratic Action (ADA). Ultimately, Wright comes to the conclusion of many other political scientists: "Of the numerous variables that influence the voting behavior of congressmen, the campaign contributions of PACs appear to take effect only infrequently. Only when other cues, such as party, are weak can PAC contributions be expected to be important."[7] In short, what PACs do is a reflection of what they are able to do The ability, in turn, stems from their own nature and the bargaining position of incumbents in the exchange.

Such conclusions run counter to the conventional wisdom, and like most academic writing on campaign finance, they fail to disturb or dislodge it. The supporters of the conventional wisdom are tireless, and they have a platform. They also have telling testimony from members of Congress that PACs do indeed change votes—always the votes of other members—with their contributions. To be sure, the testimony is notoriously unspecific; most (but not all) of it comes from liberal Democrats, some of it is ex parte or self-justifying, and some of it is little more than sophisticated scapegoating.[8] Still, congressional observations are not easy to dismiss out of hand. Insiders of any kind are at their strongest in arguments on the nature of influence in the legislative process.

The common sense of the word *access* also makes the case for the conventional wisdom. If access is indeed the goal of PAC contributions, will PACs settle merely for the "opportunity to persuade"? Won't they expect success in a certain number of instances? Will they be satisfied with an invitation to the gaming table if they lose every spin of the wheel? Moreover, the nature of influence in a legislative body involves much more than final roll-call votes. PACs exert influence at other points in the legislative process—in initiatives not taken, in committee amendments, or in special rules affecting floor consideration. Some academic political scientists, one should add, have long shared reservations about an exclusive reliance on roll calls.

A side-by-side illustration of studies of the PAC-committee connection, one by a public interest group and one by two political scientists, makes many of those points. In 1991 Congress Watch, the "legislative advocacy arm" of Ralph Nader's Public Citizen, studied votes in a subcommittee of the House Banking Committee on proposals and amendments to proposals that would "substantially deregulate the nation's banks." In its summary, Congress Watch reports, "On five key votes, the top five recipients of banking PAC money averaged $190,378 in receipts and voted against banking interests only 24 percent of the time. Conversely, the five lawmakers who received the least bank PAC money averaged $35,521 in receipts and voted with consumers and against the banking industry 76 percent of the time."[9] The data suggest that the bank PACs are clearly mixing their contribution strategies, and that by and large they give much more money to committee members sympathetic to them. One has no hint, however, of how to unravel the problem of simultaneous cause. Is there anything more here than decisions by a number of bank PACs to contribute to House members who had proven themselves sympathetic to the banks' interests and policy positions?

Political scientists Richard Hall and Frank Wayman begin the report of their research on PAC money and House committees by reconstructing the logic of what PACs seek with their contributions. "First, we suggest that in looking for the effects of money in Congress, one must look more to the politics of committee decision making than those of the floor.... Second, and more importantly, our account of the member-donor exchange leads us to focus on the *participation* of particular members, not on the votes.... If money does not necessarily buy votes or change minds, in other words, it can buy members' time. The intended effect is to mobilize bias in congressional committee decision making."[10] Hall and Wayman focus, therefore, on three House committees and three different issues before them—and on the effects of PAC contributions to members of the committees. Instead of using votes in committee as the dependent variable, Hall and Wayman construct a measure of various kinds of participation in the business of committees (such as speaking in committee or offering amendments during markup). In each of the three cases they found that PAC contributions had a moderate but significant degree of influence, explaining more than 55 percent of the variance in participation by individual members. PAC money, therefore, mobilized already like-thinking members to more active support of the PACs' interests in committee. Their conclusion about one of the cases applies to all three: "The more money a supporter received from the dairy PACs and the stronger the member's support, the more likely he or she was to allocate time and effort on the industry's behalf (e.g., work behind the scenes, speak on the group's behalf, attach amendments to the committee vehicle, as well as show up and vote at committee markups). Alternatively, money may have diminished the intensity of the opposition."[11] Regardless of why the PACs give, they seem to get heightened activity and support from their congressional sympathizers. We are left, however, to speculate about the ultimate results of such support and activity on congressional decisions.

A consensus about PAC influence is emerging among scholars of campaign finance. It is founded on two central conclusions. First, the influence of PAC contributions tends to be strongest on the narrower, less visible issues before the Congress. Members have long called them "free votes," free in that they are liberated from the usually dominant influences of party, district, leadership, and mass opinion. These are the votes available for less influential constituencies (such as contributors) or even for classic legislative log-rolling or horse-trading. Second, the influence of contributions can be directed at all the points of access and influence in the legislative process in the Congress. The kinds of policy refinements and strategic maneuvers crafted in committee may be important for specific interests even though they do not involve great issues of policy. The same can be said of many appointments to the courts and to executive agencies. Contributors do not necessarily seek, or even expect, to score impressive policy victories measured by final roll-call votes. In the world of reduced expectations in which PACs are forced to live, the smaller accomplishments have to suffice.

The Hall and Wayman findings narrow the gulf between the academy and conventional wisdom, but the gulf remains. In part it results from major disagreements about evidence and authority, about the credibility of participants and observers in the Congress versus the data-based analyses of scholars, and about fundamental questions of what evidence it takes to come to conclusions. In essence, the gulf reflects different wills to believe. Some scholarship, to be sure, but even more journalistic analysis, begins with deeply set convictions, rooted in the Progressive worldview, about the impact of money on public officials. The line between dispositions to believe and foregone conclusions is very thin.

Most durable are the differences across the gulf on analytical issues. One concerns the credibility of the testimony of participants, and even the weight their words carry vis-à-vis the detailed data of the scholars. Consider Charles Keating as an authority on the question of the influence of the contributor. Keating, a political pariah now, is nonetheless widely quoted as evidence of the effect of money. When asked by a Senate committee whether his contributions influenced senators to take up his causes, Keating replied, "I want to say in the most forceful way I can: I certainly hope so."[12] The conferral of authority here may reflect only the news media's fondness for campaign finance machismo, but it may reflect, too, a disposition to give great weight to the words of participants. The danger of granting authority status to participants—contributors or recipients—is that authority is conferred even on clearly self-serving conclusions merely because the authority's message is useful or congenial.

Beneath the controversies over the conventional wisdoms, there are also great differences over who carries the burden of proof. Scholars will not readily consent to demands that they accept responsibility for proving or disproving an assertion they do not make: the one about PACs' buying influence over the making of policy. Nor will they concede that any assertion is valid until it is disproven. Ultimately, however, the debate comes down to the kinds and weight of evidence that will establish the tie between money and votes or other activity in the Congress. One of the greatest strengths of any conventional wisdom is that by definition it is validated by the sheer number of people who subscribe to it. Such validation does not yield easily to the desiccated numbers and equations of empirical social science.

The conventional wisdom is vulnerable also for its assumption that PACs dominate the exchange between contributor and candidate—an analytical predisposition that comes out of the late 1970s. But we now have abundant evidence that the exchange is bilateral rather than unilateral, that candidates have leverage in it, and that the incumbents among them increased that leverage in the 1980s as their reelection rates soared. As PACs have shifted more and more to the support of incumbents, and to the search for access to them, their freedom of action has diminished. Whereas incumbents have organized with increasing effectiveness, PACs have not. Nor have they maintained their ability to enforce expectations. PAC sanctions depend on the value of withdrawn contributions, and since PACs have continued to disperse their contributions widely, the average PAC contribution amounts to well less than one-half of 1 percent of the average House incumbent's receipts in an electoral cycle. Even a major contribution of $5,000 or more accounts for only a few percent of the average candidate's receipts. Consequently, the PAC position in the 1990s is not what it was in the 1970s.

Finally, the countervailing controls of American pluralism constrain even the most determined PACs. Organizations of interests have greatly proliferated since the 1970s. The larger the number of groups (that is, PACs), the greater the offsetting and limiting effect on the political claims of any one of them. The greater the number of PACs making contributions to a specific member of Congress, the greater the likelihood that the claims of one on his or her loyalties will be opposed by the claims of another. In the words of Rep. Barney Frank, a Democrat from Massachusetts, "Business PACs invest in incumbents. It's the banks against the thrifts, the insurance companies against the banks, the Wall Street investment banks against the money center commercial banks. There's money any way you vote."[13]

A caveat to that conclusion is, however, in order. The mechanism of offsetting, countervailing group activity probably best fits policy disputes over the larger issues that are part of broader ideological positions—over issues such as medicaid funding or hazardous waste disposal. The model works less well when the dispute is single-sided, where the activity of one set of interests does not jolt another set of interests, perhaps those of consumers, into action. The nonresponding interests may be too general, too invisible, or of too low a priority to warrant political action. So, the hypothesis of countervailing interests meshes well with the conclusion that PACs have their greatest impact on the less visible politics of narrow and particularistic interests in which the conflicts, and thus the controls, of pluralism are not joined.

Critics of Tony Coelho and the DCCC raise an issue with a new twist on the money-votes relationship. If it is in fact true that the money, especially the PAC money, follows the voting records of incumbents, why can't incumbents change the record to lure the money? That, they charge, is exactly what the House Democrats did under Coehlo's leadership in the early 1980s. It is true that Democrats began to attract more business money then and that Coelho unabashedly urged the party to do so. It is also true that PACs closely scrutinize the voting records, or "scores," of incumbents. The argument suffers, however, from the monism that haunts the subject: the belief that money explains all. Why the assumption that the Democrats are politically so free to move to the center—that the influence of money rather than the mood of voters governs their political calculus? What, too, about the countervailing influence of other contributors, especially those of organized labor, that fight for a move *away* from the center? Logic and assumptions aside, however, the central factual premise of the argument does not hold up. The ratings of the roll-call positions of House members by the AFL-CIO, the U.S. Chamber of Commerce, the Americans for Democratic Action, and the American Conservative Union all give House Democrats collectively a more liberal score in 1990 than they had in 1980.[14]

That an increasingly national "contributor constituency" has entered American electoral politics seems beyond contest. Electoral politics remain local because the constituencies are geographically defined with only one representative and two senators per constituency and because the American political parties have been decentralized and local. Now PACs and other representatives of national interests find a small but measurable additional edge in electoral politics. They increasingly ally themselves with the lobbying of the interests they share, and it becomes increasingly difficult to say whether their victories come through contributing or lobbying. It is far easier to say simply that contributions have become one more limited means among many in the pursuit of policy goals—and one more piece of evidence that the localism of American electoral politics is increasingly anomalous. Campaign finance serves as a shaper of national politics as well as one of its consequences.

The Purchase of Elections

"As a general rule," Benjamin Disraeli once said, "nobody has money who ought to have it."[15] It is precisely on the maldistribution of campaign money, especially the paucity of it in the hands of challengers, that the second great argument of the post-1974 regime centers. After the alleged buying of the Congress, it is the alleged buying of the elections to the Congress that most worries Americans. Many of them are convinced that incumbents are winning reelection at such stunning rates precisely because the incumbents have too much money and their challengers have too little.

The facts are undeniable. Challenger financing has deteriorated in the 1980s by all measures. In 1980 the average House major-party challenger running against an incumbent in the general election spent $100,458 in the entire campaign; by 1990 that figure was only $109,377, and only $54,563 in 1980 dollars. The average incumbent spent $165,509 in 1980 and $399,310 in 1990 ($199,197 in 1980 dollars). Obviously the incumbent-challenger gap was opening; the ratio was 1.6:1 in 1980 but 3.7:1 in 1990. General-election challengers found it increasingly difficult to raise money from PACs; PACs gave them 25.8 percent of their contributions to House candidates in 1980, but only 6.7 percent in 1990. House challengers, in fact, became increasingly dependent on their own resources in the 1980s. Data for 1980 are unavailable, but in 1984 general-election challengers, in a combination of contributions and loans to themselves, accounted for 11 percent of their receipts. By 1990 they provided 19 percent of their receipts; PACs accounted for only 17 percent.

For mass opinion and its shapers, such data lead to an easy conclusion. Incumbents win so often because they outspend their opponents so greatly, and challengers fail to win because they lack the resources with which to mount a winning campaign. For the scholarly community the conclusion does not come as easily, for once again they see a problem in simultaneous cause. Do candidates win because they spend more money, or do they get more money, and spend it, because they are likely to win? The structure of the causal problem is much like the problem of simultaneous cause in PAC contributions and policy outcomes in the Congress: Is the financial contribution made because of expectations about the recipient's victory some months hence, or does the contribution actually buy the campaigning that shapes the election outcome? That is, do underfunded candidates fail because contributors think their fate is sealed months before election day?

The other side of the argument is equally straightforward: challengers lose because they cannot spend enough. It is a fact not only that challengers in the aggregate fail to raise and spend the sums incumbents do, but also that the challengers who spend the most collectively win the greater share of the two-party vote. The percentage of challengers' general-election vote rises as they narrow the incumbent-challenger spending ratio or as they increase their dollar spending in the campaign (table 6.1).

Before one leaps to the conclusion that incumbents win and challengers lose because of the state of their campaign resources, there are contrary bits of data to reckon with. House incumbents won reelection at rates well above 90 percent long before they established their present funding superiority; the cumulative reelection percentage of House incumbents from 1950 through 1970 was 91.8 percent.[16] Furthermore, the gen-

Table 6.1

Relationship Between Challenger Spending and Challenger Vote
Share: 1984–1988*

Challenger:Incumbent Spending Ratios	Median General Election Vote (%)		
	1984	1986	1988
up to 1:3	28	27	27
1:3 to 1:2	36	35	37
1:2 to 1:1	43	41	40
1:1 to 2:1	45	38	43
More than 2:1	46	41	39
Challenger Total Spending Ranges	1984	1986	1988
up to $5,000	24	23	24
$ 5,000 to $ 25,000	27	26	26
$25,000 to $ 75,000	32	30	29
$75,000 to $250,000	38	35	36
more than $250,000	45	43	42

*Includes only major-party, general-election House challengers
running against an incumbent in the general election.
Source: Federal Election Commission.

eral political strength of incumbents can easily be traced, not
to their campaign treasuries, but to all of the advantages of
office they enjoy. The postal frank, their easy access to the
media, their district offices, and their staffs for "servicing"
constituents all have grown in recent decades, at least partly
to buttress their reelection chances.[17] Less obviously, perhaps,
the growing difference between the receipts and the expenditures of incumbents—their larger sums of cash on hand—
suggests that contributors give to them not to help them win
but because they are going to win, a conviction that accounts
for the PACs' having reduced their support of challengers. But
all of these clues aside, the major attack on this problem in
simultaneity has come in the scholarly work of Gary Jacobson.

The problem is easily defined. The percentage of the vote

the challengers get is related to the sums they spend; the greater the dollars, the greater the votes. Money and votes are reciprocally related, however, because challengers raise money on expectations about their ability to get votes. So, how to show that the spending of challengers actually does affect the size of the vote they get? One way is through the same two-stage least-squares procedures Janet Grenzke used to stipulate the direction of cause in the similar problem of the correlation between PAC contributions and the roll-call votes of their recipients in Congress. A second is to use poll data to relate incremental changes in spending to incremental changes in probable vote stage by stage during the campaign. Both avenues brought Jacobson to the conclusion that challenger spending did indeed lead to increases in challenger votes.[18]

The dynamic that relates challenger money to challenger votes can then be outlined. Spending money in the campaign buys visibility and greater "likely support" for challengers, which also means that spending results in the rising expectations that enables them to raise even more money. As Jacobson put it, "Candidates are given money according to how well they are expected to do, but campaign expenditures have an independent effect on how well they actually do, because without them, the expectation would not be realized. The process is largely recursive because elite perceptions and strategies determine how much is spent in campaigns, and the level of campaign spending in turn determines how much is known about candidates and therefore how much support they actually receive from voters. Elite expectations about how the vote will go are only fulfilled if they do, in fact, supply enough money to the candidate."[19] The problem, therefore, is that although money *would* help them greatly, challengers have increasing trouble in raising it in the first place.

The importance of campaign funds for challengers, moreover, was highlighted by Jacobson's conclusion that incumbent spending produced no increase in the incumbent's share of the vote. In fact, the more incumbents spent, the worse they did—not because their spending lost them votes, but because they had to spend more when challengers began to encroach on their electoral margins. Other scholars have challenged that finding about incumbent spending, and the debate is yet to be resolved.[20] Nonetheless, few would argue that the effect of incumbent spending matches that of challenger spending; it seems likely, at least, that one increment of challenger spending, an extra $25,000 perhaps, has more effect on voter awareness than does the same increment in incumbent spending. If the challenger is spending at lower levels than is the incumbent, challenger spending will also be more efficacious per increment because of the decreasing marginal utility—the smaller successive impact on the vote of each increment—of campaign spending.

Incumbents continue to outspend and then to outpoll their challengers, but to conclude that incumbents "buy" reelection or that spending leads to the margin of victory misstates the problem somewhat. Incumbents build support in their constituencies largely by virtue of the perquisites of office and by reason of the visibility and name recognition they routinely achieve. Ultimately the greatest advantage the incumbents have is not their campaign money; it is the expectation early in the election cycle that they can and will win reelection. It is that expectation that makes it so difficult for challengers to raise the money by which they might effectively overcome the incumbents' advantage in the campaign and election.

For Americans who value competitiveness in elections, the issue is of the greatest magnitude. It is simply that the campaign finance system offers challengers no weapons with which to overcome the advantages of incumbency. The challengers lack money because the incumbents' reelection prospects are so strong as to discourage both the emergence of appealing challengers and the willingness of potential contributors to invest in electoral politics. The solution to the problem, therefore, rests either in reducing the advantages of incumbency or in getting money to challengers in time to entice both strong candidates and more contributors. The post-74 regime faces no greater challenge.

Artful Dodging and Skillful Avoiding

The conventional wisdom is right at last: the regulatory vessel is in fact leaking. Important activity and individuals escape its requirements for reporting, and money flows outside of its controls in swelling torrents. One need only tick off the specifics: bundling, soft money, brokers, independent spending, fund-raisers netting six-figure totals in America's urban centers. However one may wish to describe the structural flaws—as "leaks" or "loopholes"—the integrity of the post-1974 regulatory structure is at grave risk.

The assault on the structure of regulation, the statutorily defined campaign finance system, comes in various ways. There are, first, the actors and the activity in violation of explicit statutory limits. The individuals exceeding the $25,000 annual limit on contributions are the most widely publicized case; ambitious investigators now vie to find new miscreants in the computer records of the FEC. Second, there are the invisible brokers and transactions that remain only partially within the governance of the system; the money they raise, and its origins, are reported, but neither their role nor the aggregate sums they organize are. Similar are the formal bundlers, many of whom press the limits of permissible control over contributions. Third, there are the sums raised and spent outside of the limits of the system. Soft money (previously discussed) and independent spending provide the major examples. The 1974 amendments to the FECA set strict limits on the sums of money that groups or citizens could spend independently in a campaign—that is, without the control or even the knowledge of any candidate. Like everything else in the FECA those provisions have a history. Spending by groups other than the candidates had been the stock device for dodging earlier attempts to control spending and insure full reporting of all contributions. The Supreme Court, however, struck down those limits in *Buckley* v. *Valeo,* leaving only the requirement that independent expenditures be reported to the FEC.

Enter John Terrence (Terry) Dolan, founder and executive director of the National Conservative Political Action Committee (NCPAC). NCPAC surfaced for the first time in the election of 1978, but it became a household acronym in 1980 after spending $3.3 million independently in the presidential and congressional campaigns of that year. It spent $1.1 million of that total to challenge six liberal Democratic senators running for reelection: Birch Bayh of Indiana, Frank Church of Idaho, Alan Cranston of California, John Culver of Iowa, Thomas Eagleton of Missouri, and George McGovern of South Dakota. Bayh, Church, Culver, and McGovern were defeated, and NCPAC boldly took the credit. There were other less arresting explanations for the losses—the Reagan and conservative triumphs of 1980, the growing gulfs between the losers and their conservative constituencies, for example—but they were pallid stuff next to the swashbuckling of NCPAC. A potent new political tactic, independent spending, had arrived.

The post-1974 beginnings of independent spending are obscure. Record keeping at the FEC was in its infancy in 1976, and its data on independent spending in that cycle are incomplete; the best guess is that about $2 million was spent independently, with all but $400,000 spent in the presidential campaign. Another $300,000 or so was spent in the 1978 congressional elections, and then came the eye-grabbing jump to a total of $16.1 million in 1980 (table 6.2). NCPAC alone accounted for almost half of the $2.3 million spent independently on 1980s congressional races, and flushed with the successes of 1980, it exceeded that mark in 1982 with $3.1 million of the $7.1 million spent on races for the Congress. NCPAC's dominance ended slowly after that, but independent spending hit its highest level in congressional campaigns in 1986: $9.4 million. By 1990 it had fallen back to a total of $1.8 million in the House and Senate campaigns. Amid all of the ups and downs, independent spending has been constant

Table 6.2

Independent Spending in Presidential and Congressional
Elections: 1980–1988

	Presidential			Congressional		
Year	Total $	% Against	% Rep	Total $	% Against	% Rep
1980	$13.75m	5.9%	96.6%	$2.34m	58.9%	83.9%
1982	$ .19m	.8%	50.2%	$7.10m	72.5%	75.9%
1984	$17.47m	4.8%	93.4%	$5.95m	44.3%	49.7%
1986	$ .84m	5.4%	88.9%	$9.36m	14.2%	58.9%
1988	$14.13m	24.8%	94.9%	$7.21m	16.5%	64.1%
1990	$ .50m	35.1%	98.0%	$1.77m	15.7%	48.6%

Source: Federal Election Commission.

in one way: except for the congressional elections of 1984, it has been consistently pro-Republican, often overwhelmingly so (table 6.2). No other kind of spending in all of American campaign finance has so consistently favored one party by such margins.

Even at their zenith, independent expenditures on congressional elections never accounted for major sums. The record $9.4 million in 1986 was only 2 percent of the cash expenditures ($450.3 million) by all candidates in that year's campaigns. Moreover, the effective sums were greatly exaggerated. The splashiest spenders in the 1980s—NCPAC and an assortment of PACs supporting Republican presidential candidates—were PACs without parent organizations, "nonconnected PACs" in the parlance of the FEC. They raised their money in costly direct-mail solicitations; and with no parent to pay overhead, not to mention fund-raising expenses (postage, printing, computerized mailing lists), they had to absorb all of these costs out of the money they raised. Estimates vary, but shrewd and careful reports found that only 5 to 20 percent of their receipts went into campaign activity as it is usually understood—into television or newspaper ads or campaign brochures or mailings. Nevertheless, NCPAC and its siblings

systematically overstated their campaigning by reporting solicitation costs as a part of their independent spending because
the solicitation letter contained a plea for action in support of
or opposition to specific named candidates.[21]

Such scrupulous reporting to the FEC helped create a myth.
The NCPAC millions took headlines in 1980 and 1982, although totals in the hundreds of thousands of dollars might
not have. Moreover, NCPAC and Terry Dolan cultivated an
image that combined the arts of guerrilla warfare (targeting,
hit lists) and a new amoral Machiavellianism. That Dolan
should so baldly say that "a group like ours could lie through
its teeth and the candidate it helps stays clean" was titillating
enough;[22] that it should come from a thirtyish executive director with the youthful looks and seeming innocence of a
choir boy made it the stuff of sensation. NCPAC and independent spending merged to create the archetype of a ruthless
ideological, single-issue politics.

Although the great ideological PACs dominated independent spending in its palmiest years, they did not monopolize
it. A Californian by the name of Michael Goland spent $1.1
million in 1984 to urge the defeat of Illinois senator Charles
Percy, a liberal Republican. It was by far the largest sum spent
by an individual in the post–1974 regime. Percy got only 48
percent of the vote, losing to Democrat Paul Simon, but even
experienced analysts find it hard to assess the impact of the
billboards and other ads Goland bought. Closed-mouthed
about his political agenda, Goland owns up only to a concern
for animal rights and people with disabilities. Goland-watchers
add a deep concern for Israel and conservative Republicanism
to that list. Goland reappeared in the 1988 campaign, indicted
after it was over for making illegal contributions of more than
$100,000 to an American Independent party candidate for
the U.S. Senate.

It would be wrong to suggest that independent spending
has been entirely in the hands of the political buccaneers. By
the late 1980s a few large membership PACs such as the Realtors PAC and the American Medical PAC began to spend in-

dependently in congressional elections; generally their interventions were in favor of candidates, with only a few smaller PACs making the kind of "negative" expenditures NCPAC had made famous. AMPAC spent $1.6 million on behalf of 14 congressional candidates in 1986, and the Realtors PAC spent $1.7 on behalf of six; in 1988 the level of spending dropped to $.8 million by AMPAC and $1.3 million by the Realtors PAC. In neither year did either PAC spend a cent to oppose a candidate.

In the mid-1980s, in fact, it seemed that some larger PACs would incorporate such spending into their contribution strategy, putting a second arrow in the quiver. There was even talk of retreating to it if the Congress further restricted PAC contributions. But that prospect faded along with the heyday of NCPAC and its clones. Independent spending created intraorganizational problems for the PACs that tried it; some of their donors either did not approve of it generally, or they were outraged at the PACs' choice of targets. It also raised the wrath of incumbents, especially when it was spending in favor of challengers, and they quickly learned to ignite voter backlash to it. Indeed, candidates complained even when the spending favored them; none of them wanted any part of what the public sees as their campaigns to be beyond their control.

Those explorations by mainline PACs opened up another issue that had festered for some years: the meaning of independence. How, for instance, could a large PAC making contributions to congressional candidates and discussing their campaigns with them also make independent expenditures in which there was no cooperation or contact with the candidate? Or what of an independently financed media campaign supporting candidate J when the commercials are designed and placed by the same media consultants working for candidate J's campaign? And how are voters to know who is responsible for independent expenditures on television when the credit line is invisible to most viewers? Independence comes down in the end to very small but very important details.

Independent expenditures happen to exploit a gap in the regulatory system created by the Supreme Court's application of the First Amendment to it. Soft money, however, flows in presidential campaigns as a result of an intended exclusion from the system and the constitutional status of American federalism. Most of the bundling and high-stakes brokering result from the failure of the authors of the FECA, whether out of faintheartedness or lack of foresight, to place intermediaries securely within the regulatory structure. So, the natures of the leaks differ; they are far too varied in both origin and purpose to bear the single pejorative label of loophole. Calling them loopholes blurs moral and ethical distinctions in a subject in which moral and ethical judgments abound.

Such judgments are the first reason for concern about the integrity of the regulatory structure. Its impairments invite and receive public denunciation of campaigns, campaigners, and campaign finance. Americans do not take kindly to avoidance, no matter how legal or even ethical, of systems of regulation; avoidance carries the stigma of self-servingness compounded by excessive cleverness. Independent spenders may be exercising a First Amendment right in the most open and direct way, but they are not treated much more charitably than the trimmers and shavers who bundle ever more creatively to escape the statutory limits on the size of contributions. In short, breaches in the integrity of the structure give rise to blanket judgments untempered or ungraded by any fine distinctions among the kinds of breaches.

The problems, however, extend beyond those of public judgment. The breaches create massive administrative problems, especially in reporting. Again, independent spending is a splendid case in point. The only other spending in the campaign permitted by the FECA is that by the candidates and the party committees, both of which must register with the FEC and make periodic reports to it. Their officials become institutionalized reporters and trained compliers, most of them also aided by accountants, lawyers, and computer software. A

Michael Goland must report his independent spending, but he is not in the same sense institutionalized, nor is he a trained complier with the FECA. He is not registered with the FEC, and he does not have to report his contributions to actors who are. Similarly, many of the ad hoc groups making independent expenditures in presidential campaigns are transient, striking tent as soon as the election is over. It is neither a secret nor a surprise that the FEC has had to work hard to piece together full reports on independent spending in an election cycle.

On this and other matters of administration and enforcement, the FEC suffers from an uncertain authority. The placement of exchanges and flows of money on the peripheries of the regulatory system means, in effect, that they sit also on the peripheries of the FEC's authority. One need only cite the great controversies, including the intervention of the federal district court for the District of Columbia, over the FEC's handling of the soft-money controversy. It has been almost equally vexed by the bundling inventions of the National Republican Senatorial Committee. Underfunded by the Congress and kept on a short leash for 15 years, the FEC has never been able to establish its independence as a regulator; its even division between three Democrats and three Republicans has additionally made it difficult for the Commission to deal with problems that are inevitably partisan. These leaks in the regulatory system have only further embarrassed it and given its sterner critics more reason for criticism.[23]

Administrative problems are closely related to mechanisms of responsibility. The major institutionalized actors—PACs, parties, and candidates—respond to various systems of control or responsibility: voters, members, parent organizations, representative bodies, public officials, or mass opinion, as the case may be. On the other hand, brokers such as Charles Keating or a well-heeled individual contributor make no reports to the FEC, and no other institutions or responsible bodies stand behind them. With no visibility and no long-term interest in the political system, the brokers may have no political reputation at stake; often, too, they offer no target at which the wrath of voters can be directed. The political controls of reputation and the ballot box are imperfect at best, but they do work more effectively on visible, committed political actors with continuing stakes in politics.

When the integrity of the regulatory system suffers, so too do the morale and the law-abidingness of those clearly within the regulatory perimeters. Compliance with both the letter and the spirit of a regulatory structure cannot easily survive the impression that the structure catches only some of the players while others go free. The belief that "I've been playing by the rules while those guys have been getting away with murder" has a corrosive effect on compliance. And compliance is that act of self-enforcement on which all legitimate and effective systems of regulation depend.

It almost goes without saying that breaches in the regulatory system sabotage the achievement of the initial purpose of the regulation. If the purpose was to limit PAC contributions to $5,000 per candidate per election, any modus operandi that permits groups of potential PAC contributors to give their cash instead as individuals defeats both the limit and the congressional intent that their money be identified with the interest that recruited it.

Are Campaigns Too Expensive?

Each round of debates over congressional campaign finance is, in the words of Yogi Berra, déjà vu all over again. Putting a cap on campaign expenditures was high on the agenda of reform in 1974, and it still is. The Supreme Court struck down the FECA's limits on all spending in *Buckley*, and reformers have been trying to find a way of restoring them ever since. So strongly convinced are the American people that campaigns cost too much, so firmly placed on the agenda of reform is the issue, that it flourishes in the 1990s despite the stability of expenditures in congressional campaigns. Not only does the issue persist, but its rhetoric about skyrocketing and escalating expenditures remains impervious to any new realities.

It is virtually a truism that the case for spending limits rests on the premise that the costs of campaigning are too great. It is far less easy, though, to establish that they are in fact too great. For many American adults the standards for making such a judgment are implicit; the spending is just "too much"—too much perhaps by standards of middle-class personal finance, too much because of the imagined rate of runaway increase in them. Or too much perhaps in terms of value, in terms of the worth of the product or service the money produces. The campaigns, or the parts of them they happen to notice, are simply not worth those sums, just as $40 is not too much for a good steak dinner but is an outrageous price for a bad one.

The many cries of "too much" reflect negative judgments about politics and the entire public sector. Those judgments similarly govern public opinion about the salaries of public officials. Inherent in them is a double standard, one code of behavior for the private sector and another for the public sector. Political scientists are fond of making the public-private comparison in campaign finance with data on advertising expenditures, for advertising campaigns are, like campaigns for public office, an exercise in information and persuasion. Americans are shocked by total expenditures of $445.2 million in the congressional campaigns of 1990, but in that same year Sears Roebuck, the giant merchandiser, had an advertising budget in excess of $1.4 billion.

The case against present spending levels is much stronger on pragmatic or consequential grounds. These arguments are, however, not about spending per se but about the need to raise the money in order to spend it. They go this way:

- Present levels of spending are too high because in order to raise the funds to spend, elected public officials must take too much time and energy from their public responsibilities. It is now almost a commonplace that a U.S. senator must raise $12,000 a week for six years in order to amass the $3.5 to $4 million for a typical Senate campaign.

- Furthermore, the pressures to raise those sums for a Senate race, or close to half a million for a House campaign, drive candidates to seek money in large sums at a time when contribution limits are shrinking because of inflation. Initially, candidates replaced small individual contributors with large PAC contributions, and now even the usual PAC contribution is small compared to the take at a brokered fundraiser in Los Angeles. A senator can make a flying trip to a distant spot for a quick reception and return to Washington with $50,000 or $100,000 in campaign resources. Spending levels, that is, affect how money is raised, where it is raised, and with whose help it is raised.
- The ability to raise funds becomes a substantial qualification for candidates. Candidates of knowledge, experience, and even wisdom may lack the skills or the stomach for begging funds from people they scarcely know; the need to do it may discourage them from seeking office. Worse than such a shrinking of the pool of talent is the possibility that the consequence will be to recruit and elect candidates whose skills in raising money and conducting a campaign are their chief or even their only major attributes.

The problem with elevated spending levels seems to be that one needs to raise the money in the first place.

Probably the most direct and reasonable judgments about spending levels are the ones based on a stipulated minimum campaign. If the candidate needs at least to be able to do A, B, and C in order to run a competitive campaign that also honors the need for an informed electorate, then the minimum cost of A, B, and C, with appropriate staff and overhead, frames a reasonable cost for the campaign. One recent and authoritative manual for campaigners posits a budget of $600,000 for a House challenger. Its direct-mail figures total about $150,000 for only two mailings to the approximately 200,000 households of a congressional district; it also provides $100,000 for radio and television commercials, a sum that will yield three high-visibility campaigns for three television "spots" in many metropolitan markets.[24] The budget is perhaps overweighted with personnel and overhead costs, but it is hard to avoid the conclusion that a campaign of $500,000-$600,000 is something less than profligate.[25] In view of the fact that the average major-party general-election candidate spent less than half of $500,000 in 1990 and that even the average open-seat candidate spent $484,000, one can make a plausible argument that candidates spend too little, not too much, in congressional campaigns.

Leaving aside the strength of popular and reformist feelings on the point, there is a basic conceptual problem here. Not one, but two issues are entwined: the need for the money and the costs to the system of raising it. It is easier to justify the spending levels than the effort that has to go into raising the cash in the first place. So, we are raising too much money and yet not really spending enough in the campaigns for Congress. It is a paradox that recalls Mark Twain's observation about good bourbon: "Too much is hardly enough."[26]

Reality and Reform

Even the experts and activists find it difficult to reach a judgment about American campaign finance. The mass public necessarily comes to its understandings about it without any profound knowledge, often without even basic information. Citizens are compelled to watch the shadows projected on the vast wall in front of them. They take their conclusions and judgments as they see them in the dance of distorted images. Of necessity, their judgments are the judgments of those who project the images.

In the opinions on all of the major concerns about the post-1974 system, the consonances and dissonances are consistent. Whether it is the PAC-Congress connection, the impact of money on the winning of elections, or the judgments about spending levels, mass opinion and image-making opinion are in agreement. Their consensus, moreover, diverges in all three instances from much of scholarly and other expert opinion.[27]

It is hardly a novel outcome, for expert opinion is often at odds with mass opinion over the analysis of public problems and policy solutions. It is, in fact, one of the oldest and most troubling dilemmas in the governance of mass, popular democracies.

The successes and failures of the post-1974 regime present the dilemma in a heightened form. Mass opinion about campaign finance increasingly feeds a cynicism about, even a rejection of, basic democratic processes. Any threat to mass involvement in or acceptance of electoral politics threatens the essence of representative government. The resulting conflict of equities could not be more disturbing. Is one to adopt policies that address the real problems of the system, as the informed best understand them, or ought one to devise change that will lay to rest the fears and anger of a disaffected public? Can we indeed win back disaffected citizens and solve real public problems at the same time? It is the hardest of the policy questions, this intersection of image and reality, of mass politics and expert prescription—especially when the divergence is not only over ultimate policy goals, but over the reality of the problem itself.

Whether by accident or prescience, the justices of the U.S. Supreme Court recognized the dilemma in the majority opinion in *Buckley* v. *Valeo*. Congress could act to limit the constitutionally protected flow of campaign money only in the case of "corruption or the appearance of corruption," either in the instance of certifiable corruption by some unspecified standards, or in the instance of some widespread belief that institutions were being corrupted. So, Congress might apparently act on the basis of one reality or the other, on the basis of the image behind the viewer or the image projected on the wall. Is it to make no difference if one reality could meet standards of truth or validity and the other could not? The answer, in the world of democratic politics, depends on crafting reforms that serve both reality and its appearances.

Chapter 7 _____

The Agenda and Politics of Reform

Ordinarily in regulatory systems, the regulated are not also the regulators; but the FECA is no ordinary structure of regulation. Nothing colors the politics of regulating campaign finance as much as the central fact that the Congress is regulating its own electoral activity. In addition, the members of Congress regulate the activity of candidates who try to take away their seats. Tinkering with this particular regulatory system is therefore not at all like coping with satellite transmissions or the prospectus requirements for new securities. The members of Congress know campaign finance at first hand, and they know that even the slightest change in the structure of regulations may have considerable consequences for their party and their own political careers. With their political futures at stake, the reform of campaign finance easily engages their undivided personal attention.

The FECA's regulatory regime is special in another way. Since the *Buckley* decision in 1976 it deals with activity enjoying the protection of the First Amendment. Congress and the states have always legislated limits to activity protected by the First Amendment—one thinks of laws outlawing libelous speech, forcing vaccinations regardless of religious belief, and preventing campaigning in a polling place. Only in the regulation of the electronic media, however, is there precedent for a regulatory system erected and administered to govern a whole arena of protected activity. Consequently, any change in the regulatory status quo in campaign finance must meet far more severe constitutional constraints than changes, say, in the regulation of interstate trucking or the disposal of nuclear waste. The constitutional law of the First Amendment can never be far out of mind when one begins to reform the FECA.[1]

Yet the regime of the FECA shares a great deal with regulatory systems generally. They all spawn attempts to circumvent them; in that sense they all bear the seeds, if not of their own destruction, at least of their own evasion or avoidance. A veritable race of experts springs up around them to probe their limits and vulnerabilities, to help their clients learn "to live with" the law. The FECA shares with other regulatory regimes the inevitability of failure, whether partial or total, and the consequent need for adjustment, repair, or, at worst, replacement. The regulators struggle to stay a step or two ahead of the learning curve of the regulated. In the special case of the FECA, ironically, the regulators struggle to respond to their own adaptations and to anticipate their own learning.

The Politics of Campaign Finance

For all of their effort to reform the FECA in the past decade or more, the reformers have nothing to show for it. There have been no amendments to the FECA since 1979, and determined attempts at change have subsequently ended in political deadlock. Change has been held hostage by an unusually dense, complex, and multilayered politics that thwarts even the most skilled coalition builders in and out of the Congress.

Division over campaign finance begins with the division between the parties. Democrats, historically the disadvantaged party in campaign funding, still worry about the fragility of their financial base and its dependence on PAC money and, ultimately, on the party's majority status in the Congress. They tend to worry, too, about reelection threats from well-financed Republican challengers. Republicans are more confident of their ability to raise money from a naturally affluent party following, both for candidates and for party committees (where the contribution limit for individuals is $20,000 per year.) Among some of the partisans, those pragmatic differences are reinforced by philosophical differences. Democrats are more comfortable, Republicans less comfortable, with a governmental role, whether it is regulatory or as a source of campaign subsidies. The parties differ, too, over majority status: Democrats are protective of theirs, and Republicans would like to regain it. Consequently, every important vote on campaign finance proposals in either house over the past dozen years has broken along party lines. The Senate, for example, in May 1991, passed a comprehensive reform bill (S. 3); the Democrats voted 51 in favor and 5 opposed, while 5 Republicans voted for the bill and 37 opposed it.[2]

The division between the House and the Senate, however, divides members of the same party. The burdens of fundraising, especially in the last years of a term, are on the average heavier for a senator than a representative; their constituencies are larger, the campaigns far more costly, and the elections much more competitive. Their campaigns differ qualitatively, too: Senate races depend far more on the electronic mass media, and they tend also to be caught up in national issues. Differences between the two houses also reflect different patterns in funding—House members get a larger share of their receipts from PACs, senators drawing more on individual contributions, especially those from out of state.[3] Congressional campaign finance, needless to say, differs greatly from that of the presidency, in which PAC contributions are inconsequential and major public funding is available.

Surrounding these divisions is a mass opinion of equal complexity. It is reasonably intense; a poll by Tarrance and Associates for the National Association of Business PACs (NABPAC) in June 1991 found that exactly half of a national sample thought "changing the campaign finance laws" either "important" (32 percent) or "extremely important" (18 percent), while the other half thought it either somewhat important or not important.[4] Where campaign finance stands in adults' systems of priorities is harder to say. Few individuals with strong opinions base them on much knowledge of the intricacies of campaign finance beyond an awareness of its bedevilment by PACs and its exploding levels of spending. Indeed, the fact that opinion about campaign finance merges imperceptibly into opinion about negative campaigning, television spots, mudslinging, honoraria, and politics generally poses the greatest problem for the Congress. Many members of Congress see the political problem beyond the Beltway not as a question about campaign finance, but as one about the integrity of politics and politicians. Some see reform, for instance, as a way of heading off anti-incumbent revolts at the polls or, worse, demands for limits on the length of their terms of office.

Moreover, there is the division of interests between incumbents and non-incumbent candidates, only the first of whom have influence in the legislative process. Because of their legislative power, the members of Congress, especially those of the majority Democrats, have often been called an incumbent protection society. That label oversimplifies matters, for incumbents differ greatly among themselves, even leaving party and chamber differences aside. They differ in the sums they need, in their appetites for fund-raising, in their relationships with funders, and in their constituents' abilities to give money. They differ, too, in the safeness or marginality of their districts and in the reformist zeal of the folks back home. Withal, very few of them want to make it easier for a challenger to unseat them, and most are protective of colleagues who are less well funded or who are less secure electorally than they are.

All of these cross-cutting divisions respond to and are conditioned by different perceptions of reality. Widespread popular beliefs describe one reality in which PACs, special interests, and money generally hold sway and even corrupt the greedy.

Members of Congress have another reality, one of pragmatism and career protection as well as of knowledge often generalized from personal experience or even personal rationalization. And then there are the realities of scholars, experts, and experienced observers—often more detached and less enamored of simple answers or easy solutions, generally better informed about the full range of experience under the FECA. Such a profusion of realities is by no means unique to the politics of campaign finance, but the intensity of the judgmentalism that encases these realities may indeed be unique.

When such a divisive politics is exacerbated by divided party control of the Congress and the White House, deadlock has the look of inevitability. The strategies for breaking through deadlock are limited and difficult; the House and Senate have individually tried two of them recently without success. The House in 1989 tried a bipartisan task force co-chaired by Representatives Al Swift, Democrat of Washington, and Guy Vander Jagt, Republican of Michigan. The task force reached agreement on a number of the "minor" issues—the banning of leadership PACs and more stringent control of bundling, for example—but it failed to find common ground on the major issues, especially limiting PAC contributions and candidate spending. Representative Swift chalked failure up to "legitimate partisan differences" and noted that both sides were now "more convinced that the other side is not just posturing. . . . If we were just playing games, a compromise would be more forthcoming."[5]

For its part, the Senate in 1990 tried another route to consensus. The two party leaders, Senators George Mitchell, Democrat of Maine, and Robert Dole, Republican of Kansas, jointly appointed a bipartisan group of six experts, none of them members of the Congress, to propose a plan for compromise on reform of the FECA. The "Gang of Six," as they came to be called, produced a finely tuned reform package in which they tried to balance the pluses and minuses for the major interests, especially those of the two parties. Its report of March 1990 was moderate in tone—no public funding, flexible spending limits, some additional limits on PAC contributions—but it had at best a modest influence on the Senate's work. Certainly the group did not find a formula for bipartisan agreement or compromise.[6] Both experiences demonstrated the difficulty of the task, the complexity of the interests at stake, and the inflexibility of major positions. Absent a major bipartisan leadership commitment, including White House participation, such efforts appear doomed. For now, the spurs or incentives for that commitment just do not seem to be present.

Most likely, substantial change will await one of two conditions. Control of both branches of government and both houses of Congress by a comfortable margin would probably produce the votes for reform. Reform, that is, will be the reform of a single party, although neither would find it easy to achieve agreement within itself. That scenario recognizes implicitly that the interests of the parties are so real and so hardened that they transcend the other divisions that complicate the politics of campaign funding. There was indeed bipartisan support for the reforms of the early 1970s, but those were unusual times in the shocked aftermath of Watergate. In fact, they suggest a second scenario—Watergate Revisited, in which scandal is followed by reform. Such reformers as Common Cause seemed to think they had the catalytic event in the savings and loan debacle, especially in the Charles Keating link to campaign finance; the main causes of the debacle were elsewhere, however, and no one found a smoking gun or a quid pro quo in the exchanges of Keating and his associates with the five senators. Whatever the shortcomings of the post-1974 regime have been, they have not included illegality or impropriety even approaching the magnitudes of Watergate.

So, the politics of campaign finance has developed into the politics of deadlock. George Bush's repeated assertions in 1991 that he would veto any bill that had spending limits, public funding, or separate rules for the House and the Senate virtually guaranteed a veto for any bill the Democrats in the

House and Senate might agree on.[7] That knowledge has in turn produced more than the usual posturing and stand-taking for consumption back in the district. More than a few senators voted for the provision in S. 3 to outlaw PAC contributions, with qualms assuaged by the knowledge that the House would not concur. The Democratic majority in the House was neither honored nor amused to receive the passed buck. When legislators know they are not writing legislation, they write for self-protection and self-advertisement. It is an old, if not very honorable, form of symbolic politics.

Bashing and Banning PACs

Numerous voices in the PAC movement have pointed out, if tentatively and defensively, that PACs were nowhere to be seen in the Charles Keating foray into campaign finance. True enough; the maneuvering of large sums of money from thrifts to congressional candidates and their adjuncts in the latter 1980s was accomplished entirely without the use or blessing of a political action committee. PAC-bashing, nonetheless, goes on unabated, symbolized perhaps by President Bush's proposal in late June 1989 to abolish the PACs of corporations, labor unions, and membership organizations. The assault on PACs culminated in the death sentence for PAC contributions in the 1991 Senate legislation; it was in fact one of the few parts of S. 3 that both parties in the Senate agreed about.

Any number of refinements on the general proposition to outlaw PACs, some by Democrats and some by Republicans, surfaced in the Senate after the Bush proposal. The version enacted in May 1991 (S. 3) did not, in fact, completely outlaw PACs; it merely prohibited their making contributions to candidates in federal elections. The bill still permitted them to make limited contributions to party committees. Recognizing that the Supreme Court might consider such a prohibition in violation of the First Amendment, the Senate prudently included backup provisions to cut the PAC contribution limit back from $5,000 to $1,000 and to limit the total sum a candidate could accept from PACs to 20 percent of the expenditure limit provided for that campaign in another section of the bill. Although such draconian measures may have seemed the only way to rid the system of interested money, it cannot have escaped George Bush and his fellow Republicans that PAC money is more important to Democratic candidates, especially in the House. It also seems clear that Republicans would find it easier than Democrats to organize the giving of affluent individuals as an alternative to PAC activity. And by savaging PACs the Republicans also threatened the historic alliance between organized labor and the Democratic party.

So why did Senate Democrats acquiesce? Some undoubtedly went along out of convictions about eliminating special-interest money. Some of the more conservative Democrats were not adverse to weakening the party's historic ties with labor and shedding its Republican-promoted image as the party of special interests. Some concurred, however, to score points with constituencies, often the local newspaper, that had come to expect PAC-bashing as a token of political purity. Some, too, wanted to close off the issue for the next campaign, to deny a Republican challenger the opportunity of accusing them of "supporting" and "protecting" the hated PACs. And since there was a double fail-safe—the House Democrats would not agree, and the President promised a veto in any event—they could with impunity do a bit of grandstanding.

When the politics of deadlock becomes a politics of symbols and advantage, candor and consistency are bound to suffer. The press, especially that of the Washington insiders, has delighted in tales of PAC opponents stashing away large sums in PAC contributions. It is as if they revealed Carrie Nation as a closet toper. Senator Mitch McConnell, the Republican point man on the issue, continued to raise substantial sums from PACs through the 1990 cycle, as did many of the supporters of the ban on PACs; McConnell reported receiving $1,076,029 from PACs in the 1989–90 cycle, more than 26 percent of his reported receipts. Senator David Boren of Oklahoma, the driving force of the Democrats on campaign finance reform, refuses PAC contributions as a matter of policy. The insider's newsletter, *PACs & Lobbies*, reported in 1990 that Boren had collected more than $120,000 in 1989 from executives in corporations and trade associations with PACs.[8] They were by no means alone; very few of the congressional reformers spurned PAC or PAC-like money. The usual explanation was that one had to play by the customs of the game at the moment, no matter how distasteful they might be.

The politics of the issue aside, what of banning PACs or PAC contributions as public policy or, more specifically, as a major feature of a reformed FECA? To put no fine point on it, it is probably the worst reform idea of the post-1974 regime. The problems begin at the beginning, with identifying the problems the ban addresses. Some critics of PACs have objected to their overwhelming support of incumbents, others to their burgeoning, still others to their contributions of "interested money." Most frequent of all are the charges that PAC money influences public policy. That PACs give overwhelmingly to incumbents is undeniable, but individual contributors favor incumbents in almost as lopsided a way. As for PAC growth, there has been no growth since 1986, and growth until then reflected the growth of group organization and influence in American politics. PAC money is indeed interested, but so indeed is much political activity, including voting; increasing sums of individual contributions are also interested, especially the large and brokered contributions. As for the assertion of major or substantial PAC influence over public policy, the case has not been made. In short, if the analyses of this book are valid, the major premise behind the banning or crippling of PACs is simply not supported by hard data or rigorous evidence.

Equally troubling is the constitutional question. Apparently the Senate majority passing S. 3 was not confident that the ban on PACs would pass constitutional muster: else why would it have provided backup regulations in case the ban was inoperative? That in itself suggests a less than serious exercise of congressional responsibility for constitutional rights under the First Amendment. So, too, does the substance of the matter. Is political activity to be outlawed because it has grown and flourished, or because it has supported people who do not need additional support? Or worse, because it has supported the wrong people? Can it be curtailed because it has succeeded in a way most political activity aims to succeed—because it has achieved some influence over public decisions? One could outlaw lobbying by the same arguments.[9]

Even if one is uncomfortable with the arguments of equity and constitutionality, the pragmatic arguments, those of result and consequence, are just as powerful. Eliminating PAC contributions would cut the flow of money into the campaign finance system; money, even dollar for dollar, would increase in value, and so would the leverage of contributors in the exchange. Furthermore, the loss would impact candidates, states, and congressional districts differently; for many center-city House candidates, for example, there are few affluent individual constituents to tap for contributions. Furthermore, much of the PAC money remaining in campaign finance would be organized informally, a good deal of it in ways that would resemble the high-stakes fund-raising of individuals now brought together in a few metropolitan centers. Alternatively, former PAC donors might organize loosely in a communication network, with a guiding committee urging fellow donors to make contributions of their own to suggested candidates. Successful forays into networking like those of Emily's List would surely become models.

Whatever the alternative to a PAC, however, the connection or interest that brings contributors together will be far less visible and the aggregate sums they contribute far harder to compute than they are with PACs. In the words of Citizen Action:

• Eliminating PACs will hide the special interest sources of campaign contributions. The public knows which PACs contribute to their representatives because PAC disclosure works. The public has almost no idea of . . . the special in-

terest [of] large donors to their representatives' campaigns
...because it is impossible to make individual disclosure
work.

- Eliminating PACs will increase the importance of the influence industry—lawyer, lobbyists, and public-relations firms.
Lawyers and executives with these firms contributed more
than $19 million to candidates. The identity of influence
industry interests is the most difficult to determine and
strengthens the special interests who can afford to hire these
firms.[10]

Of all the dangers in banning PACs, the greatest undoubtedly
is that the lines of responsibility for money contributed would
once again be driven out of sight.

If the legislative decision for PACs is not death but only
disability, the consequences depend on the form of the disability. If it is in the form of a sharply reduced contribution
limit, one of $1,000 or $2,000, money in the system would
decline, again strengthening the position of contributors. If
PACs wanted to involve themselves in a campaign beyond the
new limit, they would have two main options. They could
engage in the bundling or pseudo-bundling of the kind described above; alternatively, they could do what they always
have threatened to do: spend additional sums independently.
Even though such spending has caused problems within PACs
in the past, it might well become more palatable to members
or donors under a more restrictive regulatory regime. One
can easily imagine PACs permitting donors to give either to
one account for contributions or to another for independent
spending.

PACs can also be curbed by limiting the ability of candidates
to accept their money. Plans for such limits have been knock-
ing around the Congress for years. In fact, one of them, the
Obey-Railsback proposal, passed the House in 1979; it would
have limited candidates for the House to accepting no more
than $70,000 from PACs.[11] In the latter part of 1991 a task
force on campaign finance appointed by Speaker Thomas

Foley and chaired by Representative Sam Gejdenson, a Democrat from Connecticut, proposed a $200,000 limit on receipts from PACs for all candidates for the House; the limit was exactly one-third of the $600,000 spending limit it also proposed. The effect would obviously be to eliminate some PAC money since major-party candidates in the House general election of 1990 received, on the average, 41.8 percent of their receipts from PACs and incumbents received more than 48 percent.

Because receipt limits on PAC giving affect the strategies of both contributor and recipient, their impacts are not easy to assess. One thing does seem clear: while sharp limits on PAC contributions would make money scarcer and thus increase contributor leverage in the exchange, limits on receipts from PACs by themselves create a surplus of money and therefore bolster the leverage of candidates. With a limit on receipts, it is not hard to imagine incumbents picking and choosing the PACs from which they would accept money or even diverting PAC money to worthy challengers or open-seat candidates. For the exchange and its terms, that is, it makes a difference whether the limits are on the contributor or on the candidate. Finally, receipt limits raise constitutional issues. The Supreme Court has never considered their constitutionality, and since logic places them somewhere between the permissible limits on contributions and the unconstitutional limits on expenditures, their status is uncertain.[12]

Lost in all the calculations of advantage and impact that would follow a crippling of the PACs is the impact on the PACs themselves. Certainly any reduction of their capacity would hit the smaller ones inordinately hard; the larger, more professional, and more bureaucratized PACs raise money earlier, often in payroll deduction plans, have both the time and the know-how to remain flexible, and stand to develop informal networks more easily. Their ability to adapt even to abolition guarantees greater concentration in the PAC movement. Among the losers, too, would be nonconnected PACs, because they raise money later in the heat of the campaign, and labor

PACs, because they are larger and give contributions in larger average amounts. Each one of those likely mini-impacts has its special reverberations for specific kinds of candidates.

In sum, proposals to ban PACs or to cripple them fail by whatever criterion one wishes to employ. They are a politicized solution in search of a major problem. They do violence to fundamental constitutional rights. And they would return much of American campaign finance to the old regime by reducing public information and public accountability for organized giving. They would give away one of the triumphant successes of the FECA: the fullest record of organized and interested giving in the experience of the Western democracies. So, a likely two-decade scenario travels from the past and into the future. Watergate revelations shock Americans, Congress requires PACs to report fully, PACs report fully, reports shock Americans, Americans ban PACs, Americans know less about the auspices of organized and interested giving, Americans feel better about PACs and campaign finance. Another bit of the old regime returns then, even if in the guise of reform.

PAC-bashing may be good politics, but it is bad public policy. Far more constructive would be changes in the FECA that restore the integrity of the regulatory structure and that come to grips with the problem of the declining competitiveness of congressional elections. Although these changes will not be easy either to formulate or to steer through the Congress, they at least respond to serious problems.

Repairs and Refurbishing

Every regulatory system attracts professionals specializing in creative avoidance: lawyers, accountants, and other experts help the less adept to find the gaping seams or the unregulated interstices, to locate the grey areas of permissiveness, to replace new illegalities with new legalities, and generally to develop creative responses to the regulatory environment. Their inevitable successes require a periodic patching and shoring up of the regulatory structures. As tax avoidance becomes more sophisticated, threatening both revenue yield and confidence in the fairness of the system, the Congress tinkers with the regulatory statutes and occasionally, as in 1986, gives the entire structure a thorough remodeling. The development of structural problems and the consequent need to do something about them is a sure sign of the maturity of any regulatory system.

Congress has done nothing, however, to repair or maintain the regulatory structure of the FECA since the amendments of 1979. The reasons are complex, and political deadlock is only the beginning. Any patching up of the system suffers from the curse of invisibility; since the policy issues are largely visible only to insiders, there is little political pressure to act and even less political credit for acting, although the repairs for incumbents will be inconvenient at best and threatening at worst. Reformers tend also to belittle system-tuning as an avoidance of major issues or, more serious, as a shoring up of the status quo—which it certainly is—when they would prefer to dismantle and replace it. Maintenance has also been thwarted by a peculiar loss of nerve and confidence over what one might call the dread of "unanticipated consequences."

The institutional memories of the Congress recall that very few people anticipated the explosion of PACs that the 1974 amendments triggered. It is a governing belief among insiders that the law of unanticipated reactions continues to spook the FECA, although it is not easy to find another conspicuous example of it beyond the PAC explosion. The law would hardly seem to apply to the intervention of exogenous factors such as *Buckley* v. *Valeo*, especially when the causal agent is a constitutionally coordinate branch of government. Perhaps some people have the growth of bundling and soft money in mind, but if one takes these cases and those of other creative adaptations to the FECA as examples, then the law of unanticipated consequences is a truism, a statement that the regulated are smart and adaptable and that things will not always work out as easily as the reformers plan they will. Good policymaking must include careful efforts to anticipate and predict consequences of regulation, but perfect prediction is a high standard indeed against which to hold any legislation.

Most important, the Congress does not legislate irrevocably or for all time. The regulated will eagerly explore the regulatory structure, and they will find its weak joints and thin walls. Legislatures classically solve the unanticipated problems post facto with legislation restoring the integrity of the regulatory structure; in this case that ought to be especially easy, since it is the members of Congress themselves who have learned and adapted. Growing skills at adaptation to regulation usually confront growing knowledge and ability to predict the consequences of subsequent amendments.

While some uncertainty in that interaction may still remain, Congress as regulated and regulator now confronts quite the opposite problem: many consequences are too well known, too easy to anticipate. In 1974 Congress could forge a large majority more easily *because* the results for various interests were not clear. Building a majority now is much more difficult because members can knowledgeably calculate the impacts on themselves and their parties of even the most modest remolding of the FECA. The computerized records in most congressional offices, for example, permit a quick calculation of the effect on a House member, say, of a $200,000 limit on PAC receipts or the trade-offs between subsidies for postage and television time and the acceptance of spending limits at $600,000 per campaign cycle.

Two issues stand out most prominently for their threats to the integrity of the regulatory system: soft money and brokering/bundling. Both issues illustrate how serious regulatory lapses are at the margins of a system—when, that is, they involve part-time individual activists or when they involve the system's long, unguarded borders with the much more laissez-faire regimes of the states. It is far easier to tighten the regulation of central, institutionalized actors whose activities are at the heart of the transactions regulated. In addressing what to do about either soft money or bundling, consensus favors only reporting. At that point the policy disagreements begin.

In the case of soft money, one is dealing with a great variety of funds steered to hospitable states. Belatedly or not, the FEC has begun an assault on the problem with allocation formulas that determine what part of state party expenses can be assigned to state and local purposes (and thus be paid with soft money) and what part cannot. The FEC has also begun to require disclosure by national party committees of the operations, including the sources of money, of their federal (that is, hard-money) and their nonfederal (soft-money) accounts. Both requirements might well be tightened in details, but that is a matter for bill drafters. To the FEC's start ought to be added another limitation that only statute can achieve: a prohibition of the solicitation or channeling of contributions that violate the FECA by any federal officeholder or candidate for federal office. Such a provision would end the unseemly raising of soft money by presidential candidates whether or not they have accepted public funding for their campaign. It would also end exchanges such as the Keating support for the Cranston soft-money projects to identify and register voters.

A tougher issue, and one on which both commentators and congressional reformers are more timid, concerns the wisdom of extending such a prohibition to national party committees. Such an extension would be a major limitation on the four party congressional campaign committees, always a cause close to the hearts of congressional incumbents. Moreover, the reality of the contemporary Democratic and Republican parties is that their various national committees have taken over many of the activities that their state and local parties once carried out. To cut off soft-money funding for those committees' nonfederal responsibilities would throw a great part of the operation of the parties back onto state and local units no longer able to manage them, much less pay for them. On the other hand, the threat to the perceived integrity of the FECA ought not to be minimized. Quite simply, we here confront a series of Hobson's choices, the least unsatisfactory of which is probably to circumscribe but not to end national party freedom to raise and use soft money.[13]

In other words, we can end to the greatest extent possible the raising of money that cannot be raised under the FECA by people or committees subject to the FECA. We can also take steps to make sure that soft money does not enter the channels controlled by the FECA to influence the outcomes of federal elections. To go further would require the Congress to impose a uniform system of regulation on the states; the constitutional barriers would be very high, and those of political reality even higher. There is no practical way to stop the raising of money in states with more permissive statutes than the FECA; California or Georgia parties and officeholders will legally raise money in their states—corporate money or individual contributions in five generous figures—that could not be raised under the FECA. American federalism and the rights of the states guarantee as much, whether one considers the results regulatory chaos or healthy local autonomy.[14]

Bundling and brokering present even more perplexing regulatory problems. Bundling by PACs and party committees reporting under the FECA is used to avoid their contribution and spending limits under the FECA, and an end to their bundling can most easily be justified. A number of the bills before the House and Senate in 1991 had similar language that would treat any contribution made through or arranged by an intermediary or conduit as if it were a contribution *from* the intermediary or conduit if it is a PAC or party committee.[15] Such legislation, one should add, is more than an end to current bundling by PACs and parties; in many of the reform packages it serves to forestall bundling as a fall-back strategy for PAC contributions outlawed in the same packages.

After prohibiting PAC and party bundlers, one forges into the great regulatory swamp of individual action—a swamp both because of First Amendment questions and because of administrative practicalities. The easiest to include are individuals required to register under the Federal Regulation of Lobbying Act, and a number of recent reform proposals have included them. But by including lobbyists, one has crossed a divide from committees to individuals and from those actors required to report under the FECA to those not so required. Furthermore, some of those same proposals also would extend the treatment of lobbyists to any "conduit" when the check is made out to the conduit. The distinction here seems to be whether the original contribution is "earmarked" or not,[16] regardless of whether it goes to a party, a PAC, or an individual intermediary. In fact, that distinction governs the treatment of conduits and intermediaries already in the rules and regulations of the FEC. For example: "The intermediary or conduit of the earmarked contribution shall report the original source and the recipient candidate or authorized committee to the Commission, the Clerk of the House of Representatives, or the Secretary of the Senate . . . and to the recipient candidate or authorized committee."[17] Unfortunately, reporting is very limited, and for whatever reasons the FEC has never made a substantial issue of it.[18] Yet, the harder issue remains for the reformers: the brokering of contributions that enter the treasuries of intermediaries.

So, the politically active are free to host a cocktail party for an itinerant U.S. senator with a key committee assignment, selecting the guests, persuading them to give, suggesting an appropriate contribution to the senator's campaign treasury, and perhaps even collecting the checks—checks scrupulously made out to the senator. There are manifestly difficult problems even in enforcing reporting requirements on such brokering, although brokering is qualitatively similar to individual independent spending. Quantitatively, however, it reaches the proportions of the $25,000 annual limit on millions of individual contributors, and the FEC has not coped well with that problem either. The administrative problems in any attempt to win reporting of even the most lucrative brokering are staggering. The stakes are, however, as substantial as the problems: public knowledge of the well-brokered networks that may well develop into the new "PACs" of the 1990s.

Congress began, appropriately, with the simplest regulatory

tasks in 1971 and 1974. The reporting requirements of the FECA centered on PACs, parties, and candidates; individual contributions reached the records of the FEC only as they were reported by recipients. But both soft money and brokering involve individuals guiding money through the system. At their most influential, they are functional equals to PACs, parties, and candidates. Even the limited regulatory contact with individuals so far, however, has not gone well for the FEC. Reporting of independent expenditures by individuals has been spotty, and violations of the $25,000 annual limit on individual contributions have passed without FEC notice. So, when one talks about requiring individuals to report such intermediary or conduit brokering, administrative enthusiasm will be very limited. No one is anxious to solve an old problem by creating a new one, a conservatism that reflects, perhaps, the law of too-well-known consequences. Incorporating the increasing power of the intermediary into the regime of the FECA remains the hardest of all the repairs or corrections to fashion.

These repairs of the regulatory system do not involve major regulatory changes, nor are they intended to. They are merely a periodic step in conserving the status quo, as are other proposed adjustments. (The two most common "others" are an outlawing of leadership PACs and a tightening of the statutory definition of independence in independent spending.) Refurbishing a regulatory structure whose faults we get to know better and better with each election cycle ought to be a less demanding task than designing new regulatory structures. To hold the necessary repairs hostage to a broader reform plan, even an entirely different structure, or to work against incremental changes for fear they will blunt the call for major change, is to risk the collapse both of the regulation and of popular support for it.

Very Big Money and Very Little Money

The structure of regulation the Congress completed in 1974 was a remarkably good first try at comprehensive regulation of campaign finance. The Congress may in fact have got it right the first time, but we shall never know. Two years later the Supreme Court struck down all parts of the comprehensive structure limiting expenditures. In doing so, the Court may well have cut away the most problematic parts of the act, the ones most difficult to administer and least likely to get unquestioning compliance, and thus, ironically, have increased the FECA's prospects for success.

In any event, the Supreme Court did not diminish support for spending limits, even though proposals for reinstituting them have acquired heavy baggage since 1974. First, since *Buckley* candidates must accept them voluntarily, and legislatures must therefore invent ways of inducing that acceptance. Spending limits, moreover, have since 1974 acquired scholarly baggage that suggests they work to the advantage of incumbents and the disadvantage of their challengers. Jacobson's conclusion that challenger vote was directly related to the sums the challengers spent, and that incumbent vote was not, led easily to the conclusion that challengers had to be able to outspend incumbents in order to overcome all of the advantages the incumbents enjoyed. That conclusion then led ineluctably to a judgment on spending limits; in Jacobson's words, "Campaign spending does have an important effect on who wins these elections, and it is the amount spent by challengers (and other disadvantaged candidates) that actually makes the difference. Spending limits, if they have any effect at all on competition, can only work to the detriment of challengers."[19] So, debate over spending limits and the inducements for them links with the debate over how to protect the underfunded challenger and restore some degree of lost competitiveness to congressional elections. It is a connection springing primarily from the two edges on the sword of spending limits: to achieve the control of spending seems to make the plight of the challengers worse.

The public cry for spending limits reflects a widespread, almost universal belief that the costs of election campaigns are

spiraling, skyrocketing, or careening out of control and that
the sums spent are "obscene." That is not the reality of the
FEC's data about spending in congressional campaigns since
1986, but it is potent political reality nonetheless. Within the
realm of verifiable reality, the public-policy issue is one either
of rolling back a stable level of expenditure or of preventing
any future resurgence of former growth. Whether one rolls
back or holds the present line depends, in turn, on where one
sets the spending limit. The spending limit of $600,000 for
House elections proposed by the Gejdenson task force in 1991
would be more than twice the average total of $284,000 that
major-party general-election candidates spent in 1990, and in
that same year it would have limited only the 113 campaigns
that exceeded it.

As the distance between average incumbent and average
challenger spending increases, any spending limits will apply
chiefly to incumbents. Of the 113 House candidates who exceeded $600,000 in spending in 1990, 82 were incumbents.
Of the remainder, 27 were open-seat candidates and 14 were
challengers. Thus, members of Congress are really setting
spending levels for themselves, and they tend to set fairly high
limits. In debating spending limits the House, moreover, has
always observed the fiction that all districts, given their equal
populations, must have a single, uniform spending limit.
Spending levels are no more equal across the nation than is
the cost of living, and especially when one controls for electoral
competitiveness, the cost of a campaign is higher in urban,
metropolitan districts.

Spending limits by themselves curtail spending in some
campaigns and put a cap in place to deflect any future pressures upward. Those pressures are apt to happen only with
a blossoming of competition in congressional elections, however, and such a springtime of competitiveness is an uncertain
season. The chief gain would be one of perception for the
mass public, a gain hard to measure except in resulting gains
in confidence in the campaign finance system and more generally in representative institutions. But spending limits are

linked to inducements, and one must consider the effect of the inducements, too.

The initial plan post-*Buckley* was to combine spending limits with direct public funding, the combination defeated in 1974 for congressional campaigns and the one still driving the public funding of presidential campaigns. That option has encountered increasing resistance in the 1980s, both as a tax-provided government subsidy for politicians and as a low-priority competitor for shrinking public funds in an era of budget deficits. Legislatures now prefer to consider public funding as a disincentive, a weapon given to the opponent of the candidate who does not agree to spending limits.[20] But substantial public funding—public funding as an incentive—was a cornerstone in the planning of the reformers. Beyond its value as incentive, it brought two other substantial assets to a reform package: it reduced a candidate's reliance on interested private money, and it limited the time and effort a candidate had to put into fund-raising.

If the up-front cash of public funding is not acceptable, and if the bill drafters want positive incentives as well as disincentives for spending limits, *and* if they want incentives that will serve other missions, ingenuity finds a way. Democrats in the Congress have been imaginative in devising such non-cash subsidies as discounted postal rates, free or less expensive radio or television time, or tax credits for individuals contributing to the candidate's campaign. Each one of those inducements in turn becomes a policy issue in itself. Most of the tax credit proposals apply only to in-state contributions—hence the policy issue of encouraging local money and discouraging distant money. Some of the media proposals, to take another example, would not provide reductions for thirty-second spot commercials; reform of campaign finance becomes reform of media campaigning per se. And some of the incentives raise the question of who bears the cost; the media subsidies would be borne by broadcasters as a price of receiving a federal license. It is a hall of mirrors: policy issues exist within policy issues in an almost infinite regress.

The task of overseeing the spending of more than 1,750 candidates for Congress—about 875 of them Democratic or Republican candidates in the general election—has never been undertaken, and it is certainly a valid reason for qualms about spending limits. The FEC's difficulties with the state-by-state spending limits in the public funding of presidential candidates for the party nominations is never out of mind. Nor is it clear that a Congress not willing even to permit random auditing of candidate reports would give the FEC the funding and the authority it needs to do the job. From its earliest days Congress has kept the FEC on a short leash and on even shorter budgetary rations, and one can hardly be confident that spending limits would be accompanied by a change in that disposition. There is far too little confidence in the campaign finance system already for it to withstand widespread and unresolved assertions that candidates are spending beyond the limits.

The constitutional issues are no less troubling. The central question is straightforward enough: When does a package of incentives or inducements for accepting spending limits become so compelling, so coercive that the acceptance is no longer voluntary? The Minnesota law of 1990 attempting to limit the expenditures of congressional candidates is illustrative. If a candidate decides not to accept the expenditure limit and his or her opponent does, the opponent receives state funds matching small contributions up to a figure that is 25 percent of the spending limit and, in addition, the opponent is also freed from the spending limit.[21] Or, under the provisions of the 1991 Senate bill S. 3, the expenditure limit of candidates originally accepting the spending limit rises by the amount by which their non-accepting opponents spend or obligate themselves to spend above the limit. The price of voluntary choice is no longer just giving up benefits; it now involves the substantial advantaging of one's opponent. There are penalties for non-choice as well as incentives for choice. It is not the kind of voluntary option the Court approved in accepting the spending limits attached to presidential public funding in 1976, and it might well fail in a future Court test.

The greatest cause for concern about spending limits, however, is the great unknown. Since we have no experience with them in elections as vast and expensive as congressional elections, and since candidates would still get their money largely from private sources, their consequences are not easy to anticipate.[22] How will the fast learners adapt to them? Would spending in congressional campaigns move off the books of the campaign? One can imagine PACs mobilizing, endorsing, even spending independently rather than making contributions to candidates. Might ad hoc PACs begin to run campaigns for a few candidates of their choice, even independently of the campaign of the candidate? Might some expenditures of a candidate's committee be made before the formal organization of the committee or before the election-year cycle? Now that an expert and experienced elite is in place in campaign finance, political learning would likely eclipse in speed and acuity the learning that took place after 1974.

Eventually, any discussion of spending limits returns to the plight of the challengers. Equality of spending between incumbents and challengers, that is, appears to have unequal consequences. If that argument is correct, then there is a further corollary: the harm to challengers will increase the lower the spending limits are set. If an increase in challenger competitiveness is a desideratum for campaign finance reform—and it is for most observers—then the argument is a potent one. It has as well become a major weapon in the arsenal of congressional Republicans, who, as the minority party, accuse the majority Democrats of espousing spending limits as a way of further entrenching themselves in power. If spending limits work to the advantage of incumbents, they also advantage one party's incumbents more than the other's.

A great deal has happened since the Jacobson study, however. The average House incumbent's campaign in 1978 cost only $111,247; translated into 1990 dollars that is about $223,000. But in 1990 the average House incumbent spent

$398,462. If the marginal utility of each additional increment
of spending declines, then the need to be able to outspend
the incumbent declines as the level of spending rises. Enforced
equality today at $500,000 or $600,000, the range of spending
limits under discussion, is less debilitating to challengers than
equality at $398,000 or especially at $223,000. Moreover, it is
spending limits without public support, or some other early
"stake" in the campaign, that most threatens challengers. If
they are to spend competitively with incumbents, they must
raise the money in the first place. If the assistance were early
and substantial, it might even help challengers break out of
the downward spiral of expected defeat. An early promise of
funds and a cap on incumbent spending might raise the quality
of challenging candidates, who in turn could raise more
money, get more attention, and ultimately stage a campaign
that would break the dynamic of failure.[23]

It is the minority party in the House, the Republicans, that
most fears the consequence of spending limits. But the average
Republican challenger in the 1990 general elections for the
House spent only $110,000; only eight of them spent more
than $600,000, only one of whom was a winner. Indeed, sup-
port for Republican challengers has waned generally in the
1980s, even in the spending of the NRCC. They are a very long
way from spending themselves to victory—so far, indeed, that
it is hard to see how generous spending limits would hurt
them. Gary Jacobson argues that the Republicans' problem is
elsewhere than in campaign finance, that it is in finding good
candidates to challenge Democratic incumbents; he suggests
that the problem centers on the unwillingness of Republicans
to commit to a career in a government of which they disap-
prove and which they may prefer to dismantle.[24] But if there
is, in addition, the factor of expectations about the funding
of a race at work, the value of even partial public funding
would appear to be a plus in challenger recruitment.

In short, reasonably generous spending limits accompanied
by a substantial public subsidy might not greatly hurt challengers. The Democratic bill in the House in 1991 (H. 3750),

for example, offered any candidate up to $200,000 in match-
ing funds from the U.S. treasury in return for a spending limit
of $600,000. The usefulness to challengers would have been
greater had there been no matching requirement; for many
of them, matching means less money coming more slowly. But
all of this is merely trying to put the best face on a program
not intended to help challengers. The need is not for "non-
harmful" reforms but rather for those programs designed to
increase the number of competitive races for Congress.

The strength of incumbents in their races for reelection, as
I argued earlier, springs not from their larger campaign treasuries but from their incumbent status per se and from the
advantages in it that permit them to help their constituents,
to win their gratitude, to be known to them, and to get their
faces and messages before them. Their electoral position
springs not from money but from a politics that is candidate-
centered and in which party labels and energies are less important. That position could be challenged directly by cutting
congressional staffs, by limiting the postal frank, or by reducing travel budgets.

Another contemporary movement would achieve the result
even more directly by limiting the number of terms incumbents could serve; the movement is gathering momentum in
the states, and it cannot be long before it moves to the national
arena. Whatever its other shortcomings, it is hard to imagine
anything that would raise the level of competitiveness quite
as surely. Term limits would in effect mandate the holding of
open-seat races periodically in every congressional district;
they would also attract good challengers to run in incumbents'
last campaigns to ready themselves for the open-seat campaigns. As direct as all such solutions might be, though, majorities of incumbents would have to vote for them. It is better
to look elsewhere for answers.

If hope for the starving challengers is to come from within
the system of campaign finance, incumbents must still legislate
an improvement in their own challengers' fortunes. The major

options are clear. First, one could fashion programs of incentives for challengers. Nowhere is it written that all candidates must be treated equally; separate grants or subsidies for challengers only—seed money grants or media discounts—would address their plight directly. Such plans are also, need one say it, the least likely to appeal to incumbent legislators. In their heart of hearts many scholars of campaign finance would choose a second option: public grants or subsidies *without* spending limits, the option they call "floors without ceilings."[25] Such a plan would help challengers most of all; the public grants would be an early incentive in the recruitment of promising candidates and enable them to build support while not denying them the possibility of outspending an incumbent. But political scientists can count votes, too, and this is not the kind of public funding that the Congress, Common Cause, and the nation's editorial writers have in mind.

So, we look to politically viable options. Most feasible, perhaps, would be any shoring up of the national political parties. They alone have an interest in maximizing the number of party seats in the House and Senate; that commitment in turn makes them the logical funders of challengers and open-seat candidates, and it is a role they increasingly assumed in the 1980s. How best to aid the parties? Republicans have long favored expanding or removing the limits on party contributions or on-behalf-of spending; Republican party committees, however, have long raised more money than the Democrats, and they alone press against the limits of the FECA. Democratic acceptance of an enhanced party role would improve if some modest raising of the party spending limits were accompanied by incentives for contributing to the parties— perhaps a small raise in the limits on individual or PAC contributions to party committees.[26]

More effective might perhaps be tax credits for small contributions to party committees. Larry Sabato has argued convincingly for a reinstatement of the pre-1986 federal tax credit on contributions of up to $50 a person, with one change:

limiting the credit to contributions to party committees. "Such a move would clearly encourage small donations that have few if any real strings attached; the parties would not only remain unincumbered by the perceived obligations that come with large contributions, but both parties would have an exceptionally valuable tool to use in expanding their donor and membership base."[27] Less likely politically, and perhaps less useful to the parties, would be limited federal grants to the national parties specifically for aid to candidates. It is not a strange or preposterous idea; public subsidies of the major parties are already in place in at least eight states.

Whatever form any help for the challengers takes, however, it is hard to be optimistic about it. Funders—whether they are individuals, PACs, or parties—do not spend their money on challengers because they will not win. Getting money into their hands or encouraging them to give will promote their campaign giving, but legislation cannot make them give to challengers. Contributors pursue their political goals with their contributions; their giving, therefore, is heavily governed by the need to win elections. Even political parties, whose interests ought logically to extend even to long-shot challengers, find it hard to favor them over the more competitive open-seat candidates. In sum, it is difficult to see how a system of voluntarily contributions can break the dynamic of poor electoral prospects, middling candidate quality, and shortage of money. Voluntarily given money rarely precedes candidate quality and chances of winning; the risks are too great and the benefits too remote for the rational contributor. No other lesson of the post-1974 regime is clearer than that one.

New Dollars for Old, Interested Dollars

The displacement of interested money has ranked high on the agenda of the reformers for at least four decades. In fact, failure to achieve public funding for congressional campaigns in the 1974 amendments to the FECA was their only important failure. They did win at least half a loaf by eliminating the lavishly contributing fat cats, and they looked forward serenely to a funding regime led by the less interested small sums of local, individual contributors at the grass roots. The quick proliferation of PACs in the 1970s soon ended that dream and set off a renewed search for more benign sources of campaign money.

The solution that failed in 1974—full public funding of congressional elections—soon became far less feasible politically. Philosophical and taxpayer objections to the use of public money for the costs of campaigning stiffened, both because of the revolt of taxpayers and because of the growing disfavor of politics and politicians in the nation.[28] Moreover, continuing budget deficits pit the use of public funds for campaigns against other frustrated claims for public support—for medicaid, education, child care, and unemployment compensation, for example. In such rhetorical and political arm wrestling, public funding of campaigns has been the predictable loser. In just a little more than 15 years the struggle to replace interested money has shifted from the simple, all-encompassing solution of 100 percent public funding to a variety of less sweeping interventions. The most popular have had one feature in common: they seek to reduce the role of PACs in campaign funding. The most direct of them I have already discussed—banning the PACs, outlawing their contributions to candidates, reducing their $5,000 contribution limit sharply, or imposing on candidates a limit on their aggregate receipts from PACs. In whatever form, they remain solutions to an exaggerated problem, solutions likely to generate even greater problems than the ones they are intended to solve.

The less drastic alternative is to make candidates less reliant on interested money. Most of the packages of incentives for accepting spending limits also include incentives for displacing interested money. The Gejdenson task force proposal (H. 3750) provided direct federal funding for as much as a third of a candidate's receipts. Cheaper media and postal rates and vouchers for free television time as incentives for choosing spending limits also diminish the candidate's reliance on interested money to the extent they replace PAC and larger individual contributions. And they do so quietly, almost serendipitously, for attention is focused on the spending limit. Even encouraging a greater party role accomplishes the same displacement. Party monies, even those funds the party gets from PACs, are to some extent cleansed of their original interests; the party's agenda replaces the agenda of the original donor.

The same rationales apply to shoring up the position of individual contributors in the campaigns. The methods are straightforward: tax credits up to $100 per individual, an augmented contribution limit of $2,000 or more, higher annual limits for aggregate individual giving. One can, alternatively, force candidates to go to smaller individual contributions with public-funding programs that require matching, the kind of program in force during the presidential primaries. The assumption is probably true that the level of interestedness is lower in individual contributions, especially the smaller ones, than it is in PAC money.

Whatever step one proposes, however, it is beset with political problems. Any strengthening of the individual or party roles collides with the reality that Republicans are better than Democrats at raising such money. Congressional districts also differ widely in their fertility for such cultivation, the urban districts of many Democrats having the least promising soil. As for public funding, the Treasury Department will not sit idly by while proposals that will reduce tax revenues move through the Congress, and proposals to spend public monies raise the predictable issues of the deficit and of budget busting. And there are always the same grass-roots critics, the ones that tormented the members of Congress over pay increases and their bank overdrafts, waiting to convert the issue of replacing interested money into a simple issue of congressional greed. In the reforming of campaign finance there are layers and layers of political complexity beneath seemingly simple solutions.

The search for disinterested money only recently has

turned local. Several of the 1990–91 proposals for reinstituting the tax credits that had been in effect until the 1986 revision of the tax codes would limit the new credits now to
in-state or in-district money. The rationale seems to hinge on
a conviction that local interestedness is more benign than interests from other states and that, if it is not, it is at least
preferable because it is indigenous. It is the campaign finance
variation of the old saw about the inept local congressman:
he may be an S.O.B., but he's our S.O.B. That such proposals
ignore the diminishing localism and regionalism of American
politics is obvious; they are indeed frankly advocated as reforms that might reverse that dangerous nationalization. It is
at points such as these that reform of the campaign finance
system tries to become the reform of all of American politics.

Ultimately the search for disinterested sources of money
rests on two suspect assumptions. The first is that interested
money, particularly that from PACs, exerts a major and perhaps controlling influence over decisions in American legislatures. It is an assumption that rejects both the logic of
pluralism among contending interests and the systematic evidence of the best scholarship. The second assumption is that
somewhere out there one can find enough innocent, pur-
poseless money, money with no political goals or interests
behind it. At worst it is a position not unlike the stork theory
of human reproduction. It is also a denial of the group rev-
olution and the growing power of political organization that
so clearly marks the last generation of American politics. The
search for money without interests remains, as it has always
been, a search to find again a golden age of simpler, grass-
roots, citizenly politics. The problem is that this golden age,
like all others, never existed except in our nostalgic longings.

The Current Status of Reform

Reform proposals moved sequentially through the houses of
Congress in 1991, but to a very uncertain end. In May the
Senate passed its bill (S. 3), and the House passed one of its

own (an amended H. 3750) just before adjourning for the holidays in late November. Attempts to reconcile the two very different bills awaited the return of the Congress in late January 1992. Even if the two bills were reconciled in conference and the compromise version passed by both houses, presidential approval seemed unlikely. George Bush had promised to veto any bill containing spending limits or public funding, and each bill contained both. The most likely outcome some time in early 1992 was no outcome.

All of the ingredients of deadlock were, predictably, present and operative through 1991. Both bills were, first of all, Democratic bills. They passed with overwhelmingly Democratic majorities in both houses; Republicans provided only five of the 56 votes for passage in the Senate and only 21 of the majority of 273 in the House. More substantively, both bills contained the two features anathema to the Republicans: spending limits and public subsidies. Each bill set spending limits for its chamber, that for House candidates pegged at $600,000 and the one for Senate candidates on a sliding scale up to $5.5 million for California candidates.[29] As for the public funding of campaigns, the Senate bill provided for reduced postal rates and publicly financed vouchers for television time worth 20 percent of the candidate's spending limit after the candidate achieved eligibility by raising small individual contributions. The House version provided up to $200,000 per candidate in public funds to match money up to $200 raised from individuals. The Senate bill also mandated that the electronic media offer time to eligible candidates at sharply reduced rates. Republican bills in both houses featured Republican preferences; the House GOP leadership bill, for instance, would have cut the PAC contribution limit back to $1,000 and required candidates to raise at least half of their money from within their districts.

Moreover, each bill was tailored to the campaign finance of its chamber. S. 3 outlawed PAC contributions to candidates, leaving Senate candidates to the mercies of individual contributors; while that might inconvenience some senators, most have by now tapped into out-of-state networks of individual contributors. Their challengers have not. House 3750 placed a limit on receipts from PACs at $200,000, a generous figure and fully one-third of the spending limit. Other provisions, too, were chamber-specific. Subsidies for the electronic media played a big part in inducing senatorial candidates to accept spending limits; they obviously reflected the far greater role of the media in campaigns for the Senate. For their part, House Democrats wrote a receipt limit of $200,000 for individual contributions over $200 into their bill, a reflection of the lesser role the new fat cats play in House campaigns. Even the politics of reform exacerbated differences between the Senate and House; the impression lingered in the House that some of the Senate support for eliminating PAC contributions rested on the assumption that the House would undo the deed.

To be sure, there were points of contact, even agreement, between the two bills. Both outlawed leadership PACs (that is, personal PACs), both attempted to get soft money and bundling under greater control, and both provided reduced postal rates. But the two major points of difference were so substantial as to suggest the possibility that they would not be reconciled. The different stances on PACs was one—the difference between forbidding their contributions to candidates absolutely and placing a $200,000 limit on any candidate's receipts from them. The other major difference was over public funding. The senators chose to induce acceptance of spending limits by subsidizing campaigning via the U.S. mails and the electronic media; direct grants were available only for candidates whose opponents refused the spending limits. The House plan, however, made direct grants available to all candidates in a matching basis up to the total of $200,000.

It was that matching feature, in fact, that almost derailed H. 3750. As the bill of the Gejdenson task force, it approached the problem of funding the public matching grants very gingerly; the original bill suggested three sources for that money: a fund financed by a voluntary income tax add-on, the repeal of tax deductions for lobbying, and a registration fee for PACs.

Even with such a politically attractive set of funding options, the bill lacked the votes for passage until all proposals or suggestions except the voluntary income tax add-on were stricken. Moreover, the largely Southern Democratic hold-outs insisted on another concession: wording in the bill to require incentives (tax credits) for small contributions. So, the issue of how to pay for public funding was postponed to another day, a day that might not come for a long time. The Senate bill also finessed the mechanism for providing the money, noting only that it was the sense of the Senate that it should come from repealing the tax deductions available, largely to corporations, for the costs of lobbying and running a PAC. For now, therefore, there appears to be a majority for limited and matching direct public grants or subsidized media campaigning, but no majority for financing them out of what the Congress's constituents call the taxpayers' money.

With the road to legislation apparently blocked by party differences and the threat of a veto, the two bills and the debate over them inevitably looked to the 1992 campaigns. Democrats could claim that they had passed reform bills that curbed spending and diminished PAC power. House Democrats ventured further toward public funding, shielded by a Southern fig leaf against the inevitable charge they planned to use taxpayer money to finance their campaigns. Republicans, for their part, had proven they could hit the PACs harder and that they had flirted less with public resources in any form. House Republicans also established themselves as enemies of out-of-district funding. The lines were drawn for the campaign debate over campaign finance—if the public wanted it to be an issue.

And how is one to evaluate S. 3 and H. 3750? Many observers of congressional campaign finance have taken the House bill more seriously, and with good reason. By the criteria discussed in the preceding chapter, the House bill was superior:

- In help for challengers and more generally the fostering of competitive elections, the House bill provided early funds for challengers, although the matching feature made the help less dramatic than straight grants would have been. The Senate bill offered challengers substantial free media time, but it probably hurt some of them, especially Democrats, by denying them PAC support.

- Both bills would have restored some of the tattered integrity of the regulatory structure; both limited soft money and outlawed leadership PACs, for instance.

- Both bills controled spending, both with caps set at relatively high levels, although the Senate formula probably achieved a greater rollback. Although that disappointed more militant reformers, the legislated limits, especially those of H. 3750, minimized the harm to viable challengers battling entrenched incumbents.

- On the replacement of interested money, H. 3750 outscored S. 3 by a good margin. The banning of PAC contributions in S. 3 would probably fall in the courts; the backup new $1,000 contribution limit (bolstered by a stringent limit on PAC receipts) would almost as effectively drive present PAC money into invisibility. The House limit on receipts sacrificed none of the gains in openness achieved under the FECA, and it would also have created a smaller pool of unused and dislocated political money.

The chief lesson of 1991 and 1992, however, was not in any comparison of alternatives as much as it was in the sharp differences in both houses on many of the issues. The interests at stake are deeply and directly felt in the Congress and the White House, and they have so far defied the most diligent attempts at compromise or accommodation.

The deadlock in legislated change since 1979 reflects more than a dreadfully complex politics of cross-cutting political interests. It reflects epic disagreements over the realities of contemporary campaign finance and, ultimately, over the agenda of problems and solutions to them. Those disagreements in turn pose one of the most poignant policy dilemmas. Should not the flickering on the wall of the cave guide public-policy decisions, especially when they are the only reality that great majorities know? Should not one encourage or support new restrictions on PACs, for example, because they will elevate confidence in and acceptance of American politics? The case is an appealing one. Yet do we wish to concede that the myth-shapers can and will shape the contours of public policy? Are we prepared to sacrifice the ability of policy to address, even solve, the problems that the "real" reality defines?

This is merely campaign finance's version of the old problem of the place of expert knowledge in a mass democracy. The pull and tug between expert analysis and mass beliefs works itself out in the way such conflicts are always resolved in a mass democracy: by the politics of democracy itself. The flickerings on the wall of the cave create political impressions and beliefs, even political pressures and demands. Members of Congress are always responsive to grass-roots opinion, especially intense local opinion and opinion concerning themselves and their personal and political perquisites. If the public believes that PACs have achieved dangerous levels of influence, that belief becomes a potent force in shaping legislative reform packages in the Congress. Even Democrats who depend on PAC funds more than Republicans do, both as candidates and as a party, will march to the beat of the public drums and drummers. Popular images do not always create an agenda or pressures for action; more commonly they generate the reactions that elected officials fail to anticipate at their great peril.

Exactly those expected reactions have shaped the debate over the future of the post–1974 regime in recent years. They account for the absence from the debate of the major alternative to the status quo: comprehensive public funding. Even the limited public funding the House Democrats proposed in 1991—levels that would yield about 25 percent of most candidates' receipts—occasioned wariness among Democratic members and mass opposition among the Republicans. Even the House leadership admitted that limited public funding would be a hard sell in Washington and back home. In the ambivalent opinion environment, they seemed to think that opposition to public funding for whatever reason—ideology, appearance of self-aggrandizement, higher priorities for public funds—would in the end win out over support for capping expenditures and replacing private, interested contributions.

So, the debate goes on without the only major alternative in a public discourse curiously removed from the heated criticisms of the present regime. On the one hand, public funding is politically risky in modest amounts and unthinkable in large sums; on the other, it is the only alternative that addresses the major complaints on this most political of all subjects. It alone would replace interested money, fund candidates to order to achieve competitiveness rather than because they had achieved it, and solve or minimize many of the compliance issues with the present regulatory system. It is clearly an idea whose time has not come, or has not come again. One suspects, however, that if public concerns about the campaign finance regime do not abate, its time will come. When it does, the rationale will be the same one that justified the public treasury assuming the costs of printing ballots and administering elections. It will be necessary to protect the integrity of popular democracy's most sacred and important business.

A reform movement that sustains its life and passion for several decades often does so by exaggerating the benefits of reform. In this instance, the conviction that money is the root of all evil leads to the wish that reforming the flow of money will materially change the nature of representation and policymaking in American legislatures. But often the vision of the future is a vision of the past. Proposals to ban PACs in effect try to repeal the revolutionary growth in group politics over the last few decades. Proposals to sharply restrict the flow of campaign contributions across state lines seem bent on reversing the increasing nationalization of our politics, our political discourse, and our political interests and issues. The illustrations are varied and virtually endless.

A way of funding campaigns reflects, even mimics, the electoral and party politics it serves. It reflects as well the institutions of government within which it operates. Moreover, the broader political universe does not yield easily to changes in the system of campaign finance; more likely, it shapes and molds even the changes we devise. Reformers who pay too little attention to the very stubborn causes of the practices they seek to change run the risk of standing, like King Canute, in the rising tide they had commanded to recede.

Chapter 8 _____
_____
_____

_____

The Future of Campaign Finance

The sheer detail of the candidate, PAC, and party reports under the FECA has become a wonder of the democratic political world. Nowhere else do scholars and journalists find so much information about the funding of campaigns, and the openness of Americans about the flow of money stuns many other nationals accustomed to silence and secrecy about such traditionally private matters. The rolls of microfilmed reports at the FEC's Washington headquarters offer mute testimony to the new levels to which the FECA brought openness and information about campaign finance. And although the best of the state reporting systems do not match the productivity of the FECA's reporting mechanisms, they yield much more information than do any of the European democracies.

Reporting and information for what? For journalistic reporting certainly, and through it for greater public knowledge of key transactions, of the sources of money, and of its distribution among candidates. Publicity, however, does necessarily mean greater understanding, even explanation. The truth is that although we may know a great deal about the movement of money in the post-1974 system, we do not necessarily understand it or, indeed, understand campaign finance regimes generally. If I were to try to project a future for the FECA in the 1990s, I would be hard put even to produce credible speculation. Debates in the Congress and its committees over reform proposals are largely barren of any analytical framework with enough power to rise above short-term projections based on recent personal experience. As for anything we might honestly call a theory of campaign finance systems, it is too early.

Perhaps with more time and greater experience the post-1974 regime will yield more of its secrets. By 1992 its less than two decades have provided too narrow a range of experience and too few of the natural experiments one needs for framing explanations. To be sure, there has been change and adaptation in the system—far more than the critics and myth-makers have acknowledged—but the broad outlines of the post-Watergate regime have been virtually unchanged since the *Buckley* decision and the amendments to the FECA that followed it. And its political environment also has remained fairly fixed: a politics of fragmentation and deadlock with reduced initiatives in the public sector, and candidate-dominated campaigns in an informational environment increasingly fed by images from the electronic media. That is why the prospects for 1992 excite so many imaginations—an election in which one key variable in the mix, the degree of competitiveness of the elections, may be significantly altered. But first to the money supply and then to 1992.

The Supply of Money

The amount of money available to candidates for the Congress, for all candidates indeed, seems to be governed by its own dynamic. It rose almost inexorably to a peak in the mid-1980s and then fell back a bit into stability by 1990. It seems to grow from its own internal causes—from the willingness, the need, the urge of individuals to put their money into political play. The supply of campaign money, that is, appears

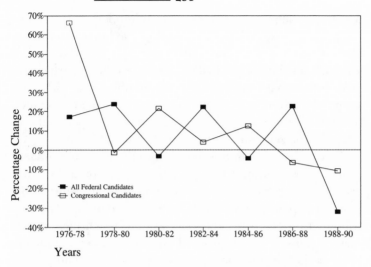

Figure 8.1
Percentage Change in Total Receipts of All Federal and
Congressional Candidates (Constant Dollars): 1976–1990

to be relatively inflexible, and it seems in the aggregate not
to reflect the other side of the exchange—the importunings
of candidates, their need for campaign money, and the competitive opportunities their campaigns offer. For evidence,
one need only look at the patterns of congressional funding
to note that they peak in the off years, the years of no presidential election (fig. 8.1). The presidential campaigns apparently siphon off funds in the presidential years, and the
suppliers do not, or cannot, adjust the supply of money to
fund the congressional candidates at their off-year levels.

Like everything else in campaign finance, the determinants
of the volume of money are both complicated and somewhat
contradictory. To a considerable extent, the money available
reflects repeated, habitual giving, even a budgeted and institutionalized giving by repeat contributors, many of them stimulated periodically by PAC, party, and candidate solicitations
or even by regular billing systems or payroll deduction plans.
The numbers of candidates seeking money does make a dif-

ference in the presidential pre-convention period; the record total contributed to those campaigns in 1988 reflected the one election since 1974 without an incumbent and thus with a scramble for the presidential nominations in both parties. But in congressional elections the total numbers are fairly constant, and differences seem largely to affect the distribution of money among incumbents, challengers, and open-seat candidates—the zero-sum game of congressional finance.

So, the decisions to put money into the campaign finance system have been individual; often, though not always, they are removed from strategic considerations or any sense of the political opportunities an approaching cycle offers. The contributor to a PAC gives generally without much idea of how many open-seat campaigns or how many vulnerable incumbents beckon in the coming election. Much more important for donors are their levels of interest in politics or the images of American politics and campaigns the media transmit, the stories of congressional pay raises or perks abused or of arrogant PACs spending wildly. Even more, perhaps, general beliefs about the political usefulness of contributing, the assessment of its efficacy as a political act, matter in the decision to give. The exchanges of the candidates and the purposeful contributors—PACs, the party committees, the affluent individuals and their brokers—is thus somewhat removed from the considerations that generate the money in the first place. With relatively fixed resources in the system, the direct parties to the exchange play something of a zero-sum game. It is precisely because they need a buffer against the inflexibility of the money supply that the incumbents work so hard to build cash reserves.

The people, the motives, and the processes that recruit the money in the first place are not the same ones that allocate or distribute it subsequently. Moreover, with the increasing organization of contributions in the post–1974 regime, the separation increases. It is the mechanism of the marketplace in campaign finance and its many exchanges by which the supply of money is allocated, and that marketplace is driven by the pursuit of electoral victory. The ability of incumbents to reduce competitive opportunities for contributors triggered a massive reallocation of funds in the 1980s, and what the incumbents gained, the challengers lost. Incumbent power, moreover, is heightened by the redistribution; incumbent gains would have been reduced if a rising tide of money had raised all vessels. And so, incumbent success in the zero-sum realities of American campaign finance has come, in a time of steady state resources, to mirror their success in another zero-sum game, that of voter choices in elections.

As the economy of campaign finance stops growing and the money supply levels off, the zero-sum nature of the marketplace intensifies in the competition for funds among incumbents, challengers, and open-seat candidates. It was evident even in 1982, when the supply was still growing. In that election the recession of 1982 threatened Republican incumbents in the House, many of whom would have ordinarily been vulnerable as freshmen who won in marginal seats in the Reagan landslide two years earlier. In addition, the number of open seats was at its usual post-reapportionment high. Despite all of the resulting opportunities, the total money raised by House candidates was not much higher than in past election years (fig. 8.1). Moreover, its distribution was only modestly altered from 1980 to get more money into the hands of the beleaguered Republican incumbents and hopeful Democratic challengers. The mechanisms that raised the money and then distributed it responded imperfectly even to the very electoral opportunities that govern voluntary political activity.

So, two basic mechanisms are at work to channel money to the candidates. One mechanism generates it, and one distributes it. To be sure, they are not completely separate; some contributions from individuals directly to candidates are certainly both generative and distributive. That is especially the case with small sums from individuals. Even as separate mechanisms, however, they share a common sensitivity to the state of electoral politics. The strategic decisions about distribution depend heavily on the quantity and quality of competition in elections and on all the things, such as incumbency and the quality of candidates, that affect it. The generative decisions depend more diffusely and distantly on elections—on assessments of the quality and content of campaigns, of the importance of elections in making political choices, of the efficacy of participating in them, even of their ability to serve the broader purposes of representative democracy.

These days Americans generate no larger supply of money than they did several election cycles ago, and we have no more than a general idea of the possible reasons why we have reached stability. The end of the frenzied growth of political money could perhaps be a cause for celebration if one did not suspect that it results from troubling causes. It is hard indeed to escape the conclusion that the new stability of the money supply reflects the poor health of American electoral politics— and perhaps of some of the rest of American politics, too. The gravity of the illness is now graphically portrayed, even exaggerated, by reporters and image-makers, but it is not a figment of their imaginations. The effect on campaign finance is similar to the effect on voting, except perhaps that citizens are driven by the internalized norms of good citizenship more to vote than to contribute money for campaigning.

Given the current level of knowledge about the dynamics of a regime, it is not surprising that one sees very few attempts to calculate the impact of statutory modifications on the flow of money in the system. One may speculate loosely that PACs might put surplus money into independent expenditures or into party committees; might some of their money also dry up or flee politics? Or might it find outlets in new forms of brokering networks? All of those questions are simply variants of the one fundamental question: what will the newly established equilibrium between input and outgo look like? It is the hardest policy assessment of them all, as well as the most important.

The optimism of the 1970s about the efficacy of electoral politics is perhaps best reflected in the fact that organized groups, through their PACs, sought so wildly to enter them.

That optimism, however, seems almost as quaintly dated as the earlier eras of urban bosses and compliant fat cats. Now it is all too easy for political activists to conclude that the important battles in American politics are being fought not in elections but in the politics of legislatures, presidencies, bureaucracies, and courts.[1] That, indeed, is the decision that PACs and many politically sophisticated individuals have made. It follows, then, that any repair of American electoral politics, any trend that will return them to their earlier importance, may ironically fuel a resumption of the growth of money available for American campaigning.

The 1992 Elections and Political Opportunity

Washington insiders and their magazines were abuzz with speculation in late 1991 about the possibility that competitiveness would return in the 1992 elections. Some very wise people predicted, despite dissenters, that there would be between 40 and 50 open House seats, a result of new seats created in the post-1990 reapportionments, normal retirements, and additional retirements for a number of special reasons: avoidance of hard races in restructured districts, fear of a Republican landslide, and desire to be able to convert surpluses in campaign treasuries to personal use.[2] In addition, the 1992 Senate races offer Republicans a possibility of recapturing a majority. Of the 32 incumbents running for reelection, 19 are Democrats, 11 of whom won their last election with less than 60 percent of the general-election vote; of the three open seats, only one (Alan Cranston's) was held by a Democrat. And everywhere there is the impression that incumbents will be more vulnerable than usual in the face of voter unhappiness.

In short, a natural experiment looms. Political scientists, like astronomers, cannot manipulate the subjects of their research; they wait for a major change in the system to occur and then hurry to observe the changes that result. If we do have a great resurgence in competitiveness in 1992, what impact will it have on the campaign finance regime? Is it possible that heightened competition will draw new resources into congressional campaign finance? Ordinarily, in a presidential election year candidates for the Congress would expect hard times, but 1992 may be an exceptional year in that respect, too, with an incumbent president suppressing competition in the Republican party and slow-starting Democrats raising little more than pittances in late 1991. If the supply of money does not increase greatly, some of the money for the competitive House races may come from the underfinanced presidential-primary races. And then? There is not much to be harvested from challengers' accounts, especially since some of them will also enjoy improved opportunities as a result of incumbent unpopularity and of redrawn districts with which the incumbent is only partially familiar. And certainly the rising interest in the Senate campaigns rules a diversion of their resources to House races.

That leaves the incumbents and a possible replay of the 1982 scenario. Incumbents can dig in, use their power in the exchanges to sustain their fund-raising, and deny their own party's challengers and open-seat candidates the resources they might more efficiently turn into party seats. And their power in the exchange is greater now than it was in 1982. At this point, how much flexibility have PACs and interested individuals left in redistributing their contributions? Have their commitments to incumbents over the past decade left them irrevocably committed to and fearful of spurned incumbents? Has their legislative strategy become a permanent alliance? Or, alternatively, can the revived party campaign committees play a stronger allocative and arbitrating role than they were able to in 1982?

The possibilities of the natural experiment of 1992 all explore facets of the one great possibility: that a resurgence of competition will transform or reenergize the campaign finance regime. Such a transformation would probably be only for the short run because the competitiveness would largely reflect the predictably turbulent politics of the first House election

after the decennial census. As a once-in-a-decade phenomenon its effect might well be muted, moreover, by incumbents
drawing down their cash on hand. One election may, in fact,
be too short a time for change to develop and solidify. Certainly only the quick of foot and wit will be able to move artfully
enough to take advantage of it.

All of the other influences making for stability would remain in place. Deadlock between Republican presidents and
largely Democratic Congresses, the stifling effect of massive
budget deficits on domestic initiatives, a separation of legislative and congressional electoral politics, the continued weakness of the parties in the electorate—all this and more lay
behind the stability of the FECA system. In fact, the whole
abandonment of electoral politics for an across-the-board support of incumbents makes sense only in a legislative setting
in which no great issues are at contest and where incremental
actions or non-actions are the chief products of the process.

Major change in the present campaign finance regime, in
other words, probably awaits changes in the basic contours of
American politics and policy-making. One need only look
around the American states to note that the electoral strategies
of private money are stronger and more important in states
in which control of one or both houses of the legislature are
within reach of either party. In those states, too, legislative
campaign committees or caucuses tend to be more effective.
The congressional campaigns of 1992 will also illustrate differences between House and Senate campaign finance that
reflect the far greater vulnerability of the Democratic majority
in the Senate. In short, the campaign finance system is a part
of the politics of a country—its parties, its other ways of organizing influence and interests, its ways of building majorities
and consensus. As they change, it changes.

But those are relatively small caliber changes. Consider another scenario: the many changes in electoral politics that
would follow a party realignment approaching the scope of
the one in the 1930s. Incumbents would lose reelection in
dramatic numbers, and power in their exchanges with con-

tributors would shift away from them. A new majority party would take control of the House and Senate. The whole structure of competitive opportunities, even the prospects of challengers, would be permanently recast. Or take a less disruptive scenario. Term limits on members of Congress would work a less dramatic but major change by mandating a large number of recurring open seats. After a term limit, however, there would remain the shadow incumbency of the locally dominant party to constrain competition in open-seat races, a constraint that would not be present in the years immediately after realignment. The point is not to predict, only to suggest the major reshaping of the campaign finance regime that would follow basic changes in the nation's electoral and representational politics.

The Regulatory Regime

We shall never know what kind of regulatory regime the FECA amendments of 1974 created because they were so drastically altered by the Supreme Court in *Buckley* v. *Valeo*. What was intended to be a closed system in which the major flows of money into and out of campaigns were fully controlled emerged as an open system of uncontrolled outlets when the Court struck down all limits on direct spending in the campaign by candidates, PACs, and individuals. A tightly constrained regulatory system became a more relaxed, open-ended one. The modifications in *Buckley* meant that the original 1974 plan would never have to meet its two severest tests: the administration of spending limits in hundreds of races and the accommodation of excess money in a system with no effective outlets. Instead, the crippled FECA affected chiefly the recruitment of money, ending the freedom of the fat cats and encouraging the development of PACs. As inflation took its toll on the FECA's fixed contribution limits, it doubtless also contributed to the gradual leveling off of the money supply.

Behind a regulatory regime there is always an abstraction one can call a model. It is the vision or desideratum behind the legislation, the kind of little world the reformers or regulators want to achieve. To write about models, however, is to write about pure types when in reality the models in place or even contemplated are hybrids or mixtures. But real-life regimes carry the predominant characteristics of one model or another, and what's more, pure types are always useful constructs for analysis. Above all, they define the major architectural options open to the builder or rebuilder. Four of them have dominated American debate over campaign finance since 1974: a grass-roots model, one based on comprehensive public funding, a party-centered model, and the status quo of organized finance.

A grass-roots model appears to have animated the Congress in 1974. Reform focused on eliminating the fat cats and on developing a broad base of local, individual giving in relatively small sums. The main implications of the model were, first, that the funding bases would largely remain local, and the voting and funding constituencies would largely remain one and the same. Second, the money given would be less interested, the political good works of middle-class citizens supplementing their choices at the polling place with the votes of their wallets. It was a model, one should remember, that must have seemed within grasp in 1974. The previous decade had been years of unparalleled participatory democracy, all the way from new neighborhood councils to mass popular movements for racial equality and against the war in Vietnam. The populist-Progressive ideal of grass-roots democracy had never seemed so attainable.

But it was not to be. The history of the post-1974 regime can almost be written in terms of the failure to achieve the grass-roots campaign finance. The group explosion was just underway in 1974, and as it accelerated, group campaign finance in the form of PACs also took off. Giving by people beyond the voting constituency increased, as did the size of individual contributions, whether local or not. Brokers and intermediaries returned to the fray, and even individual con-

tributions were more and more committed to political goals
and agendas.

The model spurned in 1974, the second here, was one of
comprehensive public funding, although that same model was
adopted for the presidential general-election campaigns and
has served in four of them subsequently (1976, 1980, 1984,
and 1988). Its operational principles stand in sweeping contrast to Congress's choice. By replacing private with public
funding one replaces the private marketplace in funding and
the allocative power of favorable prospects for electoral victory. Money and election politics would be decoupled; money
would be generated by statute rather than by perception of
electoral politics, and it would no longer be allocated, like pari-
mutuel betting, as an investment in victory. In the purest form
of public funding, exemplified by the presidential general-
election plan, money goes to candidates by entitlement, not
by reason of their ability to raise it.

Such a fundamental recasting of the entire system, such a
replacement of both the voluntary system and the regulatory
regime in one swoop, seems at least for the short run to be
mooted for strong and insurmountable political reasons. Comprehensive public funding has always carried major political
liabilities. Although it appears to address the problems of voluntary, private funding that most worry millions of Americans—the interestness of private money and its subverting of
electoral competitiveness—it generates its own set of problems. It has always raised questions about the proper role of
government; few Republicans or Southern Democrats have
been comfortable with it. It also raises concerns about the
speedy and equitable administration of so extensive a public
program, including worries about public subsidies of political
speech and partisan contests. More recently it has become
entangled in issues of deficit spending and priorities for public
programs, not to mention the ball of snakes that is the collective question of the perks, pay raises, ethics, and imperial
manner and life-style of members of Congress.

The third of these models, the party-centered model, is a

partial one, hardly able to stand on its own but constantly available for a marriage or merger. It is the preferred model of some Republicans, some journalists, and many political scientists. For the academics it is a spin-off of the notions of party government or responsible political parties—the arguments that political parties with their mass bases, their many loyal adherents, and their power as cue-giving organizations for millions of Americans are the best organizations for mobilizing large numbers of Americans behind policy programs and issue positions.[3] Better the majoritarian political parties as political mobilizers than the narrow, fragmented, demanding interest groups in the mass democracy of contemporary America.

Any alternative that promises a way out of the interest fragmentation and the lack of serious policy initiatives in contemporary American politics will find enthusiasts. But the party-led model of campaign finance has its major liabilities, too. Its political burden is that Republican party committees have always raised more money than Democratic committees; Democrats find it hard to warm up to proposals to give greater financial leeway to the parties. More fundamental, the political parties of the 1990s have neither the mass support nor the organizational strength to carry out imposing new responsibilities, not the least of which, even with the incentives of public policy, involves raising enormous sums of money. The difficulty is clear: one cannot ask the parties to assume the role they had in the 1920s or 1930s with the machinery and loyalties they command in the 1990s.

By reduction we come to the fourth and last model: that of the contemporary status quo, one which can best be called an organizational model. It is increasingly dominated by organized giving, whether it is by PACs, by brokered individuals, or by the ever more assertive legislative campaign committees of the parties. It is a kind of campaign finance in which goals are pursued collectively and in which the marketplace of exchanges between contributors and candidates is more apt to be structured. Even the strategies for dealing with the constraints of statutory regulations are worked out among small groups of experienced practitioners. It is a model that is routinized and institutionalized, one in which networks of information and expertise are increasingly important.

The organizational model was probably never really planned or intended. It happened as a result of the failure of the grass-roots model, but more trenchantly, it happened because of political learning and adaptation and because of the empowerment of incumbents and well-established and organized political interests. Indeed, one is tempted to say it developed because of the tendency of campaign finance regimes in the United States to regress, or to evolve, to a norm, even to an inherent state. The direction of the changes in all of the campaign finance regimes of this century has been strongly determined by two influences. First, they tend to reflect increasingly the contours of the broader electoral politics of which they are a part; the post-1974 regime has not been, probably could not have been, a holdout against the rise of organized groups in American politics. Second, campaign finance regimes tend, like other regulatory regimes, to yield to the wishes of the better-organized participants and those with more at stake in its operation. Systems of campaign finance, therefore, probably tend to greater organization, efficiency, and rationality as a consequence—and thus to the increasing dominance of the more purposeful players.

Barring the substitution of an entirely new model for the post-1974 regime, one must turn to less fundamental changes in the status quo—to a rolling back of PAC contribution limits, for example, or to new limits on the ability of candidates to absorb PAC and out-of-state money, or to spending limits on candidates. Those alterations would, however, work major changes in the present regime by cutting the supply of money or by shifting its distribution. Any of them would certainly work changes in the present equilibrium between getting and spending, and any would affect in some way the evolution of the regime. But it seems safe to predict that any would also be followed by another round of evolution sparked by the adaptations of the increasingly experienced and skilled—and organized—participants themselves.

Change thus goes on without legislation. Even within a stable system such as the status quo of 1991, the flow of money erodes the regulatory barricades. Political learning—as adept always in avoiding restraints as in honing strategies—finds the new devices of avoidance, the weaknesses in the restraints, the unanticipated avenues of free action. In short, the experts begin to beat the system. But maintenance of the system can profit from the compensatory learning of the regulators; fine-tuning can narrow and constrain the options of the actors who must comply. To change the system in a major way is to discard that knowledge and to begin the cycle of learning and response all over again. The stakes are larger when one begins the cycle *ab initio*, and it is the potential avoiders who have the important first moves.

This is not to argue against all reform, only to point out that the greater the aspirations, the greater the risks. All of these cautions, too, apply only to changes in a voluntary system, especially changes that add severe constraints to a system of voluntarism and freedom of action. If one talks about substituting a system of public funding, especially one of full public funding, then the calculus changes dramatically. The entire flow of money is reconstituted, both as to its source and as to the principles on which it is allocated. The system is greatly simplified, the sum of money fixed and known and its allocation a question of statutory right. The mere fact that the quantity of money equals the amount that legally can be spent—as in the case of the general-election funding for the presidency—transforms a complex unknown into the readily knowable.

The Special Politics of Campaign Finance

The images of campaign finance in the public mind are hopelessly intertwined with the public's impressions about politics generally, about the integrity or knavery of politicians, about the nature of campaigning and campaign tactics, even about the pay and perquisites of public officials. The politics of campaign finance, therefore, features the same double standard—higher standards for the public than the private sector—that American public brings to all of the politics of representation. Just as it easily accepts salaries of more than a million dollars in corporate management while denying one of $100,000 to members of Congress, it is shocked at costs of campaigns that are easily dwarfed by everyday commercial transactions. It abhors skillful avoidance of FECA limits while at the same time employing millions of lawyers, accountants, financial planners, and tax preparers to help avoid paying personal taxes. Popular distrust of politics and politicians is an unavoidable cost of holding public office.

Much of this attitude springs from the Progressive and populist traditions. Many of the relationships of representation involve money, campaign finance most purely, and they easily validate the central proposition of the Progressive worldview: that interests, money, and influence are integrally linked and that they form the driving force behind the major decisions of the political system. Above all, Progressive images and predispositions create their own reality, and it is that reality that is the chief justification for the attack on the post-1974 status quo. It drives reform by defining what is wrong, by defining the acceptable reforms, and by defining the political rewards and punishments for action or inaction on them.

Considered more broadly, the politics of campaign finance has a number of special characteristics. It is, as I have just noted, a politics centered in a broader politics of representation and, therefore, a politics of politics. Naturally, it is a politics to which the members of Congress are enormously sensitive, for it is the politics of their reelection and political careers. It is also a politics that is almost pure populism, driven by mass fears, mass opinion, and mass voting, a politics easily inflamed whether by somber editorialists or by the demagogues of the radio talk shows. It is a politics that looks not at a member of Congress's legislative record but at personal qualities and political styles. And it is a politics complicated and heightened by the fact that the members of Congress legislate about themselves, by the fact that self-interest is central to the policies they choose.

More specifically, the intense mass concern about campaign finance can best be seen by looking at recent history. Certainly the intermittent episodes of PAC-bashing cater to popular fears, as does the rhetoric that nourishes myths of the growth of campaign money. The failure of maintenance and repair of the regulatory structures reflects the same fears, for repairs are scorned for merely propping up a discredited system, a self-serving preservation of the status quo. Ironically, even the reformers may have set in motion perceptions that come back to haunt them. Their charges about the effect of campaign money on the Congress have undoubtedly given support to opinion that rejects the use of public funds to pay for campaigns.

Even though some of the popularly held images may be in error, the issues behind them are not trivial. The politics of representation—the politics of politics, that is—is in a real sense the politics of democracy. It is the politics of who will be listened to in the American political system. One sees, for example, the "enfranchisement" of a new political constituency, a campaign funding constituency. People may disagree over the extent of its influence in the final accounting of political influence, but it would be a foolhardy soul who would assert that it had no substantial influence. The alliance of a part of the funding constituency with well-established group lobbying only gives the question greater force. Moreover, the new constituency is national and organized, and its interests are to some extent at variance with the interests of the local, grass-roots constituencies that vote and whose opinions make up mass public opinion. The rejection of PACs and their works is, therefore, an attempt to repulse foreign or hostile interests and to protect local voter hegemony.

These politics of campaign finance add a dense and complicated layer to the stratified politics that have led for more than 10 years to legislative deadlock over reforming the regime of 1974. The fact that the politics of politics are at stake pits strong and irreconcilable party interests against each other; it sets the House against the Senate, and at a time of divided control of the elected branches, it positions a president of one party against the majority party in the Congress. Deadlock, too, reflects and springs from the difficulties of making policy, even of framing policy proposals, when not only interests and opinion but even images of reality, are fragmented. Placating mass opinion becomes the first priority in a politics of representation. But there are limits to placating, for the politics of representation is often marked by an inherently destructive dynamic that leads it either to inaction or to ineffective or inept public policy that in turn creates further mass cynicism and displeasure.

Campaign finance regimes change or evolve either by legislated design or by their own internal dynamic and processes. The attempts at legislated reform go on, but political deadlock appears to doom them. Even if limited change comes, it seems unlikely that it will abandon the outlines of the regime that has evolved since 1974. Increasingly, indeed, it seems that short-term changes in the regime may come instead through changes in its political environment. That is the fascination of the 1992 campaigns. Fundamental change in the environment, however, seems as distant as a party realignment or a constitutional amendment limiting the terms of members of Congress. Perhaps, indeed, the end of the post-1974 regime will come only in the same way it was born—in the aftermath of great and disillusioning events.

Notes

Chapter 1: The First Ninety Years

1. William Safire, *Safire's Political Dictionary*, 3d ed. (New York: Random House, 1978), pp. 220–21.

2. Louise Overacker, *Money in Elections* (New York: Macmillan, 1932), p. 133.

3. Herbert E. Alexander, *Financing Politics*, 3d ed. (Washington: CQ Press, 1984), p. 11.

4. Data from Herbert E. Alexander, *Financing the 1972 Election* (Lexington, Mass.: Lexington, 1976). For fuller histories of American campaign finance before 1972, see (in addition to Overacker, *Money in Elections*) James K. Pollock, *Party Campaign Funds* (New York: Knopf, 1926); Alexander Heard, *The Costs of Democracy* (Chapel Hill: University of North Carolina Press, 1960); and Robert E. Mutch, *Campaigns, Congress, and Courts* (New York: Praeger, 1988). I also have set out a fuller but brief summary of the history in *Money in American Elections* (Glenview: Scott, Foresman, 1988), pp. 16–33.

5. F. Leslie Seidle and Khayyam Paltiel, "Party Finance, the Election Expenses Act, and Campaign Spending in 1979 and 1980," in Howard R. Penniman, ed., *Canada at the Polls, 1979 and 1980* (Washington: American Enterprise Institute, 1981), p. 232.

6. PACS, in addition to registering with the Federal Election Commission and listing a treasurer and a bank, must meet one more qualification in order to be eligible for these contribution limits. The PAC must qualify as a "multicandidate committee," getting its funds from more than 50 contributors and making contributions to at least five federal candidates. If the PAC fails to qualify, it is subject to the same contribution limits as an individual.

7. 424 U.S. 1 (1976).

8. For an excellent summary of the decisions of the Supreme Court extending such constitutional protections, see Leon D. Epstein, *Political Parties*

in the American Mold (Madison: University of Wisconsin Press, 1986), pp. 179–97.

9. Kay L. Schlozman and John T. Tierney, *Organized Interests and American Democracy* (New York: Harper and Row, 1986), p. 75. The number of national nonprofit associations rose from 10,734 in 1970 to 19,121 in 1985, according to the various volumes of the *Encyclopedia of Associations* published by the Gale Research Company of Detroit.

10. Since the Federal Election Commission did not begin to operate at full power until the 1978 elections, complete data on congressional campaign finance are not available before that election. Even then, the FEC never had the resources to edit and reconcile the data for the receipts and spending of congressional candidates in 1978; one must use a final preliminary report and its data. Worse than that, FEC data for 1976 are sketchy, and for 1974 one has to rely on the much smaller volume of data that Common Cause assembled. Consequently, although a few of the time series reported here begin in 1974 or 1976, most begin with data from 1978. In all instances the data are from official press releases, volumes, and computer files of the FEC unless otherwise noted.

11. Some of these changes in the early 1980s were spotted and reported earlier by Theodore J. Eismeier and Philip H. Pollock III in "A Tale of Two Elections: PAC Money in 1980 and 1984," *Corruption and Reform* 1 (1986), pp. 189–207.

12. If one looks at median expenditures of major party candidates for the House rather than averages (i.e., means), the stability is of longer duration. In constant dollars the median for 1982 was $170,000, against $169,000 for 1990. See David C. Huckabee, *House Campaign Expenditures, Receipts and Sources of Funds: 1980–1990* (Washington: Congressional Research Service of the Library of Congress, August 23, 1991).

13. Ibid.

14. See, for example, Larry Makinson, *The Price of Admission: Campaign Spending in the 1990 Elections* (Washington: Center for Responsive Politics, 1991).

15. The decision, by a 4–2 vote, was in an FEC response to a question posed by the Sun Oil Company and its SunPAC; see FEC Advisory Opinion 1975–23 (December 3, 1975).

16. On Common Cause, see Andrew S. McFarland, *Common Cause: Lobbying in the Public Interest* (Chatham, N.J.: Chatham House, 1984).

17. *Spending in Congressional Elections: A Never-Ending Spiral* (Washington: Center for Responsive Politics, 1988).

18. Philip Stern, *The Best Congress Money Can Buy* (New York: Pantheon Books, 1988).

19. *Public Interest Profiles, 1988–89* (Washington: Congressional Quarterly, 1988), p. 638–39.

20. For example, see Stephanie D. Moussalli, *Campaign Finance Reform: The Case for Deregulation* (Tallahassee, Fla.: James Madison Institute, 1990).

21. In 1989–90 the PACs registered with the Federal Election Commission reported total receipts of $372.4 million. Estimates of the average size of PAC contributions vary; figures in the range of $50 for all PACs are frequently bruited about. If they are correct, one divides by 50 to get a total of 7.5 million contributors; discounting arbitrarily for repeaters, one comes to a range of five to seven million individuals. These calculations do not consider the many additional contributors to PACs that function only in state or local elections.

22. For stimulating discussions of the Progressive worldview and its relation to the imperatives of mass journalism, see Herbert J. Gans, *Deciding What's News* (New York: Vintage, 1980), and Austin Ranney, *Channels of Power* (New York: Basic Books, 1983).

23. I have tried to chart major newspaper coverage more systematically in "Campaign Money and the Press: Three Soundings," *Political Science Quarterly* 102 (Spring 1987), pp. 25–42.

24. Cox is the chairman of Common Cause. The letter was undated but received in early 1991; included with it was a contribution form headed "PEOPLE AGAINST PAC$," followed by the opening line: "It's a Disgrace . . . that our United States Congress is on the auction block. . . . UP FOR GRABS to the highest bidders." The elisions and emphases are in the original.

25. An undated letter received in 1991 and signed by Susan S. Lederman, president of the League of Women Voters. The emphasis on campaign finance reform is part of the League's "historic new campaign to TAKE BACK THE SYSTEM." (In the original the all-caps name of the campaign was also in boldface type.) Is it hopeless nit-picking to note that at issue is not "spending . . . in Congress" but contributions to candidates for the Congress? In other words, the issue at hand is not lobbying or group-spending for lobbying.

26. For one of only a considerable number of examples, see the editorial "The Price of Cleaner Government," *New York Times,* May 14, 1991. For a fuller illustration of the reformist zeal that animates much of investigative reporting on campaign finance, see Steve Weinberg, "Following the Money," *Columbia Journalism Review* (July/August 1991), pp. 49–50. The article opens with a reference to an editorial in the *Boston Globe* headlined "WHY POLITIC$ $TINK$."

27. The cave metaphor can be found in book 7 of *The Republic*.

Chapter 2: The Sources and the Sums

1. The data of the NES have been made available through the Inter-University Consortium for Political Analysis. Neither the Michigan people nor the Consortium are responsible for the analysis or interpretation of their data here or subsequently in this book.

2. Herbert E. Alexander and Monica Bauer, *Financing the 1988 Election* (Boulder, Colo.: Westview Press, 1991), esp. chap. 1. Their estimate of spending in the 1988 elections, $2.7 billion, includes a number of indirect expenditures (e.g., all party expenditures, the costs of the nominating conventions, all PAC overhead and administrative costs, and organized labor's expenditures in mobilizing votes) that I have excluded to arrive at my estimate of $1.7 billion. My total, in other words, is what I believe to be the sum of the direct campaign expenditures in Alexander and Bauer's estimates of the total spending in years of the campaigns.

3. Under the FECA the PACs of unions or corporations must set up a "separate, segregated fund" into which the political contributions of individuals go and out of which political expenditures are made. A number of states, however, permit the assets of the corporate or union parent to be used politically. The case of the PACs of membership organizations is less clear; if they are incorporated, and most are, they must also maintain the separate fund.

4. Alexander and Bauer, *Financing the 1988 Election*, ch. 1.

5. For a similar but fuller treatment of the question, see Ruth S. Jones, "Contributing as Participation," in Margaret L. Nugent and John R. Johannes, eds., *Money, Elections, and Democracy: Reforming Congressional Campaign Finance* (Boulder, Colo.: Westview Press, 1990), pp. 27–45.

6. The Hatch Acts of 1939 and 1940 also forbid the solicitation of campaign contributions from U.S. government employees by other government employees, and a number of states have "little Hatch Acts" too.

7. The five organizations sponsoring the 1990 survey are the National Association of Manufacturers; the Public Affairs Council, an organization of corporate officers heading public or governmental affairs divisions; the Business-Industry PAC (BI-PAC), a leading PAC among corporate and business PACs; the U.S. Chamber of Commerce; and the National Association of Business Political Action Committees (NABPAC).

8. Richard P. Conlon, "The Declining Role of Individual Contributions in Financing Congressional Campaigns," *Journal of Law and Politics* 3 (Winter 1987), pp. 467–98.

9. For the purposes of computing the 1978 percentage, I had to estimate the sum of all individual contributions to congressional candidates since the FEC did not aggregate all individual contributions until the 1983–84 cycle. The total is derived from a formula of 0.94 times total receipts (the 6 percent reduction being the approximation of loans and interest) minus total PAC and party committee contributions.

10. David Johnston, "Charities Seek Strategy as Contributions Decline," *Los Angeles Times*, March 22, 1985.

11. *Giving and Volunteering in the United States*, 1990 ed. (Washington, D.C.: Independent Sector, 1990).

12. For example, see the conclusions about the American political culture in the most influential study of it: Gabriel A. Almond and Sidney Verba, *The Civic Culture* (Princeton: Princeton University Press, 1963).

13. State and local estimates are from Herbert E. Alexander, *Financing the 1980 Election* (Lexington, Mass.: Lexington Books, 1983) and Alexander and Bauer, *Financing the 1988 Election*.

14. It is logically possible, of course, that expenditures for overhead costs are declining by the same sum that state and local political spending is increasing, but I know of no reports that suggest that PACs are carrying fewer of their overhead costs now than they did some years ago.

15. *Hidden Power: Campaign Contributions of Large Individual Donors, 1989–1990* (Washington, D.C.: Citizen Action, 1991), esp. pp. 11–14.

16. A study published just a month later in the *Los Angeles Times* comes up with totals pretty much the same as the basic totals of the Citizen Action study. See Sara Fritz and Dwight Morris, "California Campaign Cash May Stay Home Next Year," June 10, 1991.

17. Janet Grenzke, "Comparing Contributions to U.S. House Members from Outside Their Districts," *Legislative Studies Quarterly* 13 (February 1988), pp. 83–103.

18. Richard Morin and Charles R. Babcock, "Out-of-State Donations to Candidates Are on the Rise," *Washington Post*, July 31, 1990.

19. See, for example, Peter Applebome, "Carolina Race Is Winning the Wallets of America," *New York Times*, October 13, 1990.

20. Conlon, "Declining role.".

21. Sara Fritz and Dwight Morris, "Federal Campaign Donors' Limits Not Being Enforced," *Los Angeles Times*, September 15, 1991.

22. *Hidden Power*, p. 15.

23. *Hidden Power*, p. 18.

24. The question of whether such brokers do in fact violate the rarely enforced legal constraints in the brokering of earmarked contributions is addressed in chapter 7.

25. Since soft money is a phenomenon mainly of presidential campaign finance, it awaits a fuller discussion in chapter 5.

26. Alexander and Bauer, in *Financing the 1988 Election,* estimate that groups (primarily unions) spent $42.5 million mobilizing voters in all phases of the 1988 race for the presidency.

Chapter 3: The Grand Exchange

1. The phrase *the best Congress money can buy* has been widely used in the last decade or more by print journalists, television reporters, members of Congress, and public interest groups, as well as by Philip Stern as the title for his 1988 book. I have no idea who originated it.

2. The data through 1988 are from two publications of the Congressional Research Service (CRS) of the Library of Congress, both of them by David C. Huckabee: *Reelection Rates of House Incumbents: 1790–1988* (Washington, D.C.: CRS, 1989) and *Re-election Rates of Senate Incumbents: 1790–1988* (Washington, D.C.: CRS, 1990).

3. Data through 1988 come from Norman J. Ornstein, Thomas E. Mann, and Michael J. Malbin, *Vital Statistics on Congress, 1989–1990* (Washington, D.C.: CQ Press, 1990), pp. 59–60.

4. Raymond A. Bauer, Ithiel de Sola Pool, and Lewis A. Dexter, *American Business and Public Policy* (New York: Atherton Press, 1963), p. 455. See also Kay L. Schlozman and John T. Tierney, *Organized Interests and American Democracy* (New York: Harper and Row, 1986) for a similar advocacy of bilateralism.

5. On the market analogy I have found especially useful Gerald Keim and Asghar Zardkoohi, "Looking for Leverage in PAC Markets: Corporate and Labor Contributions Considered," *Public Choice* 58 (July 1988), pp. 21–34.

6. A PAC is not easy to define; the phrase *political action committee* does not appear in federal statutes. It is a nonparty, noncandidate political committee that is also a multicandidate committee (i.e., it receives funds from more than 50 people and makes contributions to at least 5 federal candidates).

7. See, for example, Theodore J. Eismeier and Philip H. Pollack III, *Business, Money, and the Rise of Corporate PACs in American Elections* (New York: Quorum Books, 1988), and J. David Gopoian, "What Makes PACs Tick? An Analysis of the Allocation Patterns of Economic Interest Groups," *American Journal of Political Science* 28 (May 1984), pp. 259–81.

8. Marick F. Masters and Gerald Keim, "Determinants of PAC Participation among Large Corporations," *Journal of Politics* 47 (November 1985), pp. 1158–73.

9. Center for Responsive Politics, *PAC on PACs: The View from the Inside* (Washington: Center for Responsive Politics, 1988), pp. 39–40.

10. Michael Malbin, *Money and Politics in the United States* (Chatham, N.J.: Chatham House, 1984), pp. 278–79.

11. One set of PACs had of course already adopted those strategies and characteristics: the labor PACs. On the predictions, see, for example, Edwin M. Epstein, "The PAC Phenemenon: An Overview—Introduction," *Arizona Law Review* 22 (1980), pp. 355–72; and Frank J. Sorauf, "Political Parties and Political Action Committees: Two Life Cycles," *Arizona Law Review* 22 (1980), pp. 445–64.

12. Theodore J. Eismeier and Philip H. Pollock III, "The Tale of Two Elections: PAC Money in 1980 and 1984," *Corruption and Reform* 1 (1986), pp. 189–207 at 206–7.

13. Laura I. Langbein, "Money and Access: Some Empirical Evidence," *Journal of Politics* 48 (November 1986), pp. 1052–62.

14. Robert H. Salisbury, "The Paradox of Interest Groups in Washington—More Groups, Less Clout," in Anthony King, ed., *The New American Political System,* 2d ed. (Washington, D.C.: American Enterprise Institute, 1990), pp. 203–29.

15. The entire question of influence, especially the ability of PACs to influence the making and direction of public policy, receives much fuller treatment in chapter 6.

16. All of the data of this paragraph come from Larry Makinson, *Open Secrets: The Dollar Power of PACs in Congress* (Washington, D.C.: CQ Press, 1990), pp. 44, 52. The book is the result of a project of the Center for Responsive Politics, of which Makinson is the research director.

17. The comparisons can go back no further than 1984 because that was the first cycle in which the FEC aggregated and published data on individual contributions.

18. On the 1982 experience and on the Democrats' failure to capitalize fully on their opportunities, see Gary C. Jacobson, "Party Organization and Distribution of Campaign Resources: Republicans and Democrats in 1982," *Political Science Quarterly* 100 (Winter 1985–86), pp. 603–25.

19. For details see Peter Bragdon, "St Germain Out, but Incumbents Still Strong," *Congressional Quarterly,* November 12, 1988, pp. 3266–70.

20. Jonathan S. Krasno and Donald P. Green, "Preempting Quality Challengers in House Elections," *American Journal of Political Science* 50 (November 1988), pp. 920–36.

21. As a practical matter one really has to accept the FEC definition of an open seat. In addition to the districts in which no incumbent runs at the regular time, it also includes all special elections since they too are by definition without an incumbent candidate. It does *not* include elections in which there is no incumbent because the incumbent was defeated in the primary; the FEC considers both general election candidates in such a circumstance to be challengers.

22. More precisely, perhaps, more Democrats than Republicans had opponents whose spending did not reach the $5,000 threshold that compels a candidate to file spending reports with the FEC.

23. Gary C. Jacobson notes and discusses the same phenomenon in *The Electoral Origins of Divided Government: Competition in U.S. House Elections, 1946–1988* (Boulder, Colo.: Westview, 1990), esp. chap. 6.

24. California gets seven, Florida four, Texas three, and Arizona, Georgia, North Carolina, Virginia, and Washington one each.

25. Data from Harold W. Stanley and Richard G. Niemi, *Vital Statistics on American Politics* 2d ed. (Washington: CQ Press, 1990), p. 183.

26. See Janet Hook, "Will the Flood of Retirements Arrive in 1992? Maybe Not," *Congressional Quarterly,* January 12, 1991, p. 72–79. In 1989 the Congress set a 1993 deadline for the personal use of campaign funds by incumbent

members; earlier legislation had permitted that conversion only for members of the Congress elected before 1980. The 1989 law removes the possibility of conversion for this "grandfathered" group of incumbents at the end of 1992. As of early 1991, 166 House members qualified as "grandfathers", but their intentions about conversion are not known, except that almost 100 of them have pledged not to convert the money to personal use if they depart before 1993.

27. Despite shifting numbers of open seat races, the percentage of major party candidates falling into the 40–60 percent range of the general election vote also remained constant. The totals for 1980, 1984, and 1988 are these: 61, 69, and 61 percents.

28. Data come from Ornstein, Mann, and Malbin, *Vital Statistics on Congress, 1989–1990*.

29. The 125 challengers filing reports in 1990 and the 137 in 1988 were, conversely, low figures for the same period.

30. At least five states permit larger contributions to candidates for the upper house of the state legislature than to candidates for the lower house: Connecticut, Michigan, Minnesota, Montana, and New York. For these and other summary data on state regulation of campaign finance, see Carl Brown and Joyce Bullock, *COGEL Blue Book*, 8th ed. (Lexington, Ky.: Council of State Governments, 1990).

31. See, for example, Charles R. Babcock, "The Senator and the Special Interest," *Washington Post,* November 6, l990.

32. That Citizen Action study, *Hidden Power,* is reported at some detail in chapter 2.

Chapter 4: The Organizational Factor

1. The assumption of an average of $50 per contributor has a good deal of basis in fact. A number of association PACs report averages in the $30–$50 range, with corporate PACs averaging sums larger than that; but labor PACs report far smaller average contributions. It is likely, then, that the overall average falls somewhere between $40 and $60.

2. This brief summary by no means covers all of the extensive regulation under which PACs operate in federal elections. For a fuller explanation see Frank J. Sorauf, *Money in American Elections* (Glenview, Ill.: Scott, Foresman, 1988), pp. 34–43 and chap. 4. Furthermore, state statutes may define and regulate PACs for their elections; virtually all states subject them to less stringent regulation than does the Congress.

3. As the name Committee on Political Education (COPE) indicates, not all PACs carry the words *political action committee* in their names or titles. Those with parent organizations are, however, required by the FECA to contain a reference to the parent in their name.

4. See Everett M. Rogers and F. Floyd Shoemaker, *Communication of Innovations* (New York: Free Press, 1971), especially pp. 176–82.

5. *Time*, October 25, 1982. The text of the story, beginning on p. 20, was headed "Running with the PACs;" a subheading proclaimed, "How political action committees win friends and influence elections." The various headlines suggest that *Time* still viewed PACs as primarily electoral organizations in 1982.

6. The NCPAC campaign in 1980 featured a "hit list" of six incumbent Senate liberals (all Democrats); four of them were defeated. (I examine the NCPAC story more fully in chapter 6.) As this sentence also indicates, the so-called "leadership" or "personal" PACs of would-be presidential candidates and some of the congressional leadership are nonconnected PACs for want of a sponsoring organization. In purpose and in form they are special cases, and they illustrate one of the ways in which the nonconnected category is the most diverse that the FEC employs.

7. For examples of PAC disillusion, see Center for Responsive Politics, *PACs on PACs: The View from the Inside* (Washington: Center for Responsive Politics, 1988), esp. chap. 3. One also finds it in somewhat more muted form in Catherine Morrison, *Managing Corporate Political Action Committees*, a research report of the Conference Board (New York: Conference Board, 1986).

8. Inactivity here is defined as not making any contributions to federal candidates in the two-year cycle. The percentage is the number of PACs active in the cycle, divided by the number of PACs registered at the end of the cycle. Some FEC volumes report higher rates of inactivity as a result of using as a divisor the total number of PACs registered with the FEC at any time during the two-year cycle.

9. On organizational constraints on PACs, see Theodore J. Eismeier and Philip H. Pollock III, *Business, Money, and the Rise of Corporate PACs in American Elections* (New York: Quorum Books, 1988), chaps. 2 and 4; Edward Handler and John R. Mulkern, *Business in Politics: Campaign Strategies of Corporate Political Action Committees* (Lexington, Mass.: Lexington Books, 1982), chap. 4; Frank J. Sorauf, "Who's in Charge? Accountability in Political Action Committees," *Political Science Quarterly* 99 (Winter 1984–85), pp. 591–614; and John R. Wright, "PACs, Contributions, and Roll Calls: An Organizational Perspective," *American Political Science Review* 79 (June 1985), pp. 400–14.

10. Eismeier and Pollack, *Business, Money*, p. 67.

11. Wright, "PACs, Contributions, and Roll Calls," p. 411.

12. Of the 275 PACs, 200 gave their funds overwhelmingly to Republican candidates, 75 to Democratic candidates.

13. Sorauf, "Who's in Charge?"

14. Generically or collectively the committees are sometimes called the Hill Committees (for Capitol Hill).

15. Gary C. Jacobson, "Party Organization and Distribution of Campaign

Resources: Republicans and Democrats in 1982," *Political Science Quarterly* 100 (Winter 1985–86), pp. 603–25.

16. Coordinated expenditures are also known as 441a(d) or "on behalf of" expenditures; they differ from conventional contributions in that the party committee may retain control over the final spending of the funds. And unlike the "independent expenditures" of PACs, these expenditures, available to party committees only, may be made with the full knowledge and cooperation of the candidate.

17. Frank J. Sorauf and Scott A. Wilson, "Campaigns and Money: A Changing Role for the Political Parties?" in L. Sandy Maisel, ed. *The Parties Respond: Changes in the American Party System* (Boulder, Colo.: Westview, 1990), pp. 187–203.

18. Coelho finally resigned his House seat in mid-1989 amid a controversy over personal investments financed by loans from a wealthy donor to party causes. For a less than flattering view of Coelho and his days at the DCCC, written before Coelho's final troubles, see Brooks Jackson, *Honest Graft* (New York: Knopf, 1988).

19. Chuck Alston, "A Political Money Tree Waits for Incumbents in Need," *Congressional Quarterly,* June 30, 1990, pp. 2023–27.

20. Clyde Wilcox, "Share the Wealth: Contributions by Congressional Incumbents to the Campaigns of Other Candidates," *American Politics Quarterly* 17 (October 1989), pp. 386–408.

21. Candidates are free to transfer funds from their own campaign committees to other candidates; in doing so they are governed by the limit of $1,000 on individual contributions. If they establish a PAC, they may use none of the funds of the PAC for their own campaigns; but if they meet the qualifications of a multicandidate committee, the contributions they make to other candidates are governed by the $5,000 limit on PAC contributions.

22. Tom Kenworthy, "Collaring Colleagues for Cash," *Washington Post,* May 14, 1991.

23. Malcolm E. Jewell and David Breaux, "The Effect of Incumbency on State Legislative Elections," *Legislative Studies Quarterly* 13 (November 1988), pp. 495–514.

24. Ronald E. Weber, Harvey J. Tucker, and Paul Brace, "Vanishing Marginals in State Legislative Elections," *Legislative Studies Quarterly* 16 (February 1991), pp. 29–47.

25. Jeffrey Stonecash, "The Significance of Campaign Finance for Control of the House: New York, 1986–1988," *Comparative State Politics* 12 (April 1991), pp. 6–15.

26. See Rob Gurwitt, "How to Succeed at Running a Legislature: Pack a Mighty Wallet," *Governing,* May 1990, pp. 26–31. For a report on the growth

of party campaign support in the Texas legislature, see Robert Harmel and Keith E. Hamm, "Political Party Development in a State Legislature: The Case of the Texas House of Representatives" (Paper given at the annual meeting of the Midwest Political Science Association, Chicago, April 1991). As for transfers in California and the legendary success of Speaker Brown, such transfers from one legislative candidate to another were invalidated in a proposition (Proposition 73) passed by a majority of the California electorate in 1988; it was held invalid for violating the protections of the First Amendment of the U.S. Constitution in 1990 by a U.S. District Court judge in Sacramento.

27. Anthony Gierzynski and Malcolm E. Jewell, "Legislative Party Campaign Committee Activity: A Comparative State Analysis" (Paper given at the annual meeting of the Midwest Political Science Association, Chicago, April 1989.

28. On this development see Stephen E. Frantzich, *Political Parties in the Technological Age* (New York: Longman, 1989), and Paul S. Herrnson, *Party Campaigning in the 1980s* (Cambridge, Mass.: Harvard University Press, 1988).

29. Tom Loftus, "The New 'Political Parties' in State Legislatures," *State Government* 58 (Fall 1985), p. 108.

30. The percentages in the text, are for the funds these business PACs gave directly to candidates.

31. On this ill-fated prediction, see my article and that of Edwin M. Epstein in *Arizona Law Review* 22, no. 2 (1980), devoted to campaign finance. The view was also prevalent within the PAC movement; labor's COPE remained the goal and model for some corporate PAC managers into the early 1980s.

32. See especially Chuck Alston, "Breaking Free of Spending Limits," *Congressional Quarterly,* September 29, 1990, p. 3091. The ever-inventive NRSC was found guilty in the spring of 1991 of violating the contribution limits in 1986 with its bundling on behalf of 12 Senate candidates.

33. Names are mentioned in two articles: James A. Barnes, "Giving More Than Advice," *National Journal,* December 16, 1989, pp. 3052–54; and Neil A. Lewis, "Legal Skills and Legislation: Washington Growth Industry," *New York Times,* December 29, 1989.

34. Sara Fritz, "Keating Affair Offers Rare View of Campaign Funding," *Los Angeles Times,* December 23, 1990. The emphasis is in the original.

35. In terms of the debates within academic political science, the strength of legislative parties, especially their campaigning arms, cannot be seen as a sign of a return to party government or party responsibility. There is no point of responsible contact with the party organization, the executive party, or the organs in the party taking positions or writing platforms.

Chapter 5: The Fifth Source

1. This summary relies in part on the data in Council on Governmental Ethics Law, *COGEL Blue Book*, 8th ed. (Lexington, Ky.: Council of State Governments, 1990). None of the "modest to negligible" state programs dispersed more than $500,000 in reported elections; Florida and Rhode Island are, however, just beginning public-funding programs. North Carolina apparently is also embarking on a limited program of public funding. This list does not include those states that channel public money to the political parties rather than to candidates.

2. On the localities, see Herbert E. Alexander and Michael C. Walker, *Public Financing of Local Elections: A Data Book on Public Funding in Four Cities and Two Counties* (Los Angeles: Citizens' Research Foundation, 1990).

3. These features are, of course, the result of the Supreme Court's holdings in *Buckley* v. *Valeo* that the acceptance of public funding and/or spending limits must be voluntary.

4. The 25 percent cut-off reflects the Congress's desire to exclude minor-party candidates from automatic eligibility. They achieve eligibility for funds only *after* the election by polling at least 5 percent of the popular vote; their vote as a percentage of the average of the vote of the two major-party candidates fixes the percentage of the major-party funding they acquire post facto. But that success, or partial success, qualifies the party for a similar partial share at the next presidential election. John Anderson, an independent candidate in 1980, was paid $4.2 million after the election as a consequence of polling 6.6 percent of the popular vote. Even though his 1980 eligibility also assured an up-front payment of that sum in 1984, Anderson chose not to run in that year.

5. That sum of $8.3 million per party is the result of a formula that provides two cents (in 1974 pennies) for every voting-age American, adjusted upward to account for changes in the CPI. In addition the statute also permits candidates to raise money privately to cover legal and accounting costs.

6. In coming to that total I have counted a candidate each time he or she ran and qualified for funding. Among the 33 Democrats are candidates not ordinarily considered Democrats but who filed with the FEC as Democrats: George Wallace (1976), Ellen McCormick (a right-to-life candidate in 1976), and Lyndon LaRouche (1980, 1984, and 1988, for a total of about $1.85 billion in federal funds).

7. Candidates are limited to using $50,000 in personal and family resources. In addition, they may also raise and spend a total not to exceed 20 percent of the aggregate limit ($2 million in 1974 dollars) to cover the costs of fund-raising.

8. Herbert E. Alexander and Brian A. Haggerty, *Financing the 1984 Election* (Lexington, Mass.: Lexington Books, 1987), p. 208.

9. A number of states have experimented with funding public financing by tax add-ons. The taxpayer, that is, adds a sum to his or her tax liability, and that sum then goes into a separate account for the funding of campaigns. Those programs have either folded or become inconsequential for lack of the necessary funds; whether that was the intention of the devisers of the tax add-on I cannot say. The system is in effect a publicly managed program of private funding.

10. The percentage is of the income tax forms filed, whether the one-dollar box or two-dollar box (for joint returns) was checked.

11. FEC, *Record* 17 (July 1991), pp. 1–2.

12. Market Decisions Corportion, for the Federal Election Commission, *Presidential Election Campaign Fund Focus Group Research* (Washington: FEC, December 1990), pp. iv-v.

13. Ibid., p. vi.

14. This and the polls which follow immediately are described in report 91–346 of the Congressional Research Service of the Library of Congress, *Campaign Financing: National Public Opinion Polls,* April 12, 1991. This particular poll was taken by the NBC News/Wall Street Journal Poll in December 1990.

15. Greenberg-Lake/The Analysis Group, "Money and Politics: A Survey of National Opinion," from February of 1990.

16. Ibid.

17. ABC/Washington Post Poll, January 1990.

18. These polls results are nothing new. The same phenomena of the volatility depending on the question and the support for full public funding when combined with spending limits can be seen in poll data from the early and middle 1980s. I dealt with those data in a chapter, "Public Opinion on Campaign Finance," in Margaret L. Nugent and John R. Johannes, eds., *Money, Elections, and Democracy: Reforming Congressional Campaign Finance* (Boulder, Colo.: Westview Press, 1990), pp. 207–24.

19. I certainly cannot claim that this is the only current definition of soft money, but I think it is the "consensus" definition. As an alternative, that of Tim Curran in *Roll Call* (May 20, 1991) seems to me too general and imprecise: "...a term for loosely regulated funds that are donated by corporations, wealthy individuals, and unions to party organizations rather than directly to candidates. The money, however, ultimately benefits individual contenders for office." Not even the term *soft money* is universally accepted; the *New York Times,* at least in its editorials, persists in rejecting soft money as a euphemism for what it prefers to call sewer money or, less frequently, dirty money.

20. Under the new rules of the FEC soft-money transactions by PACs and party committees must be reported to it, and the commission issued its first report on the soft-money transactions of national party committees in a press release of August 6, 1991.

21. Herbert E. Alexander and Monica Bauer, *Financing the 1988 Election* (Boulder, Colo.: Westview Press, 1991), p. 37.

22. The reporting of "political communications" goes on, and the FEC publishes reports of aggregate data on them. They remain the least-known data of American campaign finance, largely because the substantial exceptions even to the reporting requirement make the data less than useful. The great majority of the reported expenditures for political communications are those of organized labor.

23. David Ignatius, "Return of the 'Fat Cats,' " *Washington Post*, November 20, 1988.

24. Fred Wertheimer, "Bush and Dukakis Took Illegal Money," *New York Times*, February 1, 1989.

25. *Common Cause* v. *FEC*, 692 F. Supp. 1391 (D.D.C. 1987).

26. There is a lucid summary of the rules in a statement by the chairman of the FEC, John W. McGarry, in *COGEL Guardian* (newsletter of the Council on Governmental Ethics Laws of the Council of State Governments), April 30, 1991.

27. 424 U.S. 1 (1976).

28. There are alternative carrots available, but they have not been widely used. The U.S. Government, for example, might have tied a candidate's acceptance of spending limits to the benefit of tax credits for contributors to the candidate. Minnesota did so, but by combining it with the other incentive of public funding, it made it very difficult to measure the independent effect of the tax credit incentive.

29. *Book of the States: 1990–91* (Lexington, Ky.: Council of State Governments, 1990), p. 123. The data are generally from 1989, with two states (New Jersey and Virginia) reporting for 1990. The total of 98 legislative chambers excludes Nebraska, whose one house is nonpartisan.

30. There have been no general-election gubernatorial candidates in Michigan and New Jersey who did not accept public funding. The level of funding in those two states, significantly, is higher than it is in Minnesota or Wisconsin.

31. Under the Minnesota law an indirect state subsidy does remain even if both the candidate and the opponent accept the spending limit. Because they accepted it, their individual contributors can secure a state refund of up to $50 for making a contribution to a candidate accepting spending limits.

Chapter 6: If It's Not Broken... Or Is It?

1. This quotation and the ones that follow are from the network "rush transcript" of the *NBC Nightly News* for Sunday, April 21, 1991.

2. *Newsweek*, December 1, 1986, p. 49.

3. "Political Bribery and the Intermediate Theory of Politics," *UCLA Law Review* 32 (April 1985), pp. 784–851, at p. 848. Philip Stern, in *The Best Con-*

gress Money Can Buy, stops just short of that position, noting that "the line between a campaign contribution and a bribe is only, as one senator put it, 'a hair's breadth' " (p. 18).

4. Amitai Etzioni, *Capital Corruption: The New Attack on American Democracy* (New York: Harcourt, Brace, Jovanovich, 1984). See pages 56–57, for example.

5. Janet M. Grenzke, "PACs and the Congressional Supermarket: The Currency Is Complex," *American Journal of Political Science* 33 (February 1989), pp. 1–24. For another study coming to a similar conclusion, see William P. Welch, "Campaign Contributions and Legislative Voting: Milk Money and Dairy Price Supports," *Western Political Quarterly* 35 (December 1982), pp. 478–95.

6. John R. Wright, "PACs, Contributions, and Roll Calls: An Organizational Perspective," *American Political Science Review* 79 (June 1985), pp. 400–414, at p. 411. The five PACs are the American Medical PAC, the PAC of the American Bankers Association (BANKPAC), the Realtors PAC, the Associate General Contractors PAC, and DEAC, the PAC of the National Automobile Dealers Association. It may well be that Wright's conclusions about organization apply more forcefully to PACs of large, federated membership organizations than they would to some other PACs; to say that, however, is not to say that other PACs do not have their own particular kinds of organizational imperatives.

7. Ibid., p. 412.

8. After Senator Alan Cranston was found by the Senate Ethics Committee to have engaged in "improper and repugnant behavior" in soliciting funds from Charles Keating, he defended himself on the floor of the Senate by asserting that, had he been forced to defeat a censure motion, he could have cited "example after example of comparable conduct" on the part of fellow senators to show that he had violated no Senate norms. "Cranston Accepts Panel's Reprimand, Offers Defense," *Minneapolis–St. Paul Star Tribune,* November 21, 1991.

9. Congress Watch, *Banking on Influence: Bank PAC Contributions and Subcommittee Votes on Bank Deregulation,* June 17, 1991, p. 1. The quotations earlier in the paragraph are from the title page and p. 1, respectively, of the same report.

10. Richard L. Hall and Frank W. Wayman, "Buying Time: Moneyed Interests and the Mobilization of Bias in Congressional Committees," *American Political Science Review* 84 (September 1990), pp. 797–820 (emphasis in the original). The article has an especially lucid review of the scholarship on the influence of campaign contributions on legislative decisions.

11. Ibid., p. 810. Hall and Wayman also consider the possibility of simultaneous cause, "that in allocating contributions to committee members during the previous election cycle, a group may attempt to anticipate who the principal players will be on issues it cares about" (p. 809). They deal with the

problem by estimating their model of participation using the two-stage least squares procedures.

12. David J. Jefferson, "Keating of American Continental Corp. Comes Out Fighting," *Wall Street Journal,* April 18, 1989.

13. Quoted in Robert Kuttner, "Ass Backward," *New Republic,* April 22, 1985, p. 22.

14. The specific scores of the liberal groups rose: the AFL-CIO score rose from 67 in 1980 to 82 in 1990, the ADA score from 57 to 71. The acceptability scores of the conservative groups dropped in the same span of years; the Chamber's score went from 59 to 34, the ACU score from 30 to 20.

15. The aphorism is cited in Lawrence J. Peter, *Peter's Quotations* (New York: Morrow, 1977), but its source is not given.

16. That is, 4064 of 4428 incumbents seeking reelection were successful. Data from Norman J. Ornstein, Thomas E. Mann, and Michael J. Malbin, *Vital Statistics on Congress, 1989–1990* (Washington: Congressional Quarterly, 1990), p. 56.

17. Generally on the use of congressional perquisites for developing constituent support, see Morris A. Fiorina, *Congress: Keystone of the Washington Establishment* (New Haven: Yale University Press, 1977).

18. Gary C. Jacobson, *Money in Congressional Elections* (New Haven: Yale University Press, 1980). See also Jacobson's restatement and reconsideration in "Money and Votes Reconsidered: Congressional Elections, 1972–1982," *Public Choice* 47 (1985), pp. 7–62. For another review of the theoretical problem and additional poll data, see Jacobson, "The Effects of Campaign Spending in House Elections: New Evidence for Old Arguments," *American Journal of Political Science* 34 (May 1990), pp. 334–62.

19. Jacobson, *Money in Congressional Elections,* p. 162.

20. Contra the Jacobson conclusion, see Donald P. Green and Jonathan S. Krasno, "Salvation for the Spendthrift Incumbent: Reestimating the Effects of Campaign Spending in House Elections," *American Journal of Political Science* 32 (November 1988), pp. 884–907.

21. For example, the researches of Michael J. Malbin on the subject are reported in Ronald Brownstein, "On Paper, Conservative PACs Were Tigers in 1984—But Look Again," *National Journal,* June 29, 1985, pp. 1504–9. The rules of the FEC require that letters raising money for a specific candidate or candidates be treated as independent expenditures themselves; it is not clear to me that all of the indirect costs in getting that letter to the reader must also be reported.

22. Quoted in Myra MacPherson, "The New Right Brigade," *Washington Post,* August 10, 1980.

23. See, for example, Brooks Jackson, *Broken Promise: Why the Federal Election Commission Failed* (New York: Priority Press, 1990).

24. For the Minneapolis-St. Paul television market, by no means one of

the country's most expensive, one pays about $100 a "rating point" for television advertising (i.e., $100 for reaching 1 percent of households once); so, for a single ad campaign $30,000 will yield approximately 300 points, or 80 percent of households three or four times.

25. S. J. Guzzetta, *The Campaign Manual: A Definitive Study of the Modern Political Campaign Process*, 2d ed., rev. (Alexandria, Va.: Political Publishing, 1987). The proposed budget is on p. 83.

26. I am indebted to Charls Walker for the Twain quotation. Neither he nor I know the occasion on which, or the essay in which, Twain made the observation.

27. I want to be clear that in referring to scholarly opinion I am talking about more than my judgments. I have cited examples of scholarly opinion about the first two issues; as for the question of spending levels, see, inter alia, Larry J. Sabato, *Paying for Elections: The Campaign Finance Thicket* (New York: Priority Press, 1989), especially chapters 2 and 3.

Chapter 7: The Agenda and Politics of Reform

1. Members of Congress have from time to time introduced constitutional amendments (that is, joint resolutions proposing an amendment) that would in effect repeal the limitations the Supreme Court placed in *Buckley* v. *Valeo* on Congress's power to regulate campaign finance. They have not attracted much support in either House; there appears to be little desire in the Congress to push an amendment that would in effect curtail a First Amendment freedom.

2. Four of the five dissenting Democrats were from the Deep South (Shelby of Alabama, Breaux and Johnston of Louisiana, and Hollings of South Carolina); the fifth was Burdick of North Dakota. Three of the dissenting Republicans came from the maverick or moderate regions of the party (Cohen of Maine, Jeffords of Vermont, and Pressler of South Dakota), and two had recently endured hearings on their ethics (Durenberger of Minnesota and McCain of Arizona).

3. On the effects of the differences between the two houses, see Chuck Alston, "One Chamber's View of Reform Is Anathema in the Other," *Congressional Quarterly* (June 29, 1991), pp. 1727–31.

4. From a letter to members of Congress from Steven F. Stockmeyer, executive vice-president of the National Association of Business PACs, dated September 12, 1991.

5. Kim Mattingly, "Campaign Task Force Can't Reach a Deal," *Roll Call*, September 11–17, 1989.

6. The six included three professors of political science (Herbert E. Alexander, David B. Magleby, and Larry J. Sabato) and three lawyers with party and other political experience (Jan W. Baran, Robert F. Bauer, and Richard

Moe.) Their report of March 6, 1990, was entitled simply *Campaign Finance Reform* and subtitled *A Report to the Majority Leader and Minority Leader of the United States Senate by the Campaign Finance Reform Panel.*

7. See, for example, the Bush letter to Senator Mitch McConnell of Kentucky, the Republican point man on campaign finance in the consideration of S. 3 in 1991; it appears in the *Congressional Record* of May 23, 1991, S6489–90.

8. *PACS & Lobbies,* vol. 11 (February 21, 1990).

9. The constitutional looseness is not limited to this issue. There have been proposals for financing limited public funding by taxing PAC contributions, and among the states New Hampshire, for example, has financed its limited funding of campaigns by increased fees or charges for filing for a position on the ballot.

10. Citizen Action, *Hidden Power: Campaign Contributions of Large Individual Donors, 1989–1990* (Washington: Citizen Action, 1991), p. 3.

11. The bill, which also included a reduction in the PAC contribution limit from $5,000 to $3,000, carried the House with the votes of 188 out of 262 Democrats and the support of 29 of the 124 Republicans. It died in the Senate, the victim of a threatened Republican filibuster.

12. Several states have receipt limits on their statute books. The only test of their constitutionality of which I am aware was decided by the Wisconsin Supreme Court in a unanimous decision upholding them; see *Gard* v. *Wisconsin State Election Board,* 456 NW2d 809 (1990).

13. The ad hoc panel appointed by senators Mitchell and Dole in 1990 approaches the problem very thoughtfully in its report, *Campaign Finance Reform.* It concludes by recommending limits on the soft-money portion of spending by national party committees on generic party spending.

14. The reasons for repairing the leakages in the regulatory structure are set out in chapter 6.

15. For example, S. 3, the bill that passed the Senate in May 1991.

16. Under the rules and regulations of the FEC, "earmarked" means "a designation, instruction, or encumbrance, whether direct or indirect, express or implied, oral or written, which results in all or any part of a contribution or expenditure being made to, or expended on behalf of, a clearly identified candidate or a candidate's authorized committee." 11 CFR 110.6 (b)(1).

17. 11 CFR 110.6 (c)(1)(i).

18. The FEC has, however, pursued cases of the abuse of earmarking in which PACs or party committees have claimed funds were earmarked when the FEC believed them to have entered the control of the bundler.

19. Gary C. Jacobson, *Money in Congressional Elections* (New Haven: Yale University Press, 1980), p. 186. A longer treatment of Jacobson's arguments and publications can be found in chapter 6.

20. The politics of public funding is discussed fully in chapter 5.

21. The issue will soon reach the federal courts. The Minnesota Republican party is, in the autumn of 1991, asking the federal courts to hold the Minnesota statute invalid. The courts may well decide the case on the grounds that Congress preempted the legislative field with the FECA and not reach the constitutional question of coercion and voluntary choice. The Minnesota statute, now at Minn. Stat. 10A.40–51, does not specify the sum of the second, penalizing incentive. Only Minnesota and New Hampshire have, to the best of my knowledge, attempted to regulate the finance of campaigns for the U.S. Congress.

22. Minnesota and Wisconsin alone among the states have substantial public funding of legislative elections linked with spending limits, but the scholarly community has not written systematically about the political consequences or the administrative problems of their programs.

23. Quality is a very slippery concept when applied to candidates. It refers usually to their political attractiveness, skills, and visibility—their electibility, in other words. Political scientists most often measure it in terms of previous public offices sought and held; some scholars also add indices of personal qualities such as celebrity and occupational status.

24. Gary C. Jacobson, *The Electoral Origins of Divided Government: Competition in U.S. House Elections, 1946–1988* (Boulder, Colo.: Westview, 1990), esp. chapter 6.

25. I am not sure who originated the phrase, but many political scientists will associate it with Herbert Alexander, who has long espoused the option.

26. The present limits on contributions to national party committees are $20,000 a year for individuals and $15,000 a year for multicandidate committees. It is the only place in the entire regulatory network of the FECA, I believe, in which individual limits are more generous than those on PACs.

27. Larry J. Sabato, *Paying for Elections: The Campaign Finance Thicket* (New York: Priority Press, 1989), p. 51.

28. Only some of the decline is apparent in the data of public-opinion polls. See the discussion of poll data on mass attitudes about public funding in chapter 5.

29. The Senate bill, however, did provide for exceeding the spending limit for the state by as much as 25 percent if the candidate raised additional individual contributions of $100 or less from citizens of the state.

Chapter 8: The Future of American Campaign Finance

1. For a somewhat stronger statement of this thesis, see Benjamin Ginsburg and Martin Shefter, *Politics by Other Means* (New York: Basic Books, 1990).

2. Funds contributed to the campaign committees of members of Congress must be used for political purposes; they may not be used for personal purposes. However, members sitting in the House in 1980 were exempted

("grandfathered") from that legislation until 1993. No member sworn in in 1993 will be able to convert funds to personal purposes—thus the possible extra incentive for retirement in 1992.

3. The academic literature is abundant, but the classic sources go back more than a generation, and both involve the great prophet of party government, E. E. Schattschneider. See his book, *Party Government* (New York: Rinehart, 1942). Schattschneider was also a member of the Committee on Political Parties of the American Political Science Association, whose report, *Toward a More Responsible Two-Party System* (New York: Rinehart, 1950), is the classic statement of the "party responsibility" position. David Broder's position in a number of writings seems to me also to share these commitments; see, for example, his "Bogus Campaign Finance Reform," in the *Washington Post,* June 2, 1991.

Index

Access. *See* PACS
Ad Hoc PAC Coalition, 22
Adaptation. *See* Political learning
AFL-CIO, 173. *See also* COPE
Aitkins, Joan, 50
Alexander, Herbert E., 3, 29, 32,
    147–48, 247n4, 251nn13,26,
    258n2, 258–59n8, 263–64n6,
    265n25
Almond, Gabriel A., 251n12
Alston, Chuck, 256n19, 257n32,
    263n3
American Conservative Union, 173
Americans for Democratic Action,
    167, 173
American Independent Party, 182
American Medical Association PAC,
    22, 34, 182–83
Anderson, John, 258n4
Applebome, Peter, 251n19
Arizona, 161
Assembly Campaign Committee
    (Wisc.), 120
Assembly Democrats (Calif.), 119
Assembly Republican PAC (Calif.),
    119–20

Babcock, Charles R., 251n18,
    254n31
Baran, Jan W., 263–64n6
Barnes, James A., 257n33
Bauer, Monica, 29, 32, 147–48,
    251nn13,26

Bauer, Raymond A., 252n4
Bauer, Robert F., 263–64n6
Bayh, Birch, 180
Berra, Yogi, 186
Beverly Hills, Calif., 126
Bilateralism. *See* Exchanges
BIPAC, 121–23
Bliley, Thomas J., Jr., 121–22
Boesky, Ivan, 162
Boren, David, 198–99
Boschwitz, Rudy, 85
Brace, Paul, 256n24
Bragdon, Peter, 253n19
Breaux, David, 256n23
Broder, David, 266n3
Brokers: excluded from FECA, 53–
    55; interests, 125–26; organizers
    of individuals, 124–27;
    presidential, 140; Senate fund-
    raising, 89–91. *See also* Bundling;
    Keating, Charles H.
Brown, Carl, 254n30
Brown, Willie, 119
Brownstein, Ronald, 262n21
Buckley v. *Valeo*: Congress, power
    of, 189; consequences, 138;
    First Amendment, 191; indepen-
    dent spending, 56–57, 179–80;
    public funding, 152, 258; spend-
    ing limits, 10, 186; uncon-
    stitutionality of FECA,
    11–12
Bullock, Joyce, 254n30

267